PARLIAMENT AND CONSCIENCE

PARLIAMENT AND CONSCIENCE

BY

PETER G. RICHARDS

Professor of British Government
University of Southampton

London

GEORGE ALLEN & UNWIN LTD

RUSKIN HOUSE MUSEUM STREET

FIRST PUBLISHED IN 1970

© *George Allen and Unwin Ltd. 1970*

ISBN 0 04 340006 X

PRINTED IN GREAT BRITAIN
in 10 point Times Roman Type
BY BILLING AND SONS LTD
GUILDFORD AND LONDON

Preface

The House of Commons elected in March 1966 has differed from its predecessors in that it has devoted more attention to social questions which have strong moral overtones. These are commonly described as 'issues of conscience'. Members vote according to personal convictions for no party discipline is applied. The whips take no action even to encourage Members to attend the debates. This freedom imparts greater vigour and greater uncertainty to the work of Parliament. How does the British political system work when party leaders and the Civil Service tend to step aside? Is it desirable for legislation to be passed in this atmosphere of abnormal liberty? These are the central questions I try to answer in the following pages.

The core of the work is the half dozen case-studies of issues raised through major private Members' Bills. I am most grateful to the Social Science Research Council for the financial assistance which enabled me to organize this research. My research assistant, Mrs Margaret Fuller, has given invaluable aid, collating the detailed material, interviewing, and commenting upon my early drafts. Chapter 9 is based entirely on her detailed study of division lists: it is, indeed, but a preliminary statement of the results of her research, and I hope that other more specialized aspects will be published subsequently elsewhere.

I am grateful to the Gallup Poll and the National Opinion Poll for permission to reproduce results of their surveys.

I owe a debt of gratitude to many other people. Members of both Houses of Parliament who have played a leading role in the controversies over issues of conscience have been kind enough to spare time to talk to us. So also have the officials of various voluntary bodies concerned with this legislation. Occasionally a civil servant was consulted. The list of people interviewed would be too long to reproduce here. Dr David Butler of Nuffield College, Oxford, gave us access to his files containing information about the social background of MPs, and Mr Rex Walford allowed us to use the data he has collected on the religious affiliations of MPs. At the University of Southampton, Mrs Powell and Mrs Tearall helped with the typing; Mr Liam O'Sullivan made valuable comments on Chapter 1; Miss Diana Marshallsay, B.A., Dip. Lib., Librarian of the Ford Collection of Parliamentary Papers, has once again rendered great assistance by providing the Index. At home, Lesley has worked on the calculations (other than Chapter 9) and my wife, once more, has prepared the final draft for the printer.

As much of what follows is controversial, it is perhaps necessary to make the formal declaration that I alone am responsible for the opinions expressed.

PETER G. RICHARDS
University of Southampton
February 1970

Contents

Contents

Chapter 1

Conscience, Law and Morality

explanation of conscience [handwritten]

Conscience is a complex term, embracing many shades of meaning. It required three and a half columns of description and explanation in *The New Oxford Dictionary*.[1] Essentially, conscience implies a moral sense, a knowledge of right and wrong arising from one's innermost thoughts. It is used in religious, ethical and political discussions, and most commonly where these fields overlap. Shakespeare was very fond of the term. Milton used it in powerful verse to uphold the right to religious liberty:

> 'Help us to save free conscience from the paw
> Of hireling wolves, whose gospel is their maw.'
>
> *To the Lord General Cromwell, May 1652*

Areopagitica makes his plea for political freedom: 'Give me the liberty to know, to utter, and to argue freely according to conscience above all liberties.' The word can also be used to indicate a political testament as in the title of Senator Goldwater's book, *The Conscience of a Conservative*. Especially is it a term used to justify one's actions. It earns easy approbation. To deny another man's conscience is to deny his integrity, his freedom of thought and individuality. In a democratic society a man who suffers for his conscience will earn some respect. The tendency to ignore individual conscience in an authoritarian community, be it state or church, arouses wide condemnation from those who sustain liberal values.

The quotations from Milton show that in this country the theme of conscience had close associations with puritanism. The puritan himself embodies a conflict between individualism and authority. He *Puritanism* [handwritten] rejected the claim of the priest to interpret the will of God and the right of the state to impose religious conformity upon him. Instead, he imposed on himself another authority by insisting upon the fundamental truth of the Bible and by subjecting himself and his family to a severe regime of restraint, sobriety and religious observance. Puritan values condemned the venality and corruption of public life. Devotion to hard work and self-discipline, that led to almost

[1] Vol. II (Oxford University Press, 1893).

automatic saving, steadily strengthened the economic position, and ultimately the political influence, of the tradesmen and artisans who attended chapel regularly. Their demand for high standards of morality in all forms of behaviour was impossible to denounce and difficult to ignore. The consequent dilemma for the established order of society was neatly summarized by George IV: 'The non-conformist conscience doth make cowards of us all.' Disraeli's Taper accepted the importance of the puritans in cynical fashion: 'I am all for a religious cry. It means nothing and, if successful, does not interfere with business when we are in.' Taper, of course, was wrong. The newly-enfranchised electors enquired increasingly into the opinions of parliamentary candidates and expected their performance to match their opinions. Meanwhile, puritan, liberal and non-conformist attitudes were changing. The belief in a minimum of state action, in *laissez-faire*, was eroded by the recognition that social and economic improvement demanded some measure of government intervention in affairs. Yet the non-conformist insisted that the new forms of state provision must permit an element of choice, the right to dissent or opt out, wherever an issue of personal or religious freedom was involved.

During the latter half of the nineteenth century the claim that conscience should provide a legitimate exemption from the normal requirements of social policy was formally accepted in legislation. The Education Act, 1870, created local School Boards for the purpose of providing schools financed from public funds; the establishment of state schools necessarily provoked an outcry over the character of the religious instruction to be provided. The Act therefore contained a conscience clause to permit parents to withdraw their children from religious instruction if they so desired. Since the teaching provided was in sympathy with the beliefs of the Established Church, the conscience clause was of vital concern to the dissenting denominations. Another example is vaccination against smallpox. This was made compulsory in 1853, although the law was not enforced everywhere for many years. As more measures were taken to make the law effective, so resistance to compulsion grew. Agitation developed in many parts of the country and the imposition of penalties by the courts for non-compliance generally served to inflame opinion even more. Much of the support came from non-conformist and co-operative circles. Objections were made on medical grounds, that the practice was dangerous; the principle of freedom was also invoked, that parents should be able to decide what was to be done to their children's bodies. After long years of struggle the anti-vaccinators were successful. An unexpected Liberal by-election victory at Reading in 1898, where the Liberal candidate had opposed compulsory vaccination, provided a final spur to change; the Vaccination Act of that year allowed for the exemption of children whose parents could satisfy a court of their conscientious objection.[1] The operation of this particular conscience clause was short-lived as compulsory vaccination ended in 1907. The most recent application of the principle of conscientious objection has been in relation to military service: in both world wars it was accepted that those who could satisfy the authorities of the genuine nature of their beliefs should be excused combat duties.

These three cases are similar in that conscience provides a relief from compulsion, but otherwise they raise wholly separate issues. Objection to a particular form of religious instruction was a legitimate corollary to the principle of religious toleration which had been secured in the seventeenth century. The argument over vaccination, whether a parent should be entitled to insist on a course of action that might cause his child to die through disease, lost its interest as outbreaks of smallpox became rare.[2] The military service issue is more complex. It raises a variety of ethical and practical problems. Should a man be required to kill others if he feels it wrong to do so? Should a man be compelled to fight for a cause in which he does not believe? Is is possible to force a man to fight? What is the effect on the morale of an army of pressing into it many men who are basically opposed to military effort? Alternatively, if it is made easy to escape military duty, will it be possible for the state to organize forces of sufficient strength to preserve itself? In practice, the way taken through these opposing considerations was to admit the principle of conscientious objection, but for the tribunals dealing with individual objectors to be unsympathetic.[3] Conscientious objectors also suffered an amount of social ostracism in wartime. With the end of compulsory military service this problem disappeared.

Yet these conscience clause issues form but a small part of the challenge that individual conscience presents to legislators. Constantly they have to decide how far the state should regulate human conduct and how far each person should be allowed to act as he sees fit. Common agreement exists that certain types of anti-social

[1] For a full description of this controversy see R. M. Macleod's account: *Public Law* (1967), pp. 107–28, 189–211.

[2] Similar issues do still arise today in the case of parents, e.g. Christian Scientists and Jehovah's Witnesses, who object to all medical treatment for their children or to particular types of treatment.

[3] For a critical account of tribunal procedure see R. S. W. Pollard: *Administrative Tribunals at Work* (Stevens, 1950), Ch. I.

conduct, e.g. murder, arson, rape, must be prohibited by law and prevented wherever possible. On other forms of behaviour there is less agreement: there can be dispute over whether the state should prohibit them or, indeed, whether they are intrinsically evil. All the case-studies in this book relate to determination by the state of frontiers of permissible behaviour; other quite separable frontiers may be imposed by religious bodies, employers, schools, friends, etc. One case-study – on capital punishment – is distinct in that the question of permissibility applies to the state rather than to the individual. With this one exception, the issues raised could be put into a single all-embracing question: how far should the state impose its conscience on that of individuals? Yet to put the problem thus is unacceptable because conscience is essentially personal. This will be disputed by those who wish the state or any other organization to act in accordance with their own moral imperatives. But if an institution acts in a way dictated by a moral urge, it does so at the command of its dominant members. The collectivity itself cannot have a conscience. Baron Thurlow expressed this idea in a cynical form: 'Did you ever expect a corporation to have a conscience, when it has no soul to be damned, and no body to be kicked?'

Liberal opinion has insisted that respect for the individual demands that the concepts of law and morality be kept separate. Henry Sidgwick, a late Victorian writer, explained the evolution of Liberal thought in this way: 'Partly the belief came to be widely held that in matters of morality, speaking broadly, any one honest man is as much an expert as any other, and that it is his duty to exercise his own judgement and follow the light of his own conscience. Partly – so far as some further enlightenment of a plain man's conscience was felt to be a desideratum – experience was thought to have shown the danger of trying to obtain this enlightenment from the industry and ingenuity of systematic moralists.'[1] There is also a practical difficulty, noted by Sidgwick, that faces anyone who contends that a court of law should be a court of morals: what scale of values should the law try to enforce? Any democratic response to this challenge must make some reference to public opinion. But public views on morality are less definite than the legal code applied by judges and magistrates. Law must be precise, otherwise no one can know what is illegal. Such a degree of definition cannot be obtained from any reference to popular attitudes on moral questions since these embrace a variety of opinion based on the exercise of personal judgement.

The basic problem about the proper extent of human freedom was given a classic answer by John Stuart Mill in his essay *On Liberty*:

[1] *The Elements of Politics* (Macmillan, 1891), p. 196.

'As soon as any part of a person's conduct affects prejudicially the interests of others, society has jurisdiction over it, and the question whether the general welfare will or will not be promoted by interfering with it, becomes open to discussion. But there is no room for entertaining any such question when a person's conduct affects the interests of no persons besides himself, or needs to affect them unless they like (all the persons concerned being of full age and the ordinary amount of understanding). In all such cases, there should be perfect freedom, legal and social, to do the action and stand the consequences.'

Unfortunately this distinction between self-regarding action and other-regarding action produces acute difficulties of interpretation. If anyone wishes to take noxious habit-forming drugs, e.g. heroin, should he be stopped? Two separate reasons can suggest an affirmative response. First, the state may be said to have a paternalist function which provides justification for preventing people from harming themselves: *per contra* it can be argued that paternalism is an impertinent interference with the individual for which no adequate justification can be produced. Second, anyone who renders himself incapable of work can become a burden on the state welfare services and, therefore, on the whole community. This would make drug-taking other-regarding action and so liable to social control, although in Mill's day this conclusion would be less certain since the modern welfare services had not been developed. Indeed, the growth of community welfare provision has substantially reduced the area of human action that has no effect on others. If a couple have a large family, perhaps because of their particular religious beliefs, they may be unable to support it and will make heavy demands on the social services. Are parents to be prohibited from producing children they cannot support, at least at the standard that society expects? It is clear that in modern conditions Mill's doctrine, instead of being a claim for freedom, could be used to justify state interference with what are considered intimate personal matters.[1]

Few actions can be regarded as wholly self-regarding and the dividing line is always open to argument. To take another example:

---

[1] Counter-arguments can, of course, be presented to this theme. Men are not equally worthy; they will not make equal contributions to or equal demands on the resources of the state. This we must accept as a basic reality and as a price of liberty and humane social policies. Alternatively, one could deal with irresponsible social action not by compulsion to conform to an approved pattern but by the withdrawal of support. Thus the delinquent (but not his dependants) would lose the right to benefit from the social services. Here other problems arise, e.g. the definition of irresponsible social action.

should people be prohibited from going to a theatre on Sunday because other people find such behaviour offensive and feel that the values they uphold will be harmed if such behaviour is permitted? For the strict Sabbatarian, the more recreation and entertainment are allowed on a Sunday, the more society offends against his principles and the more will his conscience be troubled by the widespread flouting of his interpretation of the Fourth Commandment. Can this degree of harm possibly justify interference with the liberty of those who wish to attend a theatre on Sunday? If so, cannot the potential theatre-goer claim that he is harmed by the organization of religious services which tend to breed such intolerance of mind as to lead to objections to Sunday theatres? In practice, obviously, no action should be banned unless the amount of harm caused to others is substantial, otherwise the only forms of conduct permitted would be those which secured general approval. This would produce either a colourless community held down to a strict regime of social conformity or alternatively, if no concensus could be achieved, the society would break up into warring parts. Toleration is a social cement.

Mill did not assert that all other-regarding action should be subject to social control – he merely noted that the question of control was a legitimate subject for discussion. In each case the balance of advantages must be considered. A calculation of various factors is required: how far other people are adversely affected; whether the behaviour concerned is in public; whether the harm done to others is a matter of fact or opinion; whether the danger is to adults, who can appreciate the risks, or to children who may not. In assessing the final balance great weight should be given to the value of individual freedom. To justify interference with personal liberty it must be shown that the harm resulting from freedom must be greater than the harm coming from restrictions. A form of cost-benefit analysis is required, based as far as possible on scientific objective evaluation of the consequences of alternative forms of action. Of course, such measurements are difficult to make. On which side the balance falls is a matter which everyone, including each member of a legislature, must decide for himself. Ultimately it is a matter of conscience. And conscience, as Harold Laski argued: 'for most of us is a poor guide. It is perverse, it is foolish, the little knowledge it has is small alongside the worth of the social tradition. But perverse, foolish, ignorant, it is the only guide we have.'[1]

Not everyone agrees that such questions should be settled within the framework of philosophical radicalism for they prefer, to use

[1] *Liberty in the Modern State* (Allen & Unwin, 1930), p. 76.

Laski's phrase, the worth of the social tradition. The Wolfenden Report stimulated afresh the discussion on whether the regulation of morals was the concern of the state. Lord Devlin was critical of the report's acceptance of the distinction between sin and crime.[1] Professor Hart attacked Lord Devlin's views[2] and others have joined in the controversy.[3] It is not possible in a brief summary to do full justice to the full range and splendour of the argument, but some description is essential since the issues raised have a vital bearing on the case-studies of parliamentary behaviour that form the core of this book.

The crux of Lord Devlin's position is that the state has a duty to uphold moral standards because these are essential to the maintenance of society. If the state does not concern itself with morality, we face the decay of the community. Lord Devlin accepts that not all immoral actions are, or should be, crimes. What, on this view, should determine the limits of what the law will allow? The judge's answer is a mirage beloved by lawyers – the reasonable man, the man on the Clapham omnibus or twelve of them seated together in the jury-room. If such people are moved to intolerance, indignation and disgust by particular conduct, then such conduct should be banned. Lord Devlin recognies that the limits of tolerance shift; much that was scandalous to the Victorians or even the twentieth-century Georgians would not raise an eyebrow now. He agrees also that privacy should be respected as far as possible, although he rejects any distinction between public and private morality.

With some exceptions, Lord Devlin does not indicate how he would apply these principles to particular issues: indeed, he is prepared to leave decisions to the jury. But his criticism of the Wolfenden Report produced a reaction based on the assumption that he was defending the legal *status quo*. Those with progressive, reformist ideals denounced his approach. Indeed, the fear of judicial conservatism was greatly strengthened by the case of *Director of Public Prosecutions* v. *Shaw*,[4] in which judges acted both as law-makers and as custodians of public morals. Shaw was convicted on three charges after having published a directory of prostitutes, one of which was 'conspiracy to corrupt public morals'. By reference to antique precedents the House of Lords were able to decide that such

[1] *The Enforcement of Morals* (O.U.P., 1959).
[2] *Law, Liberty and Morality* (O.U.P., 1963).
[3] *Inter alia*, B. Mitchell: *Law, Morality and Religion* (O.U.P., 1967); D. Rostow: *Cambridge Law Journal* (1960), p. 174; G. Williams: *Criminal Law Review* (1964), p, 253; R. Wollheim: *Encounter*, November 1959.
[4] (1962) A.C. 220; (1961) 2 W.L.R. 897; (1961) Crim. L.R. 468.

an offence does exist in English Law. There are no clear limits to or definition of this crime. To engage the services of a prostitute is not illegal: thus a conspiracy to corrupt public morals can include the encouragement or facilitation of actions which in themselves are perfectly legal. The doctrine could presumably be invoked against anyone who assisted homosexual or lesbian behaviour. Any behaviour that a prosecutor and a jury find sufficiently unpleasant could conceivably be punished under this broad rubric. *Shaw* aroused much controversy in legal circles and no further charges of conspiracy to corrupt public morals have been reported. Certainly, it represented broadly Lord Devlin's view of what should be the relationship between law and morals.

Professor Hart has suggested that Lord Devlin regards social morality as a seamless web so that all its provisions are essential for the preservation of society.[1] This is untrue. Lord Devlin explicitly recognizes that fornication, adultery and lesbianism are not illegal and that society accepts that this should be so. He does not appear to be hostile to abortion law reform.[2] The two central criticisms to be made of the Devlin thesis concern the belief that the moral tone of society must necessarily be good and true, and that the optimum means of resolving such issues is to appeal to public opinion as reflected through the distorting mirror of the courts of law.

It is convenient to consider these matters in reverse order, and to review first the wisdom of juries. Why should a collection of men (and women) on the Clapham omnibus know which parts of social morality are essential for the preservation of society? They may fear that certain changes have a damaging effect: such fears are difficult to prove or disprove. A jury can be presented with expert evidence. Yet will the evidence necessarily be understood, especially if it is complex, technical or conflicting? One can argue that it does not matter if juries impose rules that are not essential for the preservation of society, but in this case the preservation of society becomes an inadequate justification for the moral content of the criminal law. Lord Devlin's view is that if a form of behaviour or a piece of merchandise provokes 'intolerance, indignation and disgust' in a jury, then it must be so damaging to society as to require suppression.

Juries, of course, do not determine the principles of law, they apply principles to particular situations. The moral standards of juries vary. To achieve reasonable uniformity and certainty in the legal process it is necessary for basic rules to be decided by a legis-

[1] *Law, Liberty and Morality*, p. 70.

[2] This is a matter about which 'the community is not deeply imbued with a sense of sin'. *The Enforcement of Morals*, 1965 edn, p. 24.

lature. Lord Devlin will admit this, but he argues that if a law conflicts with the moral sense of a jury they will try to avoid enforcing it and that a jury is of particular value in considering new problems on the frontiers of permissibility which have not been dealt with by Parliament. It is precisely in such matters that the decisions of juries are so unsatisfactory and contrary to the principles on which Lord Devlin rests his case. Juries have been so sympathetic to motorists driving under the influence of drink that the law had to be changed to strengthen the hands of the prosecution. The fact that increasing numbers of people were being killed and maimed by drunken drivers was something juries chose to ignore to the detriment of the preservation of society. *R. v. Quinn*[1] provides a quite different example. In this case a jury was asked to convict the owner of a strip-tease club under the terms of an eighteenth-century statute, the Disorderly Houses Act, 1751, passed in a different age to deal with a different problem. The jury had not seen the entertainment under challenge nor, unless they had been members of the private club concerned, were they entitled to see it. Although the prosecution was successful, strip-tease clubs continued to exist, and six years after the Quinn case the Greater London Council began to grant public licences for strip-tease shows. *R. v. Quinn* provides a direct refutation of the claim that a jury can be trusted to take moral decisions needed for the self-preservation of the community.

There are further objections to placing reliance on juries. They operate under substantial constraints. Normally, and this is wholly proper, they regard it as their duty to apply the law irrespective of personal convictions on moral issues. It is rare for their attitude to make a law inoperable. Further, when the law is complex and the evidence is conflicting, the decision of the jury may well be influenced by the tenor of the judge's summing-up.[2] This is well illustrated by the prosecution of two novels for obscenity. In the case of *Lady Chatterley's Lover* it may be that the liberal attitude reflected in Mr Justice Stable's directions to the jury was the determining factor. The law itself recognizes the weight of a judge's influence and insists that it be exercised equitably: the conviction of the publisher of *Last Exit to Brooklyn* was set aside on appeal because it was held that the trial judge had not presented the case for the defence adequately in his closing remarks to the jury. So a plea for the value of juries is partly a plea for the value of the influence which judges[3]

[1] (1961) 3 W.L.R. 611.
[2] This point is made by Dean Rostow, otherwise a supporter of Lord Devlin in the *Cambridge Law Journal* (1960), p. 178.
[3] Also recorders and chairmen of quarter sessions.

may exercise. It is to accept judges as custodians of morality – the same attitude as in *D.P.P.* v. *Shaw* described above. Notwithstanding Mr Justice Stable, the prospect is unattractive. In view of their age, their social isolation and the unbalanced content of their experience, I query whether we should accept judges as our moral guardians.

The theory of legal moralism should be examined at a more fundamental level. The crux of the theory is that society has a right of self-preservation. It is easy to accept this as obvious and necessary so long as one accepts the fundamental postulates on which a community is based. What if your conscience impels you to treat a particular political regime as evil? Did the Nazi regime have a right of self-preservation? Nazi supporters thought it had: their opponents fought to deny this right. Inside and outside South Africa are people who regard the apartheid policy as morally repulsive. The badge of a free man is that he can stand aside and judge the quality of life as ordered by the state: if it offends him sufficiently he can protest. Broad support for a policy strengthens the position of a government, but support does not endow a policy with greater moral virtue although it makes the task of enforcement much easier. To claim that the law must uphold the moral fabric of society is a two-edged sword. Usually this is a conservative theme which assumes the morality of existing law. It can also fit a revolutionary programme that seeks basic changes in the moral fabric of society. In neither case is the equation of morality with law likely to promote tolerance. For an autocracy it can lead to a denial that the individual need or should concern himself with such basic issues. Happily, in a democratic society the arguments are normally in a lower key and liberal opinion accepts there can be a gap between what is desirable and what is permissible. Yet this greater harmony does not always remove the problem; a majority can impose unreasonable restraints on a minority and law may lag behind changes in opinion. So Lord Devlin is prepared for a jury to say that it is unwilling for certain moral judgements to be enforced by law.

In a British context there is a danger that this discussion will become unreal. While judges and juries have contributed to the development of the criminal law, the law for the most part is determined by Parliament. Had a jury trying a homosexual case in 1965 decided that the defendant must be punished, not because of the law, but because his conduct was eroding the basis of society – it would have been wrong as shown by subsequent experience. Had the jury decided to acquit because it was not greatly offended by the defendant's behaviour, the decision would have been wrong in the sense that the jury was failing to uphold the law passed by Parliament.

The discretion of the courts is, or should be, limited to the framework of the law. Thus the central question remains: what policy should a legislator adopt on the relationship between law and morals?

Lord Devlin's guidance is confusing. He has written: 'in a democracy a legislator will assume that the morals of his society are good and true; if he does not he should not be playing an active part in government. . . . But he has not to vouch for that goodness and truth. His mandate is to preserve the essentials of society, not to reconstruct them according to his own ideas.'[1] This extraordinary statement may be taken as the high water mark of legal moralism. It invites urgent questions. Why should a legislator not feel that the moral tone of society is bad in some aspects? Why should he not feel that the law should be adjusted to correspond more closely with his own ideals? Above all, why should a person with reforming instincts abstain from public life? However, later in the same article there is a more balanced exposition of how law-making should work. 'The legislator as an enforcer of morals has far greater latitude than a judge. Legislation of that sort is not usually made an election issue but is left to the initiative of those returned to power. In deciding whether or not to take the initiative the relevant question nearly always is not what popular morality is but whether it should be enforced by the criminal law. If there is doubt on the first point, the doubt of itself answers the second question in the negative. The legislator must gauge the intensity with which a popular moral conviction is held, because it is only where the obverse is generally thought to be intolerable that the criminal law can safely and properly be used.'[2]

The latter quotation pays attention to democratic principles. It prefers popular opinion to educated or informed opinion.[3] It is willing to equate sin and crime whenever the man on the Clapham omnibus tends to do so. It is basically anti-intellectual. It makes morality a fact rather than a matter for judgement or conscience. It conflates the state with society by assuming that the state must punish anything condemned by society with sufficient emphasis. It stresses the prudential element in law enforcement and demotes ethical considerations. Above all, it can be defended as a sensible, no-nonsense system for the running of a successful, stable society.

[1] 'Law, Democracy and Morality', *University of Pennsylvania Law Journal* (1962), Vol. 110, p. 639.

[2] *Ibid.*, p. 644.

[3] Whenever an appeal is made to public opinion, the question must arise whether the appeal is based on a genuine belief in majority rule or whether it is based on a belief that popular opinion happens to coincide with a personal opinion.

There is no doubt that many Ministers, senior civil servants and police officers think in this way. Sometimes Members of Parliament do as well; the following chapters contain references to opinion surveys and constituency pressures relating to moral issues on which Parliament has been asked for a decision.

If the legislator does move towards this approach, he tends to avoid enquiry by his conscience into the nature of morality. Often this is the most comfortable avenue open to him. Certainly it can lead towards a code of conduct imposed from outside rather than one which achieves positive individual acceptance. The safeguard proposed, the jury, is inadequate. Admittedly there have been cases where the jury has refused to convict because it has felt a law to be unreasonable, but in all normal circumstances a jury upholds the law. It feels a duty to do so. The law itself conditions a jury towards this point of view. It is difficult for a new pattern of conduct to become generally acceptable if it is initially illegal. The result is a neat social mechanism for self-perpetuation; it has nothing to do with justification. Yet the consequences may be wholly acceptable if, like Lord Devlin, one argues that the law should be slow to change.

As it is, the law is slow to change. Basic legal principles are decided by Parliament. For various reasons, some political, some procedural, law reform is not easily achieved on controversial aspects of human behaviour. There is a heavy in-built bias in favour of the *status quo*. The purpose of this book is to review the political processes which preceded changes in this field in the 1960s. This outburst of activity resulted from the great gap between current social thought and practice and the provisions of the law. The philosophic debate outlined above is both relevant and irrelevant to these important public discussions. It is significant in that it is concerned with the relationship between law and morality: it is unrelated in that the various policy changes could all be accommodated to the modern version of utilitarian doctrine or to legal moralism, depending upon how one chooses to interpret facts and apply principles to specific issues.

Chapter 2

The Legislative Process: Discipline, Procedure, Tactics

I

It has been shown that the idea of a conscience clause was fully familiar to the non-conformist circles from which the modern Labour Party developed. As Labour representation in the Commons increased, the concept attained fresh importance because of the Labour attitude to representation. The first Labour Members were nominated and assisted through the Labour Representation Committee, a body created to secure representation of working-class interests in Parliament: the L.R.C. obtained support from the affiliation of trade unions and other bodies. Until 1918 the Labour Party had no individual membership, and as an organization formed by the affiliation of other organizations it had a wholly different base from that of the older traditional parties, Conservative and Liberal. Labour thought of its Members as spearheads of a mass movement, dedicated to advancing the cause of a particular section of society by the promotion of appropriate legislation. Its inspiration was democratic. Specific proposals, approved by the Party, were to be placed before the electors and candidates victorious at the polls would then be pledged to do what they could to carry out the proposals. Assuming that Labour gained a majority in the Commons, the Party could then claim a mandate from the electors which provided justification for crushing opposition – for example, from the House of Lords – to the implementation of the Labour programme. The early Labour movement recognized that unity was strength. Even if electoral victory were attained, their aims would not be achieved unless Labour representatives in Parliament worked together as a cohesive group. Party discipline in Parliament was essential. Naturally, there were differences of opinion over how strictly this doctrine should be applied. In 1903 the Labour Representation Committee required its candidates, if elected, to form a separate group in the Commons and to resign if unable to support the majority view of the group.[1] Three years later the attitude

[1] R. T. McKenzie: *British Political Parties* (Heinemann, 1955), p. 387 *et seq.* The resolution is unclear whether resignation from the group or from Parliament was expected; presumably the latter was intended.

softened. Candidates were required to sign a pledge accepting the constitution of the Party and, in addition, they had to agree to abide by the decisions of the parliamentary party: there was no mention of resignation. The great Liberal victory of 1906 brought with it 29 Labour Members into the Commons, so for the first time Labour had a significant block of votes and its theory of parliamentary discipline faced the acid test of practice. An initial difficulty arose over the 1906 Education Bill.[1] Labour policy advocated secular education, but one Labour Member was a Roman Catholic and others had grave doubts about the party line, perhaps because of constituency pressure. So the parliamentary party adopted a conscience clause which gave Members who felt a serious difficulty over accepting majority decisions the right to abstain, or even to vote against, the predominant party view. So 'conscience' provided an escape route from absolute allegiance. Keir Hardie reported to the 1907 Labour Conference: 'Unity in things essential and in all things liberty, fairly expresses the disciplinary rule of the Party.'[2]

Ever since, the extent and implications of the conscience clause have been a source of controversy among Labour Members. Initially it seems to have been intended to cover such matters as pacifism, temperance and denominational education where a moral or religious element entered a political issue. Dissident Labour Members always pressed for a broader application. A clash over the operation of the conscience clause was one factor leading to the complete split between the Labour Party and the I.L.P. Over the years the attitudes towards discipline have been completely reversed. In 1903 it was the left-wingers on the Labour Representation Committee who called for strict discipline to ensure vigorous action in the prosecution of the class war; since the 1920s the left-wing have supported freedom of action, no doubt because moderate opinion has commanded a firm majority in the Parliamentary Labour Party. For the party leaders the operation of the conscience clause was potentially awkward, notably in the case of armaments. A genuine pacifist was allowed to disassociate himself from the Party's defence policy, but this toleration was not supposed to be extended to those who objected to the policy on political or non-religious grounds.[3]

The 1945 version of the Standing Orders of the Parliamentary Labour Party attempted to define the scope of conscience more narrowly. 'It is recognized that on certain matters, for example,

[1] R. K. Alderman: 'The Conscience Clause of the Parliamentary Labour Party', *Parliamentary Affairs* (1966), Vol. XIX, pp. 224–32.

[2] Conference Report, p. 40.

[3] C. R. Attlee; *The Labour Party in Perspective* (Gollancz, 1937), pp. 214–17.

religion and temperance, Members may have good grounds for conscientious scruples, and in such cases they may abstain from voting.' However, with a large parliamentary majority, Labour could afford to adopt a more flexible attitude and in 1946 the Standing Orders were suspended. They remained in abeyance until 1952 when 57 Labour Members defied a three-line whip on defence. This produced wide disquiet in the Party and a feeling that it might break up unless cohesion was restored. A new form of Standing Orders contained this sentence: 'The party recognizes the right of individual Members to abstain from voting on matters of deeply-held conscientious conviction.' Two aspects of this phraseology are significant. First, conscience was firmly restricted to individuals. What had alarmed the Labour Party was not merely that its Members held different views but that the minority had organized themselves, held separate meetings and planned concerted action against the majority; it appeared that a party was developing within and, in a sense, against the Party. Organized opposition was not henceforth to be permitted, but personal convictions would be tolerated to the extent of allowing abstention. The second aspect to be noted is that conscience was not limited to moral or religious issues but could be claimed apparently in relation to any item of policy. A further question that the Standing Order failed to cover was how far the revised conscience clause permitted a Member to make speeches highly critical of party policy. Left-wing Members were rarely silent about their conscientious convictions, and Lord Attlee, when still Leader of the Party, was constrained to remark that 'conscience is a still, small voice, not a loudspeaker'.

Inevitably, the reimposition of Standing Orders in 1952 failed to quell disagreement among Labour Members.[1] Standing Orders were again suspended between 1959 and 1961; subsequently a modified version emphasized that conscience 'does not entitle Members to cast votes contrary to the decision of a party meeting'. Thus abstention was acceptable but not full rejection of party decisions. Harold Wilson's election as Leader in 1963, combined with a growing prospect of victory at the polls, served to diminish disputes. The tight-rope result in 1964 required full support for the Wilson Government in face of the constant threat that Ministers would be defeated in the Commons. Disciplinary problems revived with the secure Labour majority achieved in 1966, but the Government Chief Whip, John Silkin (Deptford), was determined to follow a liberal

[1] For more detail, Peter G. Richards: *Honourable Members* (Faber, 2nd edn, 1964), pp. 148–52.

policy with rebellious back-benchers; indeed his policy was too lenient to please some 'loyal' Members who protested that the 'rebels' avoided the odium of voting for unpopular Government measures and escaped without any penalty for their conduct. In November 1966, the Parliamentary Labour Party established a new code of conduct which condemned personal attacks on other Labour Members and required any organized groups of Members to be registered with the Chief Whip: in return for these restrictions it was agreed that a broader interpretation be placed on the traditional conscience clause. This new and undefined freedom soon produced sharp conflict. 37 Labour Members voted against the Government's attempt to enter the Common Market while a further 50 abstained. Silkin then notified the rebels that the right to abstain on a matter of conscience did not extend to voting against the Government on an issue of confidence supported by a three-line whip. Almost immediately afterwards another revolt took place on prices and incomes legislation. In January 1968, 25 Labour Members abstained on a vote of confidence relating to cuts in government expenditure. The Chief Whip thereupon suspended the 25 from party meetings but subsequently rescinded this decision after the back-bench officers of the Parliamentary Labour Party complained that the Chief Whip had no power of suspension. Next month the P.L.P. adopted a new code of discipline by 116 votes to 18: the vital clause reads, 'while the Party recognizes the right of Members to abstain from voting in the House on matters of deeply held personal conviction, this does not entitle Members to vote contrary to the decision of a party meeting or to abstain from voting on a vote of confidence in a Labour Government'. Although the Chief Whip could reprimand Members, the power of suspension was to be exercised through the liaison committee of the P.L.P., a body elected by Labour Members which encompassed most shades of opinion within the Party. However, the lenient policy continued and Labour Members enjoyed *de facto* a greater freedom than ever before. Disputes and rebellions became a common occurrence. Major issues included prices and incomes legislation, the Parliament Bill, industrial relations and the increase in selective employment tax in the 1969 Budget. Suddenly, in April 1969, Silkin was replaced as Chief Whip by Robert Mellish (Bermondsey). It was clear that the Prime Minister had decided that liberal discipline was placing the programme of Government legislation in jeopardy. The change had little effect.

The Conservative Party does not experience such acute disciplinary problems. Its attitude towards representation differs from that of the Labour Party because it does not accept the mandate theory to the same extent.[1] A party accustomed to power rather than to opposition is likely to view precise commitments with disfavour. Conservative principles are applied empirically to problems as they emerge. Party policy is determined by the Leader of the Party in consultation with his senior colleagues, either the Cabinet or Shadow Cabinet depending upon the political fortunes of the Party. A dissident Conservative Member cannot be told to accept the majority decision of a Party meeting; instead he will be urged to show loyalty to his Party and his Leader. A vote against his Party can cause a Conservative Member to have a difficult interview with his Chief Whip, but his political career is more likely to be threatened by his constituency association than by his parliamentary colleagues. Social pressures may be exerted to encourage him to conform and his chance of ministerial office may be adversely affected. Yet Tory discipline in the Commons is flexible and it is less necessary for an independent-minded Conservative to invoke conscientious scruples as a defence of his actions.

Political parties do not always seek to command the votes of their supporters in the Commons. Free votes are sometimes permitted. An opposition may abandon whipping when it has no unified view on a ministerial proposal, as with votes at 18. The Government is less flexible because, naturally, it wishes its legislative programme to proceed smoothly. But under the Silkin regime, when whipping tended to be divorced from the threat of disciplinary action, the whip was sometimes interpreted as a summons to attend rather than an instruction to support a particular case – for example, the debate on the White Paper on industrial relations *In Place of Strife*. Such liberality on government business is exceptional. The traditional conscience issues normally enjoy a free vote even when they arise from government legislation: thus the Commons rejected the clause in the 1968 Finance Bill to authorize a national lottery by 166 votes to 76. More often conscience issues arise from private members' legislation and there is now a strong convention that whips are not used for these Bills.

Private members' time thus provides an important element of freedom for back-benchers. The Government view on back-bench measures will vary from support, qualified support, neutrality to opposition. Ministers may try to secure the acceptance of their own policy without invoking the formal party machinery. Should an Opposition Member put forward a Bill that conflicts directly with ministerial policy, one may expect it to be killed by the loyalty of

[1] A. H. Birch: *Representative and Responsible Government* (Allen & Unwin, 1964), p. 117.

government back-benchers. If a Bill does not raise any overt party issue, or if it is moved by a government supporter, the position is more complex. Should Ministers object strongly to a measure, they will try to persuade the House to reject it while adhering to the principle of the free vote. Members of the Government may be persuaded to attend and vote accordingly: the third reading of the Hairdresser's Registration Bill, 1949, was defeated in this way.[1] It will be shown below that the attempt to impose a 'ministerial whip' against the Matrimonial Property Bill, 1968, aroused such hostility that the move was abandoned.[2] Other means are available to kill off unwelcome measures. A filibuster can be arranged more or less discreetly so a Bill fails for lack of time. The promoter may be urged to withdraw a measure in return for some concession, perhaps the promise of an official enquiry, as with Mrs White's Matrimonial Causes Bill, 1950.[3] If, in spite of everything, a Bill gets a second reading, detailed ministerial criticism at the committee stage may cause sufficient amendment to satisfy Ministers. The third reading provides another opportunity to stop a Bill, as with the Hairdresser's Registration Bill noted above. Even then there remains the House of Lords: the Women's Emancipation Bill, 1919, to give the vote to women aged between twenty-one and thirty, passed the Commons in spite of Cabinet hostility before it was defeated in the Upper House. Thus even without official whipping, the obstacles facing a Bill disliked by Ministers are formidable.

There is, however, a strong tradition that some subjects, issues of conscience, are not fit matters for party decisions. Here a government is likely to be more truly neutral. If neutrality becomes benevolent neutrality, the sponsors of a Bill will not complain. Certainly, on this type of issue, Members' freedom of action is a reality. They are forced to be free. No shelter can be found under an umbrella of party loyalty. If uncertain in their own minds, or worried about constituency reaction, the only safe course is abstention. Indeed, the unexpected quality of free votes arises not so much from the unpredictable quality of Members' opinions but rather because their attendance at Westminster becomes problematic. A free vote is an opportunity to take time off, to be used for other pressing engagements. Permission for absence can be welcome and convenient.

Peers do not have equivalent problems. They are not subject to re-election; they have no constituencies; they have no local supporters to conciliate; they are not under the same pressure to attend to

---

[1] For a full description of the progress of this Bill see P. A. Bromhead: *Private Members' Bills in the British Parliament* (Routledge & Kegan Paul, 1956), App. B.
[2] p. 152, *infra*.   [3] p. 136–7, *infra*.

parliamentary business. A majority of members in the Upper House accept a party whip, but whipping has no sanctions behind it. A whip can urge his supporters to attend on a particular occasion and to vote in accordance with party policy. But there can be no question of discipline as in the Commons. So the peers are used to a broad measure of freedom; a vote in the Lords on a conscience issue is not quite such a separate, special occasion as it is at the other end of the Palace of Westminster.

II

Three separate procedures exist for the initiation of back-bench legislation. The most important is the ballot to determine the precedence of Bills in the time allocated for private members' legislation. With rate exceptions, all important back-bench measures that become law use this channel. However, the other two categories, Unballoted Bills and Ten-Minute Rule Bills, both enter into the case-histories that form the core of this book. Therefore they demand brief description.

Under Standing Order No. 37 a Member may present a Bill without the leave of the House; the Bill is read a first time and printed without any questions or debate. Such a Bill obtains no further attention unless one of three things should occur: it is allowed an unopposed second reading; the Government finds time for debate; all balloted Bills due for discussion on a particular Friday are disposed of before the end of the sitting. The first possibility could never apply to a major controversial measure and the third possibility is almost equally improbable. Leo Abse's Bill on homosexual law reform came into the second category. Cases of this kind will occur only when the Government wishes an issue to be brought before Parliament but does not wish to take the initiative itself.

The Ten-Minute Rule procedure (Standing Order 13) permits a Member to introduce a Bill at the end of question-time on Tuesdays and Wednesdays with a short speech not exceeding ten minutes. A single opposing speech of similar length may be made and then the motion for leave to introduce the Bill is put. There may or may not be a division. Unless the Bill is defeated it is then available for further consideration in the same way as unballoted Bills described in the previous paragraph. Ten-Minute Bills are limited to one a day and a week's notice must be given when using this procedure. Their value is that they give an opportunity to ventilate a problem, to secure publicity, and to obtain some indication of the feelings of Members should a vote be challenged. A favourable reception for a

Ten-Minute Bill increases its chances of sponsorship through the ballot in a subsequent session.

The main vehicle for private members' Bills, the ballot under Standing Order 5, takes place on the second Thursday of each session. Members who so wish enter their names. By convention, Ministers do not. Twenty-seven are drawn so twenty-seven Bills are introduced under the procedure on the fifth Wednesday of each session. Sixteen Fridays are allocated for their consideration.[1] The first eight of these Fridays are devoted to second readings. Since one measure may occupy the whole of a Friday, only the first eight Members successful in the ballot can be certain of a hearing for their Bills. Those who draw a number higher than eight must try to pick a Friday when the preceding Bill(s) seem so uncontroversial as to require but a short debate. Thus George Strauss, tenth in the ballot in 1967, decided correctly that the Adoption Bill would not consume much time and so would leave room for adequate discussion of his Bill to abolish stage censorship by the Lord Chamberlain. It is also good tactics, *ceteris paribus*, to choose an earlier Friday rather than a later one so that a Bill will have a higher place in the queue of measures waiting for consideration by Standing Committee. After the eighth Friday the time available is devoted to the later stages of Bills: priority is given to those which have travelled furthest along the road to the statute book. Lords' amendments are considered first; then Bills that have reached third reading; then report stages. Any time still left over is given to second readings of Bills lower in the ballot.

Inevitably many Bills fail through lack of time rather than through opposition. Controversial measures can easily suffer. Indeed, they scarcely ever succeed unless Ministers find extra time. Since 1966 the Wilson Government has accepted that time should be made available where a substantial body of parliamentary opinion is shown to be in favour of a particular change in the law. Time is obtained by permitting the House to have additional or extended sittings, not by the sacrifice of government time. Two devices are used. The normal ten o'clock rule can be suspended so the House may have an all-night sitting. A more recent and convenient arrangement is to allow the resumption of business at 10 a.m. for a maximum of four hours,[2] enough to complete a second reading but probably

[1] Before 1966 twenty Bills were introduced to be dealt with in ten Fridays. For further historical material on this procedure see Peter G. Richards: *Honourable Members* (Faber, 1964), Ch. 10.

[2] For the discussion when this procedure was introduced see H. C. Deb., Vol. 756, cols 292–332.

insufficient for a contentious report stage. Both these techniques were used to assist the Jones Divorce Bill. Four of the six case-studies in this book record some government assistance through the provision of extra time.

Even so, the difficulties are formidable. Unless a second reading vote is obtained, the views of Members remain unknown. Opponents may try to block a measure by keeping the debate going at 4 p.m., which is the end of main business on Friday. If they succeed, the Bill is talked out and no vote is taken. The sponsors can obviate this tactic by moving that the question be put, but the Speaker will not accept the motion should he feel that there has been inadequate opportunity for discussion; if he does accept the motion, it will still not succeed without the support of 100 Members. In practice the first eight Bills in the ballot can be certain of a vote on second reading unless the parliamentary timetable is totally disrupted by a major crisis or unless Parliament is dissolved so that a general election can be held. The rate of progress is variable. Sometimes three or even four Bills are considered on one Friday. At other times there is deliberate time-wasting. Inevitably, there are flukes in the process. A Bill with a poor place in the ballot may have its chances dramatically improved because a preceding Bill due for debate on the same Friday is withdrawn. The foresight or artfulness of a sponsor can be crucial. In 1957 Graham Page (Con. Crosby) introduced a Ten-Minute Rule Bill to obviate the need to endorse cheques. The Bill was non-controversial and based on the report of the Mocatta Committee.[1] Good fortune provided sufficient time for an unopposed second reading, whereupon Page moved that his measure be considered by a committee of the whole House. At that time it happened that private members' Bills were all caught in a queue waiting for consideration by Standing Committee; Page's unusual initiative enabled the Cheques Bill to by-pass the bottleneck.[2]

A controversial Bill that has passed through Standing Committee still suffers the challenge of detailed proposals for amendment at the report stage. Again, if the report stage cannot be completed in the time available, the Bill will fail. To ensure that any progress is made, the sponsors must have one hundred supporters present to vote for the motion that the question (i.e. the amendment) be now put. The corps of a hundred must be available even if their opponents are many fewer; especially in the case of all-night sittings, this requires considerable organization. When the report stage of a major Bill consumes much time on private members' Fridays, other Bills coming

[1] Report of the Committee on Cheque Endorsement 1956–57, Cmnd. 3, ix.
[2] H.C. Deb., Vol. 568, cols 1504–18.

behind it on the journey through Standing Committee may fail for lack of time even if relatively non-controversial. Between 1959 and 1964 58 per cent of balloted Bills reached the statute book; between 1966 and 1969 the proportion was 31 per cent.[1] Measures introduced since 1966 have covered more important and controversial topics. The lower success rate is an inevitable consequence.

Conservative Members are more active in the ballot than Labour Members. From 1959 to 1969, a decade of equal periods of government by the two parties, Conservatives introduced 135 Bills under this procedure as compared with 75 from Labour and 4 from Liberals.[2] Two factors explain the difference. When the Conservatives were in office the Labour front bench stayed away from the ballot, presumably on the theory that it was a back-benchers' province. The Conservative front bench when in opposition have joined in the ballot. The other reason is that many of the older trade union Labour Members do not participate because they do not feel equal to the legal and procedural complications involved in piloting a Bill through Parliament. So when Labour is in power the draw will favour the Conservatives, with ninety Labour Members excluded because they hold ministerial office and a certain category of government backbenchers willing to miss this opportunity. Here is the explanation why, in the case-studies which follow, it has often been difficult for Members who wished to press ahead with the various reforms to find someone with a really good place in the ballot to sponsor the Bills.

Balloted Bills start their hazardous parliamentary career with a formal first reading. It is not permissible for a Member to 'pick up' a Bill which has already passed through the Lords in the same session. Thus a balloted Bill once accepted by the Commons must be accepted *subsequently* by the Lords: David Steel was unable to use Lord Silkin's Bill on abortion that had already passed through the Upper House, but the favourable reception it had received was obviously of great political assistance.

Members successful in the ballot present their Bills in dummy on the fifth Wednesday of session. The three-week gap between ballot and presentation enables Members to decide how to use their opportunity to legislate. Some will have firm ideas in advance; others will not. Those with a high place in the ballot may be approached by other Members or pressure groups urging them to espouse a particular cause. So time is needed for drafting. A sponsor makes arrangements with the Public Bill Office in the Commons for his

[1] R. L. Leonard: 'Back-bench Bills' in *New Society*, January 15, 1970.
[2] *Ibid.*

Bill to be printed in time for the second reading; there is no formal timetable but Members are expected to have their Bills printed seven to ten days before the second reading debate. Not to allow reasonable time to study the text of a Bill provides legitimate source of complaint. The time needed for preliminary consultations and drafting can also affect the choice of date for second reading. A Member who has his Bill fully prepared will be keen to have it discussed as soon as possible; a Member less ready may seek a later date.

Drafting of legislation is a highly specialized art. It is a mystic rite understood only by the limited band of official practitioners. No Member unaided can hope to produce a draft Bill framed in language that will satisfy lawyers. Even highly qualified lawyers unskilled in draftsmanship fail in this task. The Matrimonial Property Bill, 1968, was prepared by some of the best legal brains in the London School of Economics, yet the quality of the drafting was widely condemned. An opponent of a Bill can score an easy point by claiming that it is defective technically. Major social measures of the type examined in this book are now commonly prepared in consultation with the official parliamentary draftsmen. But Members have no constitutional right to such assistance. It is merely made available when Ministers are sympathetic or adopt a pose of neutrality tinged with benevolence. Clearly, this is unsatisfactory. Yet if any Member successful in the ballot could claim drafting assistance as of right, then much expert, expensive and scarce skill could be wasted on measures that had little chance of becoming law, either through government hostility or lack of time. This cost of wasted effort should be met because one can never know which efforts will be wasted. A Bill with a low priority may be lucky or win a higher place in a later session: governments sometimes change their minds and sometimes are replaced. Meanwhile the drafting problem for private members has become less acute in recent years because the Labour Government has accepted that legal technicalities should not impede the achievement of reforms that are widely desired.

The absence of party discipline necessarily produces extra hazards for a Bill. A sponsor has difficulty in estimating the extent of his support and more difficulty in ensuring the attendance of his supporters. The need for a hundred assenters to secure a closure motion on the floor of the House has already been stressed. In Standing Committee, failure to provide a quorum on two successive occasions sends a Bill to the bottom of the queue of measures awaiting Committee consideration, an almost certain guarantee of lingering death. The performance of a sponsor in debate can also be crucial. A poor speech by a Minister moving a government Bill has little or

C

no effect on voting figures; a weak or ill-advised speech by the promoter of a private member's Bill can influence many uncommitted Members. The second reading division is very important because the Standing Committee nominated to consider details of the Bill must reflect the balance of opinion at second reading. Thus, if the second reading majority is substantial, the supporters of the Bill should be comfortably secure and in command of the Committee. If the majority is narrow, then the committee opinion will be more even and the sponsors must expect more trouble. It is also important that supporters should be in substantial agreement on points of detail. Should many Members vote for a second reading subject to the proviso that major aspects of a Bill should be changed, the sponsor may find himself burdened at the committee stage with some semi-friends who join him on some issues but oppose him on others. Good tactics may require an uncompromising speech from the sponsor in the second reading debate in order to deflect those who half support his views. At the committee stage it can be better to have a small but firm majority than to have bigger yet discordant support.

The formal debates on a Bill recorded verbatim in *Hansard* are but a small part of the political activity it generates. Whenever controversial issues are raised there will be a vast amount of discussion with interested organizations, lobbying among Members and consultation with Ministers. These private negotiations can do much to ensure success or failure. They often determine the tactics used in parliamentary debates. Political skill, sensitive organization and even the good temper of the promoter and his chief assistants are all vital to success. To secure the enactment of a major Bill is a great political achievement for a back-bencher.

Chapter 3

Capital Punishment

[handwritten margin note: attracted more attention than cap. punishment?]

I

None of the controversial issues discussed in this book has attracted more public attention than has capital punishment. None has consumed so much parliamentary time over so long a period. And although capital punishment is now abolished for all practical purposes,[1] the dispute is by no means at an end. The issues raised by the death penalty are both terrible and primitive; in consequence, for many people the subject achieves a compelling fascination. The terror arises from the awesome nature of death, and the primitive element derives from the retributive attitude towards punishment – now intellectually unfashionable but still widely supported. *[handwritten margin note: ST]*

The campaign against capital punishment is divisible into three parts: attempts to end it for particular offences; the efforts to end public executions; the crusade for complete abolition. Many of the early reformers, e.g. Sir Samuel Romilly, were not in favour of the complete withdrawal of the death penalty. Romilly's motives were certainly humanitarian, but the central theme of his argument was that if the death penalty were removed from a wide range of minor offences then juries would be more willing to convict. The severity of sentence ceased to be a deterrent because wrong-doers knew that they had a high chance of escaping punishment altogether. In 1811 Romilly, with the support of cloth-makers, secured the abolition of the death penalty for the theft of cloth. The following year vagrancy by a soldier or seaman ceased to be a capital offence. In 1819 a Commons' Select Committee[2] recommended the repeal of many statutes demanding the death penalty which had fallen into disuse: included in this category were such offences as being armed and disguised in any forest, park, warren, high road, open heath, common or down; unlawfully hunting, killing or stealing deer; robbing warrens; making a false entry in a marriage register; impersonating pensioners of Greenwich Hospital. The Committee proposed that other, lesser penalties be imposed for these offences. Its recom- *[handwritten margin note: Harsh conviction 4 minor offences]*

---

[1] The death penalty still remains for treason, mutiny and certain other offences specified in the Armed Forces Act, 1966.

[2] *Select Committee on Criminal Laws*, 1819 (585), vii.

mendations had some influence and in 1820 came the end of the death penalty for shoplifting. Steadily the range of capital offences was reduced, often in spite of opposition from the House of Lords.[1] In 1830 the Commons received many petitions against the death penalty from bankers and traders, not 'upon any abstract principle of religion, or upon any view of humanity (but) . . . as practical men to object to the continuance of a punishment which they found to be injurious to their trade and interests'. After the 1832 Election the pace of reform accelerated. A Commission appointed in 1833 reported three years later that the death penalty should be restricted to treason and crimes of violence that endangered human life.[2] The Commission wanted certainty of punishment to replace severity of punishment as the main deterrent to crime. In 1834 there were but 34 executions in England in spite of the long list of offences which nominally demanded the death penalty. Capital punishment was abolished for cattle, horse and sheep stealing (1832), house-breaking (1833), return from transportation (1834), sacrilege and stealing from the Post Office (1835), coining and forgery (1836), burglary from dwelling-houses (1837), rape, rioting, and embezzlement by servants of the Bank of England (1841). By the 1840s the nature of the argument was changing. It was not only a question of which crimes required the supreme penalty but whether the death penalty should remain even for murder.

The first association for the abolition of capital punishment had been formed by some Quakers in 1808. Forty years later their views obtained a regular hearing in the Commons. Three years running, 1848, 1849 and 1850, William Ewart, assisted by John Bright, tried unsuccessfully to get the Commons to accept a Bill to end the death penalty. Among the opponents of capital punishment was Charles Dickens, who argued that 'it produces crime in the criminally disposed, and engenders a diseased sympathy – morbid and bad, but natural and often irresistible – among the well-conducted and gentle'.[3] Sympathy for the abolitionist cause was strengthened by growing distaste for public executions: in 1856 a Select Committee of the House of Lords reported unanimously in favour of ending them.[4] Ten years later a Royal Commission made a similar, although not unanimous, recommendation. Public executions were abolished in

[1] For further surveys see E. O. Tuttle: *The Crusade against Capital Punishment in Great Britain* (Stevens, 1961), Ch. I; and L. Radzinowicz: *A History of English Criminal Law and its Administration, from 1750* (Stevens, 1948).

[2] Criminal Law Commissioners, Second Report, pp. 19–38; 1836 (343), xxxvi.

[3] *Letters of Charles Dickens* (Chapman and Hall, 1882), Vol. III, pp. 78–9.

[4] 1856 (366), vii.

1868. A curious feature of this aspect of the controversy is that many of the strongest supporters of capital punishment were among the firmest advocates of execution in private: perhaps they felt that public opinion would allow the death penalty to continue only if the actual slaughter was swept under the carpet and hidden from public view.

Meanwhile in 1861 the list of capital crimes had been further restricted and only five remained; murder, high treason, mutiny, piracy and the destruction of public arsenals and dockyards.[1] Another demand by Ewart for a complete end to capital punishment in 1864 led to the appointment of a Royal Commission. This Commission, as noted above, urged the end of public executions, and it also attempted to grade murder into more or less heinous offences, the former requiring the death sentence. Intermittent efforts to formulate such a distinction have been made ever since and never with success. However, public and parliamentary interest in the subject began to wane, perhaps because public hanging ended, perhaps because murder became effectively the sole capital crime and thus execution could be justified by the simple 'eye for an eye, tooth for a tooth' argument. Whenever a vote was challenged in the Commons the abolitionists were soundly defeated and further reform came very slowly. The Children's Act, 1908, stopped the execution of persons below sixteen years of age. Infanticide ceased to be a capital crime in 1922 – this had been one of the recommendations from the Royal Commission in 1866. At least since 1848 it had been uniform practice to use the prerogative of mercy in such cases.[2] This illustrates another reason why statutory change was not achieved: the public were broadly satisfied that murderers were not in fact hanged if they did not deserve to be.

To end capital punishment has long been a standard target for penal reformers. This aim was followed by the Howard Association, founded in 1866, and by the Penal Reform League, established in 1907. These two bodies were amalgamated into the Howard League for Penal Reform in 1921. However, the major drive to secure abolition came from the National Council for the Abolition of the Death Penalty formed in 1925, largely through the energies of Roy Calvert. His book, *Capital Punishment in the Twentieth Century*, first published in 1927, became a classic statement of the case for reform, and aroused increasing concern. When the Labour Party returned to office in 1929 a Commons' Select Committee was appointed to

[1] Scottish law differed until 1887.
[2] 'The Punishment of Infanticide' *The Nineteenth Century* (1877), Vol. I, p. 584.

review the question of capital punishment. But the Labour Ministers showed no enthusiasm for reform and the Select Committee was forced upon an unwilling Cabinet by pressure from Labour and Liberal Members.[1]

The Report of the Select Committee[2] prepared by its Chairman, Rev. James Barr, is an impressive document which set out the history of capital punishment in this country in a compelling style and then analysed the arguments presented to the Committee in oral and written evidence. Much material was collected on the experience of countries which had abolished the death penalty, but the balance of opinion among British witnesses favoured its retention. The basic conclusion of the majority of the Select Committee was 'that Capital Punishment may be abolished in this country without endangering life or property or impairing the security of Society'.[3] It therefore recommended abolition for a trial period of five years. In addition, the Committee made a series of conditional recommendations, to be adopted should Parliament decide against total abolition, which suggested revisions to the M'Naghten Rules.[4] The impact of the proposals was substantially weakened by the controversy that had developed over the Committee's proceedings. The Committee had met regularly from December 1929, to July 1930, and heard a large number of witnesses from this country and abroad. These hearings left no time for the preparation of a report before the end of the parliamentary session 1929–30, so the Committee reported that its work was not completed and was reappointed for the following session. At the next meeting, on November 13, 1930, the Chairman produced a draft report recommending abolition; Conservative Members on the Committee pronounced this to be unacceptable and requested that the Committee adjourn until the New Year so that an alternative report could be prepared. The Committee rejected any delay by 7 votes to 6 and the Conservatives walked out of the committee-room. Subsequently the Chairman's report was accepted and presented to the House. It is sterile now to consider which side in the squabble could claim to have acted more reasonably. But the effect of the procedural conflict was to cloud the issue and divert attention from the material in the report. The Labour Government refused to find time for a debate on the report, and the Home

[1] H.C. Deb., Vol. 231, cols 241–93.
[2] 1930–31 (15), vi.
[3] *Ibid.*, p. xcvi.
[4] The M'Naghten rules are the test of irresponsibility in English criminal law and were formulated in 1843 at the trial of M'Naghten for assassinating Sir Robert Peel's secretary.

Secretary, Clynes, appeared to be very hostile to reform. In the summer of 1931 the Labour Government disintegrated, and the subsequent election of a new House of Commons with an unprecedented Conservative majority ruled out any hope of change.

Although the political climate had deteriorated, the abolitionists continued their efforts. A Parliamentary Penal Reform Group, formed after the 1931 Election, recruited 48 supporters. A quarterly publication, *The Penal Reformer*, appeared from 1934 to 1939 and included articles opposing the death penalty, including one from Sir Gervais Rentoul who had led the Conservative walk-out from the 1929 Select Committee. Another type of protest, which caused some embarrassment to other reformers, was the organization of a demonstration outside a prison whenever an execution was to take place. These demonstrations were arranged by a wealthy lady, Mrs Violet van der Elst. Her activities attracted considerable publicity and certainly increased public discussion of the death penalty, but the National Council for the Abolition of the Death Penalty feared that her activities might associate their cause in the public mind with an image of hysterical emotionalism. Yet Mrs van der Elst may have had more positive influence than those who favoured more orthodox forms of protest. In 1938, for the first time, the Commons carried a motion to abolish the death penalty, although only for a trial period of five years: this motion, introduced by a Conservative back-bencher, Captain Vyvyan Adams, was carried on a free vote by 114 votes to 89. The total number voting in the division was not large and the vote could scarcely claim to be representative of opinion in the House as a whole. But the vote gave encouragement to reformers and established a precedent that the issue was one to be decided without party whipping. An amendment to the Criminal Justice Bill, 1939, to end the death penalty was defeated in committee by 16 votes to 7, but the Bill itself was lost in the upheaval caused by the outbreak of war.

During the Second World War the capital punishment issue faded away, but the return of the Labour Government in 1945 raised the hopes of the abolitionists. The National Council again became active, much literature was circulated and the subject was fully ventilated in the correspondence columns of *The Times*. However, major obstacles blocked the way. It was not possible to promote a private members' Bill to secure abolition because the Cabinet, determined to press ahead with its complex programme of social and economic reform, allowed no time for back-bench legislative initiative between 1945 and 1948.[1] So the matter could be dealt with only as part of a

[1] Peter G. Richards: *Honourable Members* (Faber, 1964), pp. 201–2.

piece of government legislation. The second main difficulty was that senior Members of the Cabinet became hostile to the abolitionist cause, perhaps because they were elderly and had formed their basic social attitudes in the early years of the century when the death penalty controversy was at a low ebb. The Home Secretary, Chuter Ede, had voted for the trial five-year suspension in 1938 but was known not to have strong views: in office he became convinced by his official advisers that to end capital punishment would be a dangerous experiment. The Permanent Secretary to the Home Office, Sir Frank Newsam, was thought to be a stern opponent of abolition. All the opinion polls on the subject showed substantial majorities against a change in the law.

In 1945 the Howard League initiated the formation of a new Parliamentary Penal Reform Group comprising a number of sympathetic Members. When it became clear that the Government was likely to bring forward a Bill that would make a variety of changes to the criminal law, this Group circulated all Members except Ministers to discover the extent of support for abolition. 187 Members agreed to sign a memorial to the Home Secretary to support the abolition of the death penalty for a five-year period;[1] however, all but 16 of these were Labour Members. The Government refused to include any mention of the death penalty in their Bill but agreed that a clause proposing abolition might be moved at the report stage, when all Members could participate, and that as the issue was a matter of conscience a free vote would be permitted. Subsequently it was announced that the free vote would not extend to Ministers: government policy was opposed to abolition so Ministers could not be allowed to vote against it. Members of the Government – including junior Ministers and whips, who had misgivings about the death penalty – could do no more than abstain. Thus for the Labour Members, the 'free vote' was but a partial free vote. The abolitionist cause was weakened because some of their supporters were debarred from voting in support of their beliefs. It may be that Ministers thought that this stratagem would defeat the abolition amendment and so remove a source of embarrassment. In fact, the amendment, moved by Sydney Silverman (Lab. Nelson and Colne) was debated on April 15, 1948, and carried by 245 to 222. The most senior Members of the Government, Attlee, Morrison, Bevin and Ede, voted against the clause, but no fewer than 46 Ministers failed to vote, including Cripps, Bevan and Wilson.

[1] J. B. Christoph: *Capital Punishment in British Politics* (Allen & Unwin, 1962), p. 37. This book provides a detailed study of the capital punishment issue between 1947 and 1957.

Immediately the Government was placed in an intolerable situation. The Home Secretary had agreed in advance to accept the verdict of a free vote. So he had to try to secure a change in the law, against which he had argued forcibly in public. Such confusion may always arise should a Cabinet both take a stand on an issue and also allow a free vote. On June 2nd the Conservative-dominated House of Lords strongly upheld the death penalty and struck out the Silverman clause by 181 votes to 28. This was poor comfort for Labour Ministers who were traditionally opposed to the aristocratic power to interfere with legislation that passed the Commons. There was no possibility of a peers *v.* people battle when the Lords were protecting Ministers against their own party supporters and, indeed, were reflecting the results of public opinion surveys more accurately than the Commons. To try to extract themselves from the morass, the Government put forward a compromise to retain the death penalty for certain categories of murder which implied 'express malice'. Five such categories of murder were proposed: (i) Those committed in association with certain other crimes, notably robbery and assault. (ii) Those committed while evading arrest, obstructing a policeman or when held in custody. (iii) Those caused by the systematic administration of poison. (iv) The murder of a prison officer by a prisoner. (v) Second murders, where the accused had previously been convicted of murder. This formula satisfied neither the abolitionists nor the retentionists. It is easy to imagine hypothetical cases to illustrate the anomalies that must arise from this type of distinction. In spite of criticism from all quarters the Cabinet decided to force this scheme, designed as a five-year experiment, through the Commons by the whips. The abolitionists could do no more than support the Government clause in the hope that the manifest problems thereof would force further reforms at a later date. The Commons accepted the compromise by 307 to 209 on July 15th: the Lords rejected it as impractical by 99 to 19 on July 20th. So the Labour Government was confronted with yet another difficulty: if it insisted on retaining the compromise the whole of the Criminal Justice Bill would be lost, or delayed. Further, the machinery of the Parliament Act could not be used to overcome the Lords' veto as the disputed clause had not been part of the Bill when it first left the Commons. So two days later the Government abandoned the compromise clause. Subsequently the appointment of a Royal Commission to examine the question of capital punishment was announced.

The nomination of a Royal Commission is an orthodox escape route for Ministers faced with an intractable domestic problem. It eases the immediate pressure as the subject of the Commission's work becomes, in a sense, *sub judice*. Any demands for action can be countered by the claim that decisions must wait upon the Commission's report. Of course, the postponement is temporary. When the report appears, public attention will again be focused on the subject. But by then another party may be in power or the crystallization of opinion may make the solution of the problem easier. Further, by the manipulation of a Commission's terms of reference, Ministers may hope to influence the direction of subsequent discussion: the instructions to the Royal Commission on Capital Punishment were carefully framed to preclude a straight recommendation for or against the death penalty. They were 'to consider and report whether liability under the criminal law in Great Britain to suffer capital punishment for murder should be limited or modified, and if so, to what extent and by what means, for how long and under what conditions persons who would otherwise have been liable to suffer capital punishment should be detained, and what changes in the existing law and the prison system should be required; and to inquire into and take account of the position in those countries whose experience and practice may throw light on these questions'. Sir Ernest Gowers, veteran of other official enquiries, was appointed chairman. The other members brought together a wide range of experience and none appeared to be committed publicly to a point of view on the capital punishment controversy.

Depressed by its failure to secure an amendment to the Criminal Justice Bill, the National Council for the Abolition of the Death Penalty had amalgamated with the Howard League. Thus the Howard League became responsible for putting the abolitionist case before the Royal Commission. It presented evidence to the Commission and tried to persuade others of similar persuasion to do so. In particular, the League was concerned because the evidence presented by the Home Office, the prison officers and the police was all designed to uphold existing practice; the opinions of those in official quarters who held a contrary view were not expressed. Meanwhile the Commission proceeded with thorough and painstaking work. It laboured for four years, 1949–53, and collected much information concerning penal systems abroad. It examined the relation between criminal liability and mental abnormality, the procedure at murder trials, the use of the prerogative of mercy, alternatives to capital punishment and alternative methods of execution. The report[1] contained no fewer than 89 conclusions and

[1] 1952–53, Cmd, 8932, vii. For an incisive commentary on the report see Sir Geoffrey Vickers: *The Art of Judgment* (Chapman and Hall, 1965), pp. 60–6.

recommendations. Yet its central proposal was weak and widely condemned as thoroughly unsatisfactory.

The Attlee Government had defended the evasive instructions given to the Commission on the ground that the principle of capital punishment was one to be decided by Parliament: Parliament, it seemed, did not need any help or advice on the basic principle. The Commission was pushed back on to secondary questions, notably whether there should be degrees of murder. Here the answer of the Commission was forthright. 'It is impracticable to frame a statutory definition of murder which would effectively limit the scope of capital punishment.' The Commission also stated firmly 'the outstanding defect of the law of murder is that it provides a single punishment for a crime widely varying in culpability'. The method of mitigating the penalty to fit the crime by the use of the Royal Prerogative was found to be unsatisfactory. The Commission did not accept that a judge should have discretion to impose a sentence less than death for a convicted murderer; instead it suggested that the jury should be empowered to substitute life imprisonment as an alternative penalty. This is the proposal which subsequently met a gale of criticism. Perhaps the Commission expected the idea to be unacceptable, for their recommendation No. 46 read: 'We recognize that the disadvantages of a system of "jury discretion" may be thought to outweigh its merits. If this view were to prevail, the conclusion would seem to be inescapable that in this country a stage has been reached where little more can be done effectively to limit the liability to suffer the death penalty, and that the issue is now whether capital punishment should be retained or abolished.'

Granted their terms of reference, the report was favourable to the abolitionist cause because it rejected the concept of degrees of murder. Its publication also gave fresh impetus to the death penalty issue, an interest further stimulated in 1953 by two cases which cast grave doubt on the administration of existing law. The first concerned two young men, Craig, aged sixteen, and Bentley, aged nineteen, who had broken into a warehouse. In attempting to escape from the police, Craig shot and killed a police officer. At the time of the shooting Bentley was already in police custody. Both Bentley and Craig were charged with murder because of the doctrine of constructive malice which requires that anyone who has a common purpose with someone else must assume common responsibility for whatever may happen in the pursuit of the common aim. Thus Bentley was found guilty of murder, but the jury made a recommendation for mercy. Craig could not be executed as he was below the age of eighteen. No reprieve was forthcoming for Bentley, and he was hanged. The Home Secretary's inaction caused widespread astonishment. There was no evidence that Bentley had incited Craig to use a gun. As the army had rejected Bentley for low intelligence, it seems impossible that he could have understood the legal doctrine of constructive malice. Ignorance of the law is no excuse, but it is still a factor that may be taken into account when the use of the prerogative of mercy is under consideration. The second case concerned the Rillington Place murders. In 1949 a man named Evans confessed to the police that he had murdered his wife and child; subsequently he retracted the confession and accused Christie, who lived in the same house in Rillington Place. Evans was convicted and executed. Four years later it was discovered that several women had been murdered in this house in Rillington Place. Christie confessed to all these murders, including that of Mrs Evans. Had the Evans jury known the true character of Christie, it is inconceivable that their verdict would have been the same. Christie's conviction forced the Home Secretary to order a fresh enquiry into the Evans' case; this enquiry, undertaken by J. Scott Henderson, Q.C., was thoroughly unsatisfactory. It was decided that the investigation had to be completed prior to Christie's execution, so the job was rushed and completed in a few days. The proceedings were held in private. The Scott Henderson Report concluded that the conviction of Evans was fully justified and was derided at the time – and since – as Home Office whitewash.[1] (A further enquiry in 1966 by Mr Justice Brabin concluded that it was more probable than not that Evans did not kill his daughter; this was the charge for which he had been executed, so Evans was granted a posthumous Free Pardon.) Thus in 1953 two executions were the cause of major dispute. One victim had certainly not committed murder personally: the guilt of the other was open to serious doubt. Home Office reaction to both cases was essentially one of self-protection, combined with a resolve to sustain police morale. A Home Secretary is not accountable to Parliament for individual decisions made in relation to the prerogative of mercy, so why Sir David Maxwell-Fyfe refused to reprieve Bentley is not known. One suspects that he feared that a reprieve linked to the shooting of a policeman would have been resented by the police.

A third execution, in 1955, aroused even more public concern. Here the reputation of the police was in no way involved. This was a *crime passionnel*. Mrs Ruth Ellis killed one of her lovers a few days after he had assaulted her and caused her to have a miscarriage. Subsequently Mrs Ellis was convicted of murder and hanged.

[1] L. Kennedy: *10, Rillington Place* (Gollancz, 1961) contains the text of the report and a searing critique of it.

Obviously the sex of the murderer added enormously to the public interest. The Royal Commission had recommended that the penalty for murder must apply equally to men and women and no feminist would argue for other than equal treatment. But quite apart from these considerations one might have expected the earlier assault on Mrs Ellis to have provided enough element of mitigation to justify a reprieve.

Over a year elapsed after the publication of the Royal Commission's Report before it was considered by the Commons. In February 1955 the House debated a Government motion to 'take note' of the report.[1] The Home Secretary, Major Lloyd George, was critical of the major recommendations of the Commission. Sydney Silverman moved an amendment to suspend capital punishment which was defeated by 245 to 214. The Lords had discussed the report briefly in December 1953, when the principle of jury discretion was criticized severely both by peers opposed to the death penalty and by those in favour of it.

In spite of this lack of progress at the parliamentary level, a new burst of activity by abolitionists developed in the latter half of 1955. A National Campaign for the Abolition of Capital Punishment was announced and a number of publications favourable to the cause appeared, including *Capital Punishment: the Heart of the Matter*,[2] by Victor Gollancz; Sir Ernest Gowers' *A Life for a Life?*;[3] Arthur Koestler's *Reflections on Hanging*;[4] Gerald Gardiner's *Capital Punishment as a Deterrent and the Alternative*.[5] These books varied greatly in style. Gollancz and Koestler produced vigorous and emotional prose. Gowers, as Chairman of the Royal Commission, was doubtless more influential, while Gardiner's careful analysis was perhaps most persuasive to the legal profession. The hanging of Ruth Ellis, together with the Bentley and Evans–Christie cases, had heightened public interest in the issue. The obvious technique for raising the question in Parliament was through a private member's Bill. J. McGovern (Lab. Shettleston) won third ballot place in the autumn of 1955 and was expected to introduce an abolition Bill. However, he was absent from the Commons on the day for balloted Bills to be introduced and so lost his chance. Silverman thereupon introduced a measure under the Ten-Minute Rule and this was read a first time without opposition. A Bill promoted under this procedure

[1] H.C. Deb., Vol. 536, cols 2064–184.
[2] Gollancz, 1955.
[3] Chatto & Windus, 1956.
[4] Macmillan, 1957.
[5] Gollancz, 1956.

normally goes no further as no time is available for its consideration. The opponents of the Bill apparently decided to kill the Bill by silence rather than risk a vote which they might lose. Since February 1955 the parliamentary scene had changed. A general election had increased the Conservative majority, not *per se* a movement favourable to reform, but the new House had an influx of younger Members who were more favourable to abolition. Indeed, none of the events of the next two years would have been possible without the development of a group of stalwart Tory abolitionists.

Underground restiveness among some of their own back-benchers convinced Ministers that some action was necessary. In February 1956 a government motion invited the Commons to agree that the death penalty should be retained but that the law of murder should be amended. Ministers were probably influenced by a set of proposals published by the Inns of Court Conservative and Unionist Association; these proposals emanated from a committee working under the chairmanship of Sir Lionel Heald (Con. Chertsey) a former Attorney-General. The Heald Committee urged the Government to accept, perhaps in modified form, the Royal Commission's recommendations on constructive malice, provocation and diminished responsibility. These were technical issues. Nevertheless, they provided the occasion for a challenge on the central principle. The abolitionists moved an amendment to the Government motion; on a free vote they were victorious by 293 votes to 262. Forty-eight Conservatives opposed the death penalty and 8 Labour Members supported it.

Immediately the Eden Government was faced with the same dilemma as that which had confronted the Attlee Government in 1948. They had expressed an opinion, allowed a free vote and were left with a parliamentary resolution hostile to their own policy. The Government attempted to resolve the problem by providing time for the further consideration of Silverman's Bill which would not be subject to formal party discipline. This led to substantial unofficial whipping among opposing groups of Conservatives. Angus Maude[1] and Peter Kirk[2] organized the abolitionists. John Eden (Bournemouth, West) and Colonel Crosthwaite Eyre (New Forest) led the retentionists and created an *ad hoc* office in a Members' interviewing room in the Palace of Westminster; weekly whips were issued to supporters, pairs were arranged for divisions and tellers were appointed.[3] Amidst all this activity the Bill continued its passage

---

[1] Member for Ealing South 1950–58 and Stratford-on-Avon since 1963.
[2] Member for Gravesend 1955–64 and Saffron Walden since 1965.
[3] Christoph, pp. 142–3.

through the Commons and the second reading was carried by 286 votes to 262. The committee stage subsequently occupied the whole House for two and a half days when hostile amendments were discussed. In all, there were eight divisions in committee. The opponents of the Bill scored a single and temporary victory when, by a majority of 4, it was agreed that the death penalty should be retained for a murder committed by a person serving a sentence of life imprisonment; this decision was reversed at the report stage. The Bill was then defeated in the Lords by 238 votes to 95. Thus the pattern of 1948 was repeated. However, the size of the abolitionist vote in the Upper House had increased substantially. Clerical opinion was heavily in favour; two archbishops and eight bishops supported the Bill, only one bishop, Rochester, opposed it. The high total of peers taking part in the division implied that many who attended were rarely seen in Westminster. Commented the *Spectator* '. . . the retentionist army was largely composed of hitherto unknown rustics who thought, perhaps, that abolition was in some way a threat to blood sports'.

In 1948 there had been no executions during the period when the Commons had accepted legislation to end the death penalty. This precedent was followed in 1956 and, if only for this reason, the Lord's decision created a situation which could not remain unaltered. The abolitionists hoped that the Government would adhere to its policy for providing time for a private member's Bill: this could pass through the Commons again in the session 1956–57 and become law under the provisions of the Parliament Act, 1949, even if their Lordships still objected. Yet it was unrealistic to expect a Conservative Government to agree to overcome the peers' veto to secure the passage of a measure which it had itself opposed. There were also strong pressures on the Government to re-establish its authority by insisting on a compromise. *The Times*, which had vacillated on the issue, now urged Ministers to impose a middle way. Dr Fisher, Archbishop of Canterbury, had supported the Silverman Bill only because the Government refused to sponsor a compromise measure. And there was much support in the Conservative Party for the proposals of the Heald Committee. To the fury of the abolitionists, the Government announced it would promote its own Bill to permit partial retention of the death penalty. Further, the Government would not provide extra facilities for a private member's Bill on the subject: such a measure would have to take its chance in the ballot and with the limited time available for balloted Bills. When the ballot was held, Labour Members fared very badly and secured but 3 out of the 20 places; even worse, the highest place was eighth.

Then only the first six Bills were certain to be voted upon so a death penalty Bill could be talked out. The Bill, introduced by the Member with the eighth place, Miss Alice Bacon (Leeds, S.E.) duly failed through lack of time. The Bill was the second on the Order Paper for February 1 1957; the preceding measure was the Advertisements (Hire Purchase) Bill, and Miss Bacon's supporters claimed that the speeches on this topic became unduly lengthy as a filibuster to protect the death penalty.[1]

The Government's measure, which became the Homicide Act, 1957, adopted the Scottish doctrine of diminished responsibility as the test for criminal responsibility, and abolished the doctrine of constructive malice. It also did what the Gowers Commission had advised was impossible – created categories of murder. The death penalty was kept solely for offences defined as capital murders – killing in the course of theft, the killing of policemen and prison officers, killing by shooting or causing an explosion, and committing murder on separate occasions. These categories were designed to deter professional criminals and were not related to the heinousness of any particular crime. Thus the poisoner and the strangler could not be executed provided he had but a single victim, but Mrs Ellis would still be eligible to hang because she had shot her lover. Obviously, the abolitionists paraded these anomalies in efforts to change the Government Bill. The fate of the measure depended entirely on the attitude of the forty-odd Tory abolitionists in the Commons and these Members were subjected to intense pressure. Most of them were interviewed by the Chief Whip.[2] No doubt, they were exhorted to consider the merits of the Government proposals, which would substantially reduce the number of executions, and also were warned of personal political consequences if they defied party discipline and failed to support the Government. There were also pressures from the constituencies: Nigel Nicolson felt obliged to change his vote, but not his opinion, because of the reaction of his electors in Bournemouth.[3] Thus it is unsurprising that the Tory abolitionists accepted the Government compromise. The subject had been debated interminably and had become a bore. They could fairly claim to have forced a major liberalization of government policy. And it places an intolerable strain on a Member to defy party discipline and incur active constituency hostility on the same issue. So the Bill passed through both Houses unchanged. The

[1] H.C. Deb., Vol. 563, cols 1323–1414.
[2] Christoph, p. 154.
[3] N. Nicolson: *People and Parliament* (Weidenfeld and Nicolson, 1958), Ch. 4.

principles of degrees of murder was established on the statute book and became an automatic target for criticism in subsequent efforts to secure the complete elimination of the death penalty.

For a while the issue subsided. The National Campaign suspended its activities after the passage of the 1957 Act. The increased Conservative majority in the Commons after the 1959 Election was not encouraging. However, the National Campaign opened a new crusade in December 1960; leading figures in this movement included Lord Altrincham, the Earl of Harewood, Gerald Gardiner, Q.C., and Victor Gollancz. In 1961 another organization with diametrically opposed aims appeared: the Anti-Violence League sought to rally public support for increased penalties for crimes of violence and an extended use of the death penalty. This body held a number of meetings but then faded away. Far more important was the movement of opinion among religious bodies. In October 1961 the Lower House of the Convocation of Canterbury accepted a motion favouring the abolition of the death penalty or its suspension for five years, and preaching in Canterbury Cathedral the Bishop of Woolwich predicted that 'hanging will go at the next really big push'. In January 1962 the bishops in the Canterbury province, meeting as the Upper House, unanimously endorsed the opinion of the Lower House. In April the same view was adopted by the British Council of Churches without dissent. Roman Catholic theology provides no firm guidance on capital punishment; many individual Catholics actively supported reform and the hierarchy was not opposed to it.

In March 1963 the parliamentary leaders of the abolition campaign, Sydney Silverman, Chuter Ede, former Labour Home Secretary, Peter Kirk, Julian Critchley (Con. Rochester) and Jeremy Thorpe (Lib. North Devon) met the Home Secretary, R. A. Butler: according to *The Times* report, the Minister held out no hope of change in the law during the lifetime of the present Parliament, and did not want the issue left to a free vote because it was a free vote that led to the anomalies now disturbing the judiciary and the lawyers. Four days later *The Times* published a letter from Gerald Gardiner pointing out that government whips were responsible for the Homicide Act and the anomalies therein.[1] The Conservative Party still opposed change, but not unanimously. The 1961 Party Conference approved the retention of the death penalty by an overwhelming majority, yet a resolution urging abolition was carried by a Conference of Young Conservatives by a majority that appeared to be about two to one.[2]

Meanwhile a series of cases emphasized the unsatisfactory con-

[1] March 9, 1963.　　[2] *The Times*, Feb. 18, 1963.

D

dition of the law of murder as it had been left by the 1957 Act.[1]
A comparison of two murders in 1958 demonstrates inequity. A man
who was known to have a hoard of money was killed and robbed
by a fellow lodger named Collier. There was little doubt that the
murderous attack was motivated by a wish to steal. Collier was
convicted of capital murder, condemned to death and reprieved.
Another man, Stokes, battered an old woman to death and subsequently stole a wallet. Stokes was executed. Perhaps because his
victim was an elderly woman, Stokes suffered harsher treatment; in
fact, the circumstances were such that it is questionable whether
Stokes was guilty of capital murder. The old woman was to employ
him as a gardener and there had been a quarrel over the rate of pay.
Then she had bent down to get some tools out of a cupboard and he
hit her about the head and killed her. Subsequently Stokes found a
wallet in her possession and stole it; he was convicted of capital
murder because the murder was committed in furtherance of theft.
The crime was a ghastly one: one would not wish to minimize the
horror in any way. Yet there must be serious doubt about the verdict.
Is it not likely that the attack was caused by the anger generated by
the argument? Was the robbery an after-thought? It is difficult to
avoid the conclusion that Stokes was executed for theft, not for
murder.

It was also a shock, even to informed opinion, that after the 1957
Act one could be guilty of capital murder who had not intended to
kill or, indeed, had not even caused a death. The case of Gypsy
Smith caused much argument in legal circles. Smith had committed
a robbery and was escaping by car when a policeman tried to stop
him and jumped on the running-board of his car. Smith drove the
car in such a way as to make the policeman fall off and, in falling,
the policeman was killed. The defence, obviously, was that Smith
had no intention or desire to kill the policeman. However, Mr
Justice Donovan's direction to the jury asserted that the intention
of the accused was irrelevant. Smith was convicted but the verdict
was reversed by the Court of Criminal Appeal. In order to clarify the
law, the Government announced that the case would be carried to
the House of Lords but, whatever the outcome, Smith would not be
executed. The Law Lords then reversed the decision of the Court of
Criminal Appeal. Yet more disturbing was the outcome of the
Hounslow footpath murder in 1960. A gang of four young men
attacked a victim on a footpath with the admitted intention of robbery. One man, Lutt, struck the victim and knocked him to the

[1] For a further discussion see Christopher Hollis: *The Homicide Act* (Gollancz,
1964).

ground. A second man, Harris, put his hand inside the victim's pocket but, finding nothing there, then withdrew. The victim shouted for help and to silence him a third member of the gang, Forsyth, kicked him on the head and killed him. The fourth man, Darby, was merely a spectator, although an associate of the others. As a result, Harris and Forsyth were hanged. Lutt was also found guilty of capital murder but, being only seventeen, was below the minimum age for execution. Darby was found guilty of non-capital murder. The question, of course, is whether Lutt and Harris should be regarded as guilty of capital murder. In particular, the Harris case was an acute issue since he was executed and had struck no blow. The justification for the verdict rested on Section 5(2) of the 1957 Homicide Act which provides that in the case of any death falling within the categories of capital murder if 'two or more persons are guilty of the murder, it shall be capital murder in the case of any of them who by his own act caused the death of, or inflicted or attempted to inflict grievous bodily harm on, the person murdered, or who himself used force on that person in the course or furtherance of an attack on him'. The case against Harris was that he must have used an element of force in restraining the victim when he put his hand in his pocket. This seemed a slender basis on which to hang a man when other murderers were in no danger of execution.

It was never possible, of course, to obtain any explanation of a Home Secretary's decision in these cases because parliamentary debate is restricted on any matter that touches the Royal Prerogative. A general statement of criteria used in considering whether to grant a reprieve was presented to the Gowers Commission, but in relation to any particular case, Home Office lips were tightly sealed. No doubt, it would have been intolerable had Parliament been able to debate any murder case at the stage when life was at stake: when fifty Members signed a motion dissenting from the decision not to reprieve Bentley, the Speaker ordered the motion to be deleted from the Order Paper.[1] Yet whether the Home Secretary was justified in refusing to issue any explanation of individual decisions was a matter of some controversy, particularly as the consequences of the 1957 Act became apparent.[2]

Inevitably the anomalies inherent in the Homicide Act became a central feature of the abolitionist case. In April 1964, Harold Wilson, Leader of the Labour Opposition, explained the Party's attitude to the Society of Labour Lawyers: 'It is generally agreed that the

[1] H.C. Deb., Vol. 510, col. 854.
[2] See G. Marshall: 'Parliament and the Prerogative of Mercy', *Public Law* (1961), pp. 8–25.

(Homicide) Act has neither a rational nor a moral basis, and few can be found to defend the present law. We feel that, as this is an issue on which people have strong views and is to some an issue of conscience, it should be left to a free vote of the House, and we are prepared to find Government time for it. On this sort of issue the House of Commons is at its best when each member is expressing his own individual view.' It was clearly good tactics for Labour to insist that the matter should be left to a free vote because this made it virtually inevitable that the Conservative Party would have to do the same. This would make matters easier for the Tory opponents of capital punishment. After Labour had won the 1964 Election, Wilson's pledge was carried out: a sentence in the Queen's Speech read, 'Facilities will be provided for a free decision by Parliament on the issue of capital punishment'. Here was a constitutional oddity. A Bill was mentioned in the Queen's Speech on which the Government, as such, did not express an opinion and which was subsequently introduced by a back-bencher, Sydney Silverman. There is no doubt that some of the procedural wrangles that developed over the Bill were due to its curious parentage.

The Murder (Abolition of the Death Penalty) Bill received its second reading on December 21, 1964, by 355 votes to 170,[1] a substantially higher majority than that achieved in the parallel divisions in 1956. However, trouble started immediately after the second reading when a further resolution that the Bill be committed to a committee of the whole House was defeated by 229 votes to 247. The opponents of the Bill wanted the committee stage to be taken in the Chamber, rather than in Standing Committee 'upstairs', as this would embarrass the Government by consuming valuable government time and, further, it might then become easier to slip through a wrecking amendment. When this move was defeated, bitter complaints were heard that Government whips had been 'put on' to ensure that the Bill was sent to Standing Committee in spite of ministerial promises of a free vote. To this the Labour Government replied that the free vote applied solely to the principle of capital punishment, not to the use of government time in the House. At this stage the dispute began to take on a party character, for tension over the use of parliamentary time was aggravated by the minute Government majority of 5 and the virtual certainty that the next General Election could not be long delayed. This explains the disparity between the two divisions; of the 82 Tories who supported the second reading, 71 supported the motion to commit the Bill to the whole House.

[1] H.C. Deb., Vol. 703, cols 870–1010.

The Bill was considered at five meetings of a standing committee. Progress was slow but all hostile amendments were defeated by substantial majorities. Yet an unusual element of chaos entered the proceedings: on one occasion there was such confusion when a vote was taken that the result of the vote was clearly contrary to the wishes of Members and the formal record had to be revised at a subsequent meeting.[1] Then on March 5, 1965, a Conservative opponent of the Bill, Forbes Hendry (Aberdeenshire, W.), who had been successful in the ballot to move a private member's motion, used his opportunity to propose that the Bill be recalled from standing committee to the floor of the House. Normally such motions are used to initiate debates on matters of policy but it is quite legitimate, although unusual, to introduce a motion that affects the procedure of the House. The motion took Silverman and his supporters by surprise: it was debated on a Friday when many Members visit their constituencies, especially when it is known that the business consists of private members' motions. So Hendry's motion was carried by 128 votes to 120.[2]

Government reaction to this situation was to propose an amendment to the Standing Orders of the House so that the House would have extra meetings on Wednesday mornings to deal with the committee stage of the Silverman Bill:[3] with the Government whips on, and Tory abolitionists opposing the Government, this proposition was carried by 299 votes to 229. Nine Wednesday mornings were occupied in this way. The arrangement caused more inconvenience to Conservative than to Labour Members because the former have more extensive business connections and, therefore, tend to have more morning engagements away from the Palace of Westminster. During these additional sittings many detailed amendments to the Bill were debated and defeated. The proposal to retain capital punishment for a person who murders on a second occasion was lost by 138 to 237; for the murder of a policeman in the execution of his duty by 115 to 165; for the murder of a prison officer in the execution of his duty by 105 to 157; for a murder in furtherance of theft by 78 to 180; for murder by shooting or causing an explosion by 76 to 180. There was also much inconclusive discussion on the alternative to the death penalty. The abolitionists suffered a single defeat – on the proposal that the Bill remain in force for five years only and thereafter should apply only as a result of affirmative resolutions by both Houses: this was carried by the quite substantial

[1] Cf. Proceedings of Standing Committee C for Feb. 10 and 17, 1965.
[2] H.C. Deb., Vol. 707, cols 1701–1812.
[3] H.C. Deb., Vol. 708, cols 1486–1616.

majority of 176 to 128. The report stage ran over two days, one of them a Friday.[1] The House accepted that life imprisonment should be the penalty for murder and rejected by 196 to 83 that the sentence should be of indefinite duration subject only to the prerogative of mercy. (The term 'life imprisonment' is less fearsome than it sounds, for a person serving such a sentence may be released at any time at the discretion of the Home Secretary: depending on the circumstances of each case, bearing in mind especially the issue of public safety, many convicted murderers nominally imprisoned for life are released after serving about ten years.) Finally, the third reading was agreed to just after midnight on July 14, 1965, by 200 votes to 98.[2]

The House of Lords accepted the Bill by substantial majorities: the second reading was carried by 204 to 104 and the third reading by 169 to 75. The reasons for this change of heart are discussed below.[3] One hostile amendment at the committee stage was narrowly defeated by a majority of four votes, 55 to 59; this sought to make the Bill expire after the five-year trial period instead of permitting its continuance subject to an affirmative resolution in both Houses. Two amendments introduced by the Lords were subsequently accepted by the Commons without a division. They permit a judge to recommend a minimum period of incarceration for a murderer sentenced to life imprisonement and require that the Lord Chief Justice be consulted before a convicted murderer is let out on licence.[4]

II

What should be the purpose of punishment? This question lies at the heart of the controversy over the death penalty. It is commonly agreed that there are three alternative justifications for punishment-reform, retribution and deterrence.[5] The reformative theory, if it means that a criminal should be enabled ultimately to return to a normal and useful life in the community, can have no meaning where capital punishment is used. The retribution idea has at least two forms. In essence, it may be a desire for vengeance; the murderer should pay for what he had done on the basis of 'an eye for an eye, a tooth for a tooth'. Here is a simple formula with a strong appeal. It is not a concept which is so attractive to the more liberal, civilized

[1] H.C. Deb., Vol. 715, cols 2113–2209 and Vol. 716, cols 358–408.
[2] H.C. Deb., Vol. 716, cols 408–66.
[3] P. 59, *infra*.
[4] H.C. Deb., Vol. 718, cols 365–99.
[5] For an excellent discussion of their application to capital punishment, see the report of the 1949 Royal Commission, pp. 17–24.

or sophisticated mind and the Royal Commission found scant support for this attitude among its witnesses. Yet there is clear evidence that the retribution theory enjoys widespread support: a Gallup Poll enquiry in February 1965 showed that 44 per cent agreed with the proposition that the first concern of the courts when sentencing a criminal should be to punish him for what he had done to others. A rather different form of retribution theory as applied to capital punishment is that because society regards murder as infinitely more serious than other crimes it must signal this abhorrence by the imposition of a penalty of unique severity.

Without doubt, the essence of the argument is whether capital punishment is an effective deterrent. It has no effect on crimes of passion, committed in the heat of a moment, where the murderer afterwards has bitter regrets for his deed. It can have no effect where the murderer has no concern for his own life, perhaps because of mental abnormality, perhaps because of an overwhelming desire to kill. After the 1957 Homicide Act a lecturer named Walden shot and killed his girl-friend while she was talking to another man: had the murder been done with a knife, the death penalty could not have been invoked. Walden decided to use a gun because he could not trust himself to use a knife. It is also certain that the law cannot deter if it is not understood. How many people understood the doctrine of constructive malice or the complex provision of the 1957 Homicide Act which led to the execution of Harris? But if the death penalty is a deterrent, it is likely to affect professional criminals who may be expected to consider the various risks they incur. Remove the fear of death, it is argued, and these men are more likely to carry guns and kill in order to escape detection and arrest. This could lead to an explosion of violence and a demand that the police, and perhaps some security guards, should carry guns. To predict how people will react when conditions change is always risky. The Royal Commission collected information from countries throughout the world where the death penalty had been terminated; after warning that it was difficult to draw firm conclusions from the statistics as social conditions varied so greatly, the Commission accepted that there was no clear evidence that to end the death penalty was likely to cause an increase in murder. It showed that over the previous half-century only 1 murderer in 12 had been executed as the remainder had escaped detection or conviction, had committed suicide, had been insane or had been reprieved. Can a penalty deter if the chances of its imposition are so slight? After the 1957 Homicide Act the number of executions fell to about 4 a year, so 1 murderer in 35 suffered the supreme penalty. Viewed purely as a deterrent, the hangman could not seem very effective. Indeed, by 1965 the deterrence theme seemed so flimsy that one suspects that many of those who struggled to keep the death penalty did, in fact, subscribe to some form of retribution theory, although this was rarely evident because retribution is not intellectually respectable and may be classed as unchristian.

Other kinds of argument were used to support capital punishment. The police and prison staff favoured it. They are more exposed to violence from professional criminals than the rest of the community. Since, rightly or wrongly, they believed that the spectre of the hangman added to their security, it could be claimed that they should receive this support and assurance. Amendments to retain the death penalty for the murder of police or warders were voted down for they necessarily implied that the life of a policeman or a prison officer was more precious than the life of anyone else. The major hindrance to reform was public opinion. All the survey results showed a heavy majority in favour of keeping the death penalty. In June 1962 the Gallup Poll showed that 19 per cent supported the abolitionist cause; in July 1964 the figure had risen to 21 per cent, and in February 1965 to 23 per cent. In June 1966, 76 per cent thought that the death penalty should be reintroduced, only 18 per cent thought it should not, while the remaining 6 per cent were 'Don't Knows'. These figures gave Members opposed to reform the mantle of good democrats who truly represented the opinions of their constituents, and gave much encouragement to their efforts to prevent change. A further demonstration against Silverman's success came at the 1966 General Election when an Independent candidate stood in Silverman's constituency of Nelson and Colne specifically to oppose the abolition of the death penalty: the Independent, Patrick Downey, won over 5,000 supporters and 13 per cent of the total poll – an unusual degree of success for an independent at a general election.[1]

Abolitionist Members could react to the unmistakable evidence of the balance of opinion only by the assertion that it was the task of Parliament to lead opinion, not merely to follow it. The Burke theory of representation always gives comfort, or excuse, to a Member hard-pressed by his constituents. It is also easier to resist the views of others where a moral principle is at stake. 'Thou shalt not kill' is a command which, so the abolitionists argued, should apply also to the state and its servants. The hangman is a murderer, even though his action has been legitimized by the state. The

[1] Humphrey Berkeley, a Tory abolitionist who lost his seat at Lancaster in the same election, described the result at Nelson and Colne as the 'most melancholy in the whole campaign'. *The Times*, May 21, 1966.

community does not signal its abhorrence of murder by giving permission to kill. Those who believe that human life is a divine gift may well feel that to deliberately destroy human life is to act contrary to divine will. Obviously not all the abolitionist Members were motivated by religious considerations: probably all of them were profoundly disturbed by what they felt to be the antique barbarity of the actual process of execution. The detailed description of the method of execution in the Royal Commission's Report[1] doubtless strengthened the abolitionist cause. The death penalty was also open to attack because of its irreversible character: an error could not subsequently be corrected. Many people believe that British justice made a mistake over the Rillington Place murders. The abolitionists also successfully attacked the deterrence theory and after 1957 were further assisted by the anomalies in the Homicide Act.

After the 1964 Election, Silverman and his supporters were over-confident. They had a clear majority in the Commons; the Lords with its changed composition was much less hostile; the Government had promised to find parliamentary time; the attitude of the church was more favourable; a large part of the principle they sought to establish had been obtained in 1957 under far worse political con-ditions. Indeed, the passage of the 1965 Bill seemed at first to be nothing more than a minor mopping-up operation. Even the Home Secretary, Sir Frank Soskice, was in favour. Previous Home Secretaries had been hostile or unsympathetic, although they com-monly changed their minds, irrespective of party, after leaving office; the leading examples are Sir Samuel Hoare, Chuter Ede and Henry Brooke. In the past the Home Office influence, designed to conciliate the police and prison officers, had swayed its political leadership. By 1965 this influence was no longer effective.

Yet what appeared to be a simple operation ran into serious difficulties. The basic reason was public opinion. On the one hand there was strong support for the retention of the death penalty as demonstrated by opinion polls. The amount of constituency pressure on Members varied, but it was almost wholly hostile to Silverman's Bill. Opinion was inflamed by some peculiarly revolting child murders – which were strictly irrelevant to the immediate controversy since the murderers were not liable to be hanged and even before the 1957 Act might well have been reprieved. People with valuable possessions also feared robbery and objected to anything that seemed to make the law softer for criminals. So the Bill's opponents were encouraged to make a final stand. Public opinion also affected the pattern of events by producing a virtual dead-heat between the

[1] pp. 240–72.

Conservative and Labour Parties at the 1964 Election. The Government's majority of five, later reduced to three, produced a degree of political tension that gravely aggravated the procedural arguments over the Bill.

The curious constitutional position offered an easy target for criticism. Silverman's Bill was a private member's Bill for which the Government had agreed, in advance, to find time. Retentionists argued that the principle of free voting should be applied to all divisions on the Bill and protested bitterly when the Government whip was applied to send it to a standing committee: as shown above, the Government's case was that free voting applied to the substance of the measure but not to procedural motions, as these affected the use of government time. Alternatively, the critics argued that Silverman's Bill was really a Government Bill; Ministers supported it and found time for it. Therefore they should accept responsibility for it. Was not the Government using private member's Bill procedure as a device to avoid associating themselves formally with a measure they knew to be unpopular? To this Ministers could answer that free voting had become traditional on capital punishment and that the Labour Party had made clear its intentions on the subject before the previous Election.

Reginald Paget (Lab. Northampton) became the whip to co-ordinate the efforts of the abolitionists. He divided his supporters into lists and secured the assistance of a number of helpers, with each helper in charge of a list. The retentionists did not admit to having a parallel organization. They held meetings to discuss tactics and the convenor was Sir Richard Glyn (Con. North Dorset). However, they disagreed amongst themselves over how far the death penalty should be used; many wished for its application to be extended and regarded opposition to the Silverman Bill as a holding operation prior to an amendment of the law in the reverse direction. These dissentions had no significant effect on the debate as the task of the retentionists was merely to oppose. Nor were the abolitionists wholly united. Most of those who voted for the second reading of Silverman's Bill opposed the death penalty on principle, but some felt that the position created by the 1957 Homicide Act was intolerable and that to end the death penalty was the best solution available to an impossible situation. This is the chief explanation of why 42 Members who voted for the second reading also supported the clause that requires the continuation of the Bill after July 1970 to be subject to an affirmative resolution in both Houses. Nevertheless, the majority in favour of this clause, 176 to 128, was surprisingly large. The vote was taken at lunch time, after the House had sat up for the whole of the previous night discussing the Budget, and the exhaustion of Members may have had some effect on the figures. Certainly the abolitionist whipping was not effective on this occasion and it had failed also on the earlier vote to bring the Bill back from standing committee to the floor of the House. Both Silverman and Paget were absent from the division which put the Bill on trial for five years, the former being out of the country. It is also the case that Paget's status in the Labour Party was declining: although a member of the Shadow Government when the Party was in opposition he had not been given a post in the Wilson Government.

Thus, in spite of starting with excellent prospects, the abolitionists secured but an incomplete victory. No attempt was made to reverse the five-year limitation on the report stage. Even had it been possible to reverse this vote in the Commons, it seemed certain that the Lords would restore the clause. This would have involved the loss of the whole Bill, and in the uncertain political climate of 1965 there could be no guarantee of passing the Bill through the Commons in the next session in order to overcome a Lords' veto. The attitude of the Upper House had changed substantially since 1957, mainly because the active membership had been changed by the introduction of life peers. The bishops were also more favourable to reform and the law lords were conscious of the anomalies created by the 1957 Homicide Act. But in spite of a 2 to 1 majority at second reading in favour of the principle of the Silverman Bill, there remained a firm desire to place the reform on probation by imposing a five-year limit. A proposal that the Bill should expire after five years, instead of continuing subject to affirmative resolutions in both Houses, was rejected by a hair's breadth, 59 to 55. In retrospect, Silverman and his associates would have done better to wait until the 1966 Parliament, when the abolition of the death penalty might well have been accepted without the automatic reconsideration clause.

Meanwhile, the necessity to reconsider the issue provided a spur for those Members like Duncan Sandys (Con. Streatham) who wish to see the death penalty reintroduced. In November 1966, Sandys introduced a Bill under the Ten-Minute Rule to reintroduce capital punishment for the murder of a police officer; this was rejected by 170 to 292.[1] There was also a steady flow of parliamentary questions asking for statistics of murders.

Interest in the matter rose sharply in the autumn of 1969 as it was certain that Parliament would have to come to a decision during the coming session. The Annual Conference of the Conservative Party carried a motion to restore the death penalty by 1,117 to 958. It was

[1] H.C. Deb., Vol. 736, cols 1409–18.

made clear to the Conference that the vote did not commit the Party
to a policy and that MPs would be guided by individual conscience.
The Shadow Cabinet's tactic was to try to delay a decision until the
summer of 1970 on the ground that this would enable the fullest
information and the latest statistics on the five-year experimental
period to be available. The Conservative Leader and his front-bench
colleagues tabled a parliamentary motion to this effect.[1] When the
Government announced that Parliament would be asked to come to
a decision before Christmas the Conservatives put down a censure
motion to complain that Parliament was being rushed; this was duly
debated and defeated on a straight party whipped vote.[2] No doubt,
the Government wished to get the issue settled well before the general
election: the Opposition, while accepting that capital punishment was
a non-party matter, were not unwilling to try to bring odium on
Ministers for an unpopular decision.

The day after the censure motion the Commons considered the
issue itself and agreed to uphold abolition by 336 votes to 185.[3] The
abolitionists included 54 Conservatives, 11 Liberals and 2 National-
ists. The retentionists included 3 Labour Members, 2 Liberals and
2 Independents. Yet it must be stressed that the vote was not entirely
a straight vote on whether to return to the 1957 Act. The issue had
been clouded by the claim that the decision should be postponed not
simply for six months but for three years. Quintin Hogg (Marylebone),
the Shadow Home Secretary, made it clear that he did not wish to
return to the 1957 Act, although he did believe that capital punishment had a deterrent effect on professional criminals. He wanted to
postpone a decision until 1973 and voted against the motion to end
capital punishment.[4] Since his vote was cast in favour of restoring
the 1957 Act, it was contrary to his stated desire. This illustrates
the difficulties of those who supported capital punishment. Almost
no one wished to return to the 1957 Act with its attendant anomalies.
Yet to attempt to draft fresh legislation was to become entangled
with the difficulties of trying to define categories of murder – unless
capital punishment is restored for all murders, a policy which by
1970 had become politically impossible.

The House of Lords voted for the permanent abolition of the
death penalty by 220 to 174.[5] Again, the issue was confused. The
actual division was not for or against hanging; but on an amendment

[1] *The Times*, November 27, 1969.
[2] H.C. Deb., Vol. 793, cols 939–1062.
[3] *Ibid.*, cols 1148–1298.
[4] *Ibid.*, cols 1179–80.
[5] H.L. Deb., Vol. 306, cols 1106–1258, 1264–1322.

by Lord Dilhorne that the decision should be postponed until 1973. When this was defeated, the motion to end capital punishment was accepted without a division. Thus some who voted for the Dilhorne amendment may have been opposed to capital punishment: this is true of the Bishop of Exeter, Dr Mortimer, the only bishop to support Lord Dilhorne. The Archbishop of Canterbury and 18 bishops voted the other way, so the vote of the Established Church was virtually unanimous. Lord Dilhorne had the support of 137 Conservative peers, 31 cross-benchers, 3 law lords, 1 Liberal and 1 Labour peer. Apart from the bishops, the abolitionists comprised 90 Labour peers, 44 Conservatives, 42 cross-benchers, 22 Liberals and 3 law lords.[1]

One fresh element in the controversy in 1969 was the interpretation of the murder statistics following the suspension of capital punishment in 1965. The Home Office issued a report *Murder 1957 to 1968* in an appropriate red cover. It was shown that the number of capital murders, i.e. murders to which the death penalty would have been applicable before 1965, had risen sharply after that date. The average for 1958–64 was 6·6; the average for 1966–68 was 21. These figures were hailed by Duncan Sandys and his associates as justification for their campaign to revive the death penalty. His opponents claimed that the statistics could not be interpreted so simply. The figures reflected an increase in violence which had commenced before 1965 and which, in some measure, was unconnected with the 1965 Act. Further, as the Home Office survey explained, the figures pre and post the 1965 Act were not strictly comparable, because since then there had been no reliable basis for estimating the murders which previously would have been capital. The classification has to be made on 'the circumstances of the offence, on which doubt might have been thrown in the course of trial if capital murder had been an issue. This particularly applies to murder in the course of theft, which allows considerable scope for argument. The analysis suggests that juries were reluctant to convict of capital murder, and that they found to be "non-capital" a number of offences which would have been classified as "capital" if estimates had been necessary.'[2] So it was inevitable that the statistics were unsatisfactory and that their interpretation was a subject of dispute. In these circumstances the Conservative argument that the decision should have been delayed until more (unsatisfactory) statistics became available appears as no more than a political tactic.

Even allowing for the fact that the voting in 1969 was confused

[1] *The Times*, December 20, 1969.
[2] *Murder, 1957 to 1968*, para. 76.

by arguments about rushing the decision and the need for further delay, it does seem that 1969, when compared with 1965, shows some movement of Conservative opinion in Parliament towards a limited return to hanging. The public opinion polls, the concern among Conservative constituency organizations about crimes of violence, and the mammoth petition said to contain a million signatures in favour of capital punishment, each may have had some effect. And since Ministers were warmly supporting abolition, there was perhaps a stronger party flavour to the argument than in 1965. It is also the case that the discussion in 1969 did not carry the same burden of responsibility. In 1965 human lives were at stake and Parliament was asked to amend an Act ridden with anomalies. Four years later few parliamentarians really believed that hanging would be brought back immediately: voting against the abolition resolution could be interpreted as a protest against leniency to criminals combined with distaste for co-operating in any way with the Labour Government. Certainly the decision on how to vote was highly individual. There is no correlation between the left and right wings of the Conservative Party and attitudes to capital punishment. Tories voting for abolition included their Leader, Edward Heath (Bexley), Sir Edward Boyle (Birmingham, Handsworth) and Members normally regarded as right-wingers, Julian Amery (Brighton, Pavilion), Ronald Bell (Buckinghamshire, South), John Biggs-Davison (Chigwell) and Enoch Powell (Wolverhampton, S.W.).

The outcome in the Commons was never in doubt. In the Lords the result was highly uncertain. The peers experienced an unusual amount of lobbying and unofficial whipping, and this resulted in a remarkable attendance of nearly four hundred for the final vote. Mrs Undine Barker, the secretary of the Liberal peers, was the main organizing force behind the abolitionist whipping, and she was encouraged in this work by the Lord Chancellor. When the whips are off the relative importance of individuals can change dramatically.

Chapter 4

Homosexuality

I

'Thou shalt not lie with mankind, as with womankind: it is abomination' – *Leviticus xviii, 22.*

'. . . if a man lie with mankind, as with womankind, both of them have committed abomination: they shall surely be put to death; their blood shall be upon them' – *Leviticus xx, 13.*

The third book of the Old Testament provides the earliest references to the prohibition of, and punishment for, homosexual conduct. They form part of the 'Holiness Code' for the Jewish people and their origin may be as early as the seventh century BC. But for Christian opinion it is undoubtedly the story of the destruction of Sodom and Gomorrah that has had the greatest influence in promoting condemnation of homosexual behaviour. Modern biblical scholarship has cast doubt on whether the sins of Sodom were necessarily homosexual,[1] and there is clear evidence that the cities were destroyed by a natural disaster, not by a catastrophe only explicable in terms of Divine wrath. The doubts about the Sodom story are not wholly modern for they were shared by Calvin. The problem of interpretation is simple yet fundamental: the crowd in Sodom demanded 'to know' Lot's visitors[2] – is the verb 'to know' to be understood in a sexual sense? This is a matter for detailed linguistic analysis. But there can be no doubt that the common view of Sodom through the centuries has reflected a widespread revulsion against homosexual activities which thus secured both justification and reinforcement.

In England in the middle ages sodomy, along with heresy, was thought to be a matter for the ecclesiastical courts: convicted offenders were to be handed over to the civil power to be burnt. It seems that sodomists rarely, if ever, suffered this penalty.[3] An Act of 1533 empowered the justices of the peace to impose the death

---

[1] D. S. Bailey: *Homosexuality and the Western Christian Tradition* (Longmans, 1955), Ch. I.

[2] *Genesis xix 5.*

[3] F. Pollock and F. W. Maitland: *The History of the English Law Before the Time of Edward I* (Cambridge U.P., 1898), Vol. ii, pp. 556–7.

penalty for 'the abominable Vice of Buggery committed with mankind or beast'. Jurisdiction was thereby removed from the
ecclesiastical authorities as part of the campaign by Henry VIII to
assert royal supremacy as against the authority of the church. This
law remained in force for over 300 years, apart from brief intervals
in the sixteenth century. The death penalty was removed by the
Offences Against the Person Act, 1861, and replaced by penal
servitude for life; a maximum period of ten years was prescribed for
those who merely attempted to commit the abominable crime.

The scope of the law relating to homosexual conduct was extended
from buggery, or anal connection, to all homosexual practices by
Section II of the Criminal Law Amendment Act, 1885, which
provided that:

'Any male person who, in public or private, commits or is a party
to the commission of, or procures or attempts to procure the
commission by any male person of any act of gross indecency with
another male person, shall be guilty of a misdemeanour, and being
convicted thereof shall be liable at the discretion of the Court to be
imprisoned for any term not exceeding two years, with or without
hard labour.'

The original purpose of this law was 'to make further provision for
the protection of women and girls, the suppression of brothels and
other purposes'. When first introduced it contained no reference to
homosexual activity. It passed through the Lords, went on to the
Commons where the extra provision was proposed by Mr Labouchere,
a prominent back-bencher renowned for his radical sympathies. The
new clause was accepted, in the early hours of the morning, without
discussion apart from a proposal by Sir Henry James that the
maximum penalty be increased from one year's imprisonment to
two.[1] Thus a major restriction on human freedom was added to the
statute book virtually without consideration. It is not true, as is
sometimes said, that homosexual practices were made illegal in a
fit of absent-mindedness because buggery had always been regarded
as a crime of great seriousness. Yet the lack of parliamentary
discussion requires explanation. Due to the prudery of this period,
homosexuality was not a topic that could be raised in polite conversation; the subject was buried beneath an oppressive veil of silence,
ignorance, distaste and condemnation. It is perhaps unsurprising
that no MP should be willing to challenge the Labouchere amendment and so appear to condone homosexual activities.

[1] Parl. Deb., 3rd series, Vol. 300, cols 1397–8.

Nineteenth-century radical politics were commonly associated with puritanism and an acute sense of righteousness. However, Labouchere was in no sense a typical puritan if only because of his wealth and an addiction to gambling in his youth. His view of women was supremely conservative: their place was in the home where they could perform their own particular functions.[1] It was inappropriate for them to have the right to vote, but it was essential to give them protection from fornicators. This attitude explains the various amendments Labouchere moved to strengthen the Criminal Law Amendment Act. Clause 11 was just one part of a drive to raise standards of sexual morality.[2] Respectable society was desperately anxious to protect itself against the forces of vice and evil felt to be lurking beneath the veneer of civilization. Even in this atmosphere *The Times* sounded a warning.

'There may be some changes lately made in the (Criminal Law Amendment) Bill which exceed the limits of sound policy and prudent legislation; but at this stage in the discussion it is better to accept some questionable provisions than to imperil the passing of the measure. . . . We wish well to its objects and we sincerely trust that it may do some good. . . . We have never been among those who think it possible by legislation to extinguish sexual vice and crime. Our greatest hope is that it represents a movement of public feeling and public conscience in the right direction.'[3]

The paper did not specify which provisions were questionable, so it is not certain that these comments were intended to be applicable to Clause 11; equally there is no indication that they were not.

The law on homosexual practices developed in a most unsatisfactory manner. It must be a matter for argument whether Parliament in 1885 fully appreciated the significance of the Labouchere amendment.[4] The Vagrancy Act, 1898, made it an offence for a male to solicit persistently in a public place for an immoral purpose. From the discussion on this clause it seems that it was designed to prevent men from trying to obtain clients for prostitutes. In fact this power was widely used in England and Wales to stop solicitation for homosexual purposes. The use of the Vagrancy Act in this way was

[1] Cf. A. L. Thorold, *Life of Henry Labouchere* (Constable, 1913), pp. 222–4.

[2] Labouchere wrote subsequently that he took the Clause *mutatis mutandi* from the French criminal code. But the French, while protecting the young, did not consider adult private acts to be illegal. Was Labouchere misleading or misled? Cf. *The Times*, January 14, 1958.

[3] *The Times*, August 11, 1885.

[4] Cf. H. M. Hyde, *The Trials of Oscar Wilde* (Hodge, 1948), p. 6.

E

recognized by Parliament in 1912 when the penalties under the 1898 Act were increased. The Immoral Trade (Scotland) Act, 1902, intended as a counterpart of the Vagrancy Act north of the Border, has not been used against homosexual solicitation. This anomaly was noted by the Wolfenden Committee,[1] which also observed that there was some foundation for the assertion that the police had been given powers to deal with homosexual importuning quite inadvertently.

No major change in the law was made during the first half of this century; the topic of homosexuality aroused deep distaste and discussion of the problem was avoided. Then in the early 1950s the position began to change. Greater frankness on sexual matters slowly became socially acceptable. This permitted traditional attitudes to be publicly re-examined in the light of contemporary attitudes and knowledge. Automatic condemnation became less fashionable. In 1952 the Church of England Moral Welfare Council initiated a study of the problem and a small group of clergymen, doctors and lawyers was brought together, unofficially and privately, to carry out this task. The group produced a report, *The Problem of Homosexuality*; originally intended to be for private circulation, it was published in 1954. The liberal, humane tenor of this document caused much surprise. It became clear that the Established Church would welcome further official investigation of the subject. The Church of England Moral Welfare Council and the Howard League for Penal Reform both asked the Home Secretary to initiate an official enquiry. Other pressures worked in the same direction. A prosecution involving a member of the House of Lords in 1953 attracted much publicity[2] and stimulated some sympathy for the accused rather than demands for a police drive against unnatural vice. Students of criminal statistics also knew that the number of prosecutions for homosexual activities had been rising; that the homosexual offences known to the police had been rising even more sharply; that police policy on homosexuality varied greatly between areas and in the same area at different times. Police authorities have commonly exercised some discretion over the prosecution of certain types of offenders; attempted suicide, street betting and traffic offences come into this category, but none of them has such grave social consequences as a charge of homosexual actions. The uneven and spasmodic character of police energy in this field illustrated by the table below must have caused disquiet in the Home Office.

[1] Cf. Report of the Committee on Homosexual Offences and Prostitution, Cmnd. 247, 1956–57, pp. 42–3 and H.C. Deb., Vol. 43, col. 1858.

[2] One of those convicted has written his account of the case: Peter Wildeblood, *Against the Law* (Weidenfeld & Nicolson, 1955).

Homosexual Offences known to the Police
(including buggery, attempted buggery and indecency between males)

	1952	1955	1958	1960	1962	1964	1966
Bath C.B.	16	14	7	2	21	13	6
Blackpool C.B.	75	42	47	19	49	40	58
Cambridge B.	3	33	3	2	24	3	0
Hereford C.C.	12	22	3	4	9	16	36
Metropolitan Police District	633	728	582	660	661	598	657
Norfolk C.C.	56	15	38	21	15	20	13
Reading C.B.	36	22	21	10	36	40	9
Sheffield C.B.	38	65	88	79	54	45	40
Warwick C.C.	140	143	362	96	57	51	92
Wiltshire C.C.	23	29	35	46	70	63	48

Source: Criminal Statistics: supplementary tables

Parliamentary interest in the matter was growing. Iain MacLeod, Minister of Health, rejected a suggestion by Desmond Donnelly (Lab. Pembroke) that the terms of reference of the Royal Commission on the laws relating to mental disorder be extended to include homosexuality.[1] Other members, notably Kenneth Robinson (Lab. St Pancras) and Sir Robert Boothby (Con. Aberdeenshire E.) also urged the need for an enquiry. Ministerial acceptance of this demand was announced in an adjournment debate introduced by Desmond Donnelly in April 1954.[2] A parallel debate in the Lords was initiated by Lord Winterton who wished to strengthen the law in order to prevent the moral decline of the nation.[3] The traditional pattern of a reactionary House of Lords opposing reforms that are urged in the Commons seemed in 1954 to apply to homosexuality – although at this stage no votes had been taken. Ten years later this pattern was to be wholly destroyed.

The Committee to enquire into homosexual offences and prostitution was appointed in August 1954 under the chairmanship of Sir John Wolfenden. The report appeared almost exactly three years later. Initially there were 15 members on the Committee but two resigned for personal reasons before its work was completed. The members were drawn from both Houses of Parliament, both the main political parties, medicine, all branches of the legal profession and the main religious denominations in England and Scotland. The terms of reference of the Committee were stated simply:

[1] H.C. Deb., Vol. 518, col. 328.
[2] H.C. Deb., Vol. 526, cols 1745–56.
[3] H.L. Deb., Vol. 187, cols 737–67.

To consider (*a*) the law and practice relating to homosexual offences and the treatment of persons convicted of such offences by the courts; and

(*b*) the law and practice relating to offences against the criminal law in connection with prostitution and solicitation for immoral purposes.

It will be noted that the terms of reference avoid any reference to morality. 'To consider the law' could include the consideration of the moral basis of the law, but the Committee did not enter this field. The section of the report dealing with homosexuality contains a review of its nature and extent together with an examination of the operation of the law and the treatment of offenders. A critic of the Committee's recommendations could argue that they were a direct consequence of the lack of a moral dimension to the report. To this a reply might be that the report had an implied code of morality – that social problems should be judged against a rational appreciation of their causes and consequences. The Committee met in private and received a massive amount of evidence written and oral. The evidence has not been published. Presumably this stress on confidentiality was regarded as vital to secure frankness and co-operation. In retrospect the insistence on secrecy seems unnecessary. Some of the evidence presented to the Committee has been published by the individuals or institutions responsible.

By far the most influential submission to the Committee was that from the Church of England Moral Welfare Council. This document was deeply compassionate in tone and was based on a wide-ranging study of the problem.[1] It distinguished between homosexuality and homosexual acts and stressed that while not all homosexuals engaged in homosexual practices they did suffer a sense of loneliness and separation from the rest of society. The two types of sexual condition, heterosexual and homosexual, were themselves morally neutral. Homosexuality was shown to be the result of a number of social factors that were in no sense the fault of the individual. The most frequent cause was unsatisfactory emotional adjustment in childhood, perhaps due to an unhappy home, divorce, death of a parent or prolonged absence of a father on war service. Tension between parents and children arose from the inability of parents to cope successfully with normal problems of personal relationships. The evidence quoted Dr Seward with approval: 'A pervading atmosphere of happiness in the home leads to a ready acceptance of life in general

[1] It was published by the Church Information Board in 1956 as part of a pamphlet entitled *Sexual Offenders and Social Punishment*.

and sex-role in particular.'[1] There followed a careful discussion of how far sexual segregation in childhood, at boarding schools, in prison or the armed forces contributed to the homosexual condition.

Turning to homosexual practices, the evidence noted that these varied in character – as do heterosexual actions. Some homosexuals found sodomy repulsive, although desiring to show affection by other physico-sexual acts. Homosexual practices were neither more nor less harmful than heterosexual practices, and the common assumption that every homosexual was a potential corrupter of youth was mistaken. 'While we have every sympathy with those who are anxious to protect the young, it must be said that there is no ground for such an assumption as this; in itself it is productive of harmful consequences, and can cause embarrassment in the most honourable associations between man and boy.' The paederast, who sought only the young, was a separate problem not to be confused with the ordinary homosexual.

On the basis of this analysis, the Church of England Moral Welfare Council could find no justification for the existing law. Homosexuals potentially suffered severe penalties, while lesbians, fornicators and adulterers escaped scot-free. These latter categories arguably caused as much – or more – social damage as homosexuals. The Council also argued that it was not the business of the state to constitute itself the guardian of *private* morality: it was the business of the church to deal with sin. The task of the state was to prevent crime and offences against *public* morality. The Council proposed, therefore, that homosexual acts in private between consenting adults should cease to be criminal and that the age of consent be fixed at seventeen.

Essentially similar recommendations came from the Catholic Church, except that it thought that the age of consent for this purpose should be twenty-one. The Catholics also insisted firmly that homosexual activities were sinful because all voluntary sexual pleasure outside marriage is sinful.[2]

The submission from the British Medical Association[3] necessarily paid greater attention to the medical aspects of the subject and stressed that prison did not provide a helpful environment for the provision of treatment for homosexual offenders. It summarized the advantages and disadvantages of the existing situation but remained neutral on the central issue of whether the law should be reformed. The criticisms of the present law were the impossibility of equitable

[1] H. G. Seward: *Sex and the Social Order* (Penguin, 1954), p. 158.
[2] The Catholic evidence appeared in *The Dublin Review*, Vol. 230, pp. 60–5.
[3] Published in the *British Medical Journal* dated December 17, 1955.

State guardian of morality?

enforcement, the fear created among homosexuals whether practising or not, the opportunities for blackmail, the disparity in attitude towards homosexual activities as compared with other forms of extra-marital sex and the possibility that the law might encourage some people to engage in homosexual activities because forbidden fruit is always sweeter. The salutary effects were that the law instils into the public mind that homosexual practices are reprehensible and harmful, that it protected the young and that any relaxation of the law could be interpreted as a public acceptance and condonation of a fall in standards of morality.

Among youth organizations there were differing views on how far homosexual law reform was desirable. The most prestigious body in this field, the Boy Scouts' Association, had no objection to reform provided that the interests of young people were protected. Their statement to the Wolfenden Committee consisted largely of an explanation of the measures taken to ensure that men convicted of homosexual offences were kept out of their Association.

Besides Government Departments and individual witnesses, a total of 35 organizations gave written and oral evidence to the Wolfenden Committee and 11 more submitted written memoranda. Even were all this material available it would be tedious to analyse because of the inevitable repetition. Some organizations favoured reform; some were neutral. The balance of influence and argument favoured change. Indeed, it is a matter of doubt whether any of these organizations upheld the existing law on homosexuality. Some bodies known to be opposed to change, the Episcopal Church in Scotland, the Baptist Union and the Salvation Army did not approach the Wolfenden Committee.

The Committee's recommendation to withdraw the taint of criminality from homosexual acts by consenting adults committed in private was in tune with the majority of informed opinion. The Committee's attitude was based on a simple principle. 'We do not think it is proper for the law to concern itself with what a man does in private unless it can be shown to be so contrary to the public good that the law ought to intervene in its function as the guardian of the public good.'[1] It then considered whether homosexual acts affected the public good on three grounds, (i) menace to the health of society, (ii) damage to the family, (iii) danger to boys. No conclusive evidence existed to support the first and third of these possibilities. The Committee accepted that homosexual activity might disrupt family life, but since it was far more commonly disturbed by heterosexual activity not regarded as criminal, the protection of marriage could

[1] Report, para. 52.

decriminalised as considered to be a private act

not be an adequate justification for the existing law. Only one member of the Committee dissented from the central recommendation on homosexuality, Mr James Adair. In a minority report[1] he objected to any weakening of the moral force of the law and stressed that if the sanctions of the criminal law were removed a main reason which impelled homosexuals to seek medical aid would be removed. From his experience as a Procurator-Fiscal in Scotland he also believed that police inquiries into homosexual behaviour could have a useful preventive effect.

The Wolfenden Report also contained a substantial amount of information which had an important educational impact on public opinion. It discussed the nature of homosexuality and the treatment of offenders. The available statistical information was reproduced. The Committee was aware of the inadequacy of the statistics and was broadly agreed that the dramatic increase in the figures was due more to greater police activity than to an increase in homosexual behaviour. It was also shown that in most Western European countries homosexual acts by adults in private were not treated as offences against the law. In support of its chief recommendation the Committee had also to consider what was meant by 'consent', 'in private' and 'adult'. It decided that the criteria to determine consent and privacy should be the same as those governing sexual acts between males and females. But the age of consent for heterosexual intercourse, namely sixteen, it felt was too low in relation to homosexual behaviour; after some hesitation the age of consent was recommended to be twenty-one.

Public reaction to the report was mixed. The press was divided.[2] Seven national dailies, including *The Times*, the *Daily Telegraph* and the *Manchester Guardian*, gave support to the Committee. *The Mirror* was vigorous: 'Don't be Shocked by This Report, It's the Truth, It's the Answer, IT'S LIFE'. The *Manchester Guardian* was more restrained: 'A fine piece of work'. However, *The Daily Mail* and the *Daily Express* and most of the provincial press shared the doubts of Mr James Adair. *The Economist* believed that although popular distaste for homosexuality would call for retaining the present law, the views of the Committee should be heeded. Thus informed opinion and metropolitan opinion appeared to be ahead of the rest of the country.

On balance, religious opinion supported reform. Dr Fisher, Archbishop of Canterbury, wrote that one of the values of the Wolfenden Committee Report was that it drew attention to the

[1] *Ibid.*, pp. 117–23.
[2] Cf. H. Hopkins: *The New Look* (Secker and Warburg, 1963), p. 205.

distinction between crime and sin. 'There is a sacred realm of privacy . . . into which the law, generally speaking, must not intrude. This is a principle of the utmost importance for the preservation of human freedom, self-respect and responsibility.'[1] Dr Godfrey, Archbishop of Westminster, wrote in his Cathedral's chronicle in the same vein. Dr Soper, a former President of the Methodist Conference, thought that the Wolfenden Report would give a new sense of hope and a promise of justice to a great many homosexuals in Britain who were 'honestly trying to live straight and decent lives in conditions which have been almost intolerable'.[2] Catholics apart, these religious leaders did not obtain unanimous support from their followers. The Bishop of Chester told his Diocesan Conference that the present law exercised a wholesome control, recognized and accepted by society.[3] The Church Assembly approved the cause of reform, but by a narrow majority, 155 to 138, after a long debate. The Methodists also supported reform but contained a dissentient minority. Firmly against change in the law were the Episcopal Church in Scotland, the Salvation Army and Moral Rearmament. However, the Salvation Army advocated a reconsideration of methods of dealing with homosexual offenders so that more use should be made of probation and medical services.[4]

Among secular organizations, the Howard League for Penal Reform and the Institute of Social Psychiatry urged the adoption of the Wolfenden proposals. The Homosexual Law Reform Society was founded in 1958. Expert and religious opinion leaders had an impact on public attitudes but a majority was not fully convinced by the arguments for reform. Three national dailies ran opinion polls on the Wolfenden recommendations and these showed between 40 and 50 per cent in favour of reform – a much higher figure than could have been obtained a few years earlier. Certainly the public personalities who favoured reform outweighed those who opposed it, both in numbers and in authority. However, some judicial opinion objected directly to the central Wolfenden thesis. Lord Denning told the Law Society Conference that 'standards and morals are the concern of the law' in relation to both public and private behaviour.[5] Mr Justice Devlin, delivering the second Maccabean lecture on jurisprudence, said that he held the belief that separation of crime from sin would not be good for moral law and would be disastrous

[1] *Canterbury Diocesan Notes*, October 1957.
[2] *The Times*, September 5, 1957.
[3] *Ibid.*, October 9, 1957.
[4] *Ibid.*, March 14, 1958.
[5] *Ibid.*, September 9, 1957.

for criminal law.[1] Thus an element of the dispute became whether sin should be the concern of the representatives of Caesar or the representatives of God: but as a church–state controversy the situation was untypical in that the rulers of the state, the Government, adopted a negative attitude. Mr Butler, the Home Secretary, speaking in the Commons' debate on the Wolfenden Report, noted that there was a large section of the population 'who sharply repudiated homosexual conduct and whose moral sense would be offended by an alteration of the law which would seem to imply approval or tolerance of what they regard as a great social evil. Therefore the considerations I have indicated satisfy the Government that they would not be justified at present, on the basis of opinions expressed so far, in proposing legislation to carry out the recommendations of the Committee. . . . I hope that the debate will do something to educate public opinion towards the type of reform which may be generally accepted.'[2] These words show clearly that Ministers were not expressing any basic views. They were merely waiting upon public opinion.

The task of the reformers was to prepare opinion for change so that Parliament would become willing to modify the law on homosexuality either at the behest of the Government or through a private member's Bill. This task was accepted by the Homosexual Law Reform Society, and the Society was greatly assisted by the increase in the number of books and other publications on the subject which were generally favourable to its cause. Prior to the 1958 debate on the Wolfenden Report, the Society sent a deputation to see the Home Secretary, and it also sent to all MPs a copy of Dr Eustace Chesser's book *Live and Let Live*[3] together with a copy of their own pamphlet *Homosexuals and the Law*. However, the Society did not attempt a direct challenge to the Government policy of inaction; no move arose to table an amendment to the official Commons' motion to 'take note' of the report. The Society's policy was to try to gain public sympathy and understanding rather than to stir up controversy in Parliament. This tactic was urged on them by their supporters in the Commons, notably Kenneth Robinson, subsequently Minister of Health in the Labour Government. Faced with the warning that parliamentarians were more likely to be irritated than persuaded by lobbying, the Society concentrated on the wider public. It provided speakers for a large number of meetings, organized by the churches, student groups and youth organizations, where it was possible to

[1] *Ibid.*, March 19, 1959.
[2] H.C. Deb., Vol. 596, col. 370.
[3] Heinemann, 1958.

discuss problems of homosexuality under broadly favourable conditions. Contacts with Parliament were, of course, maintained and
strengthened where practicable. After 1965, when the parliamentary
battle was joined, the Society did all it could to assist the sponsors
of the private members' Bills and its headquarters became an
unofficial 'whips office'.

It is impossible to measure precisely the effect of an educational
campaign but the public attitude towards homosexuality continued
to change slowly. No longer was it merely a subject for automatic
condemnation by judges and moralists or for sniggering jokes about
'queers'. Increasingly it became a fit subject for serious conversation,
a social problem demanding urgent study both medical and psychological. In 1958 the Lord Chamberlain modified his ban on the
discussion of homosexuality on the stage. A private member's
motion in the Commons led *The Times* to restate its support for
reform of the law.[1] Doubts even began to be voiced aloud as to
whether homosexuality was *ipso facto* an evil. A pamphlet published
by the Society of Friends in 1963, *Towards a Quaker View of Sex*,
made a forceful plea for a more tolerant attitude towards sexual
deviation and especially homosexuality, and it argued that no act or
relationship should be condemned merely for the reason that it was
homosexual.[2] This suggestion was at variance with earlier statements
from other religious bodies; however liberal in tone, these had all
stressed that homosexual acts were sinful if not necessarily blame-
worthy.[3] With the changing climate of opinion, the Homosexual Law
Reform Society also gained support from some unexpected quarters.
Sir Thomas Moore, an elderly Scottish Unionist MP who had no
reputation as an advocate of progressive causes, was one convert: he
raised in the Commons the case of a young man of twenty-five about
to be married who was accused of having committed one act of
indecency ten years earlier and who, as a result, lost his job and lost
his bride.[4]

Another important development occurred in July 1964, when the
newly-appointed Director of Public Prosecutions, Mr Norman
Skelhorn, Q.C., asked chief constables to consult him before prose-
cuting homosexual acts committed by adults in private. This
represented a substantial extension of an earlier request, dating from
1958, to consult the D.P.P. on stale homosexual offences – those

[1] June 29, 1960.
[2] This publication did not necessarily reflect the official view of the Society
of Friends.
[3] Cf. *Sexual Offenders and Social Punishment*, p. 81.
[4] H.C. Deb., Vol. 693, col. 587. Sir Thomas was MP for Ayr 1925–64.

more than a year old – and those where an element of blackmail was involved. The 1964 'request' did not require or imply any change in the law. The police are not required to initiate proceedings in relation to every criminal act that comes to their notice. Officially the D.P.P. was doing no more than attempting to achieve greater uniformity in the way in which discretion was exercised, but it was widely assumed that his action would produce a more humane and liberal policy.[1]

It took almost exactly ten years from the publication of the Wolfenden Report to achieve the reform of the law on homosexuality. During this period Parliament gave slowly increasing attention to the subject. The Commons debate on the report took place over a year after its appearance[2] and was concerned with the whole of the Committee's terms of reference – i.e. prostitution as well as homosexuality. Since the Government announced its intention to introduce legislation on prostitution, homosexuality received greater attention as being the unresolved issue. The division of opinion cut across party lines and both parties had avoided any policy commitments on the issue. As no division was challenged, no clear picture emerged of the balance of opinion. One of the speakers supporting reform in this debate was H. Montgomery Hyde (U.U. Belfast North); his attitude was subsequently said to be one of the reasons for failing to obtain re-nomination by his constituency party for the 1959 General Election.

The first vote on the issue came from a private member's motion introduced by Kenneth Robinson in June 1960 calling on the Government to take early action to implement the Wolfenden recommendations on homosexuality[3]. This motion was defeated by 99 votes to 213. Labour speakers in the debate tended to support reform and Conservative speakers to oppose it. One of the most significant contributions came from W. Deedes (Con. Ashford) who confessed that he had partly changed his mind; originally he had thought any change in the law to be unthinkable but he had come to feel that it was inevitable eventually. The other notable feature of the debate is the names of the speakers on the Labour benches supporting reform: besides Kenneth Robinson they were Eirene White, Douglas Jay, Anthony Greenwood and Roy Jenkins, all of

[1] This incident also gave prominence to a constitutional anomaly. The Home Secretary is the Minister responsible for policy changes in criminal law. The D.P.P. has a general responsibility for the prosecution of offenders subject to any directions received from the Attorney-General, *not* the Home Secretary, Cf. H.C. Deb., Vol. 699, cols 1207–11.
[2] H.C, Deb., Vol. 596, cols 365–507. The Lords' debate was earlier, December 1957; H.L. Deb., Vol. 206, cols 733–832.
[3] H.C. Deb., Vol. 625, cols 1453–1514.

whom were later to hold office in the Labour Government. Ministers continued their stone-walling policy of neutral inaction while emphasizing the need for more research. However, the Home Secretary refused to inform the House how many people were actually convicted for homosexual acts between consenting adults in private: to produce such statistics would require detailed examination of case papers by the police, and the Home Secretary argued that such additional work could not be justified.[1] The criminal statistics did not distinguish between acts in private and those in public, nor did they isolate cases where the persons involved were both above the age of twenty-one. Thus it was impossible to discover how many men were convicted or prosecuted for breaking a law which Wolfenden said should be repealed; nor could any geographical breakdown of the figures available show that in some parts of the country the law – at least in relation to consenting adults – was virtually a dead letter.

The parliamentary campaign to change the law achieved full vigour in May 1965. On May 12th the Earl of Arran rose in the House of Lords to call attention to the recommendations of the Wolfenden Committee and 'to move for papers'.[2] This is a meaningless formula used in the Upper House to provide a formal basis for the discussion of some aspect of public policy. The Earl's plea for reform met a remarkable response; only 2 out of the 24 lords who joined in the debate opposed reform. No division was taken because owing to the nature of the motion before the House any vote would have been valueless. However, much encouraged by the tone of the debate the Earl introduced a private member's Bill a fortnight later; this received a second reading by 94 votes to 49.[3] Two days later Leo Abse (Lab. Pontypool) failed to get a second reading of a parallel bill in the Commons introduced under the Ten-Minute Rule by 159 votes to 178.[4] However, the battle continued in the Upper House; after a hard-fought committee stage, a further tussle on report, the Bill was read a third time by 116 to 46 and passed to the Commons on October 28th. The Commons rarely find time for a private member's Bill from the Lords: in any case the end of the parliamentary session had been reached, so Earl Arran's Bill stood no chance at all.

The next session, 1965–66, was cut short by the General Election

[1] H.C. Deb., Vol. 615, cols *215–16*; Vol. 625, cols *93–4*; Vol. 627, col. *54*. (The italics indicate written answers.) H.L. Deb., Vol. 228, col. 1008.

[2] H.L. Deb., Vol. 266, cols 71–172.

[3] H.L. Deb., Vol. 266, cols 631–712.

[4] H.C. Deb., Vol. 713, cols 611–20.

in March 1966. The Earl of Arran reintroduced his Bill in the Lords but it proceeded no further than a formal first reading. However, the Commons gave a second reading to a Bill introduced by Humphrey Berkeley (Con. Lancaster) by 164 votes to 107: this Bill was promoted under the ballot procedure and the second reading debate lasted five hours or virtually the whole of a Friday sitting.[1] The movement of opinion as compared with the vote on Abse's Bill is substantial. Yet a study of the division lists shows that only three members had changed their minds, two in favour of reform and one against; the difference is explained mainly by the change in the attendance at the two divisions. Owing to the hasty termination of Parliament, this Bill made no further progress.

Homosexual law reform was finally achieved in the following session 1966–67. No fewer than 3 private members' Bills were introduced on the subject. Earl Arran was first off the mark in the Upper House. The progress of this measure can be shown conveniently by a table.[2]

Date	Stage	Ayes	Noes
26.4.1966	Second reading	70	29
23.5.1966	Committee: age of consent 25 not 21	16	77
23.5.1966	Committee: age of consent 18 not 21	12	78
16.6.1966	Third reading	83	39
16.6.1966	That the Bill do now pass	78	60

It will be seen that opposition to the Bill slackened at the committee stage when only two divisions were forced, one seeking to raise and the other to lower the age of consent. However, the Opposition made a substantial rally at the very last stage of the procedure – the motion that the Bill do now pass – a stage which has no parallel in the Commons.

Leo Abse then introduced his Bill in the Commons. He used the Ten-Minute Rule procedure to test opinion in the newly-elected Parliament; the changed composition of the House helped to produce a victory for the reformers by 244 votes to 100.[3] Reinforced by this vote and by the support of the Lords, Abse managed to persuade sympathetic Ministers that the Government must find time to allow the wishes of both Houses to become effective. What followed depended largely upon Abse's crusading energy and his good personal relations with Ministers. As the ballot for private members' Bills for

[1] H.C. Deb., Vol. 724, cols 782–873.
[2] H.L. Deb., Vol. 274, cols 605–52, 1170–84, 1190–1207; Vol. 275, cols 146–77.
[3] H.C. Deb., Vol. 731, cols 259–68.

the 1966–67 session had been held already, the Cabinet agreed that time should be found to debate the Bill introduced under the Ten-Minute Rule. Using this opportunity, Abse produced his measure for a second time and obtained a second reading without a division: this unanimity was solely technical as the views of Members were expressed on a procedural motion, carried by 194 votes to 84, that the debate should continue after 10 p.m. Abse's Bill was similar to that accepted by the Upper House a few weeks earlier except for two points. One difference, of limited importance, concerned the extent to which the new law should have retrospective effect. The other tightened up the definition of privacy. Under the measure passed by the Lords a homosexual act was not considered to be private if it took place 'in the presence of any person other than the parties to the act'. Abse's Bill laid down that the condition of privacy was not achieved 'if more than two persons take part or are present'. This version ensures that any kind of homosexual orgy is impermissible.

Abse next persuaded Ministers to nominate a separate Standing Committee to examine his Bill so that it was not held up in the queue of measures waiting for consideration by the Committee appointed to deal with private members' legislation. The Bill passed through Standing Committee at a single sitting. Supporters of the Bill avoided prolongation of discussion and opponents made a very weak showing. Only four members of the Committee had voted against the procedural motion tantamount to the second reading vote; of these four, three were absent from the single sitting of the Committee. Other members were determined to secure the exclusion of the Merchant Navy, although in support of the main principle.[1] There is evidence to suggest that the 'hard-core' opponents expected a major tussle to develop over the Merchant Navy but were out-manoeuvred when Abse accepted its omission from the Bill.

Yet the fight was far from ended. A small group of Conservative back-benches tabled amendments and new clauses for consideration at the report stage. By now shortage of parliamentary time had become the main enemy. Other private members' Bills ahead in the queue had consumed all the time normally allotted to this category of legislation. However, the Cabinet agreed to the provision of an extra Friday, but this day failed to complete the report stage as about two dozen determined opponents of the measure kept up the

---

[1] Strong pressure for this exclusion had come from the National Maritime Board and the National Union of Seamen. It was argued that there could be no true privacy on board ship and that toleration of homosexual acts could lead to disciplinary problems.

debate.[1] Further time became necessary. Strong pressure on the Leader of the House, Richard Crossman, ultimately succeeded. Had the Home Secretary, Roy Jenkins, not been strongly favourable to reform, the Bill would probably have failed at this point. In the event, the Government agreed that the debate be resumed after 10 p.m. on Monday, July 3rd. Thus, instead of concluding business at the normal hour, the Commons stayed up until 5.50 a.m. before the Bill was finally passed. The vote on third reading was 99 to 14.[2] The total number of divisions on the report stage was no fewer than thirteen. Four times the sponsors of the Bill successfully moved the closure of debate on a particular amendment. In these divisions there were always over a hundred supporters present: opponents never exceeded forty and were usually half that number. The final attempt at obstruction came from Victor Goodhew (Con. St Albans) who moved that the debate should be adjourned, but the Speaker, acting on the terms of Standing Order 28, 'dilatory motion in abuse of the rules of the House', refused to put the motion.[3]

The Lords gave Abse's Bill a second reading by 111 votes to 48;[4] the committee and report stages were virtually formal and the Sexual Offences Bill received the Royal Assent on July 27, 1967. By this time the heat and vigour of the controversy had faded; the arguments had been repeated *ad nauseam* and nothing new was left to say.

II

How did an aspect of human conduct, traditionally regarded as unspeakable and horrific, come to be legally permissible after a campaign which succeeded in the remarkably short time of fifteen years? This question must be approached through an examination of the arguments which convinced churches and other organizations that the law should be changed – arguments which subsequently convinced Parliament.

The case for reform can be divided into four broad categories: practical, psychological, moral and political, although many of the arguments can be legitimately included under more than one of the headings. The core of the practical standpoint, which might be better described as an issue of equity, was that the existing law was unenforced and unenforceable. Criminal statistics on homosexuality

---

[1] H.C. Deb., Vol. 748, cols 2115–2200.
[2] H.C. Deb., Vol. 749, cols 1403–1525.
[3] *Ibid.*, col. 1501.
[4] H.L. Deb., Vol. 275, cols 146–77.

made unpleasant reading from every viewpoint; the number of cases increased and the cases were dealt with in an erratic fashion. Since public opinion was no longer unanimous on its attitude to homosexuality, police activity in this matter damaged relations with the public. An over-worked police force could be better employed on other crimes which were both universally condemned and more detectable. The existing law also encouraged crime by providing excellent opportunity for blackmail.

Psychological evidence asserted that homosexuals were not responsible for their own condition, that there is some propensity to homosexuality in all of us which is normally latent but which may be activated by social circumstances. The treatment by the courts of convicted homosexuals varied considerably: this was unsatisfactory in terms of equity and of results. A homosexual needs help and perhaps treatment which cannot be provided satisfactorily in a prison environment. Prison and borstal provided easy access to other homosexuals and might corrupt some young men not hitherto prone to such activities. Indeed, the punitive outlook prevented society from looking at the causes and origins of homosexuality and, therefore, obstructed preventive action. The existing law forced a misuse of social resources: social investigation was required rather than a body of prison warders. An important element in the controversy was whether change in the law would facilitate corruption of the young. The reformers argued that this was not a danger because paederasts were a limited category of men quite separate from other homosexuals; that legal prohibition tended to glamourize homosexual activity and could encourage young men to experiment with 'forbidden fruit'; that law reform would enable homosexuals to meet their own kind freely and without fear and would thus remove any need to make clandestine converts. Escape from a homosexual group would be easier if its activities were not illegal and treatment could be sought without fear.

No doubt, it was on the moral aspect of the question that the Wolfenden Report made its greatest impact. The argument that conduct should be a matter for individual conscience, provided it was not injurious to society, had firm roots in liberal traditions. On these principles the Labouchere amendment became an intolerable invasion of privacy by denying to the individual the right to determine his own moral standards. Again, why should the homosexual be singled out from others who deviate from the marriage-bond relationship? It seems that the homosexual is cast as a scapegoat to divert attention from other sexual tensions in society. Further, because marriage is respectable, homosexuals may be tempted to marry to secure a façade of normality, and thus produce tragedy for wives and possibly for children.

The fourth aspect of the reform movement, the political situation, arises from a different type of consideration, and will be considered separately below.

To turn to the views of the anti-reformers, it will be seen that the balance of their case was substantially different. They objected to the theory that the law should be concerned with crime, but not with sin, and asserted that the moral sense of the nation would be offended by any alteration of the law. Probably the most common argument, repeated in almost every parliamentary debate, was that liberalization of the law would be misunderstood as constituting approval, or at least moral condonation, of homosexual conduct, because many people obtain their basic notions of what is right and what is wrong from the criminal law, which thus provides a code of decent and proper human conduct. Further, the time was not ripe to change the law because there was too much corruption in society already. On the medical-psychological aspect it was urged that medical science was not yet able to deal with homosexuality by other than punitive means; that homosexuals were a grave menace since they tried to recruit other men to their perverted way of life; that adult homosexuals did not truly feel love and affection for each other; that reform of the law would remove incentive to seek remedial treatment. But the main burden of the retentionist case lay in the fear of what would happen were the law to be changed. The need to protect the young was constantly stressed. Adult homosexuals living openly together would be certain to have a pernicious effect on youth and other susceptible people. In addition, legitimation of homosexual acts would attract the weak and the mercenary to this form of behaviour. Such conditions would inevitably lead to an increase in abnormal human relationships. The armed forces presented a particular problem because any spread of homosexual activity would undermine discipline. The reformer's argument about blackmail was countered with the claim that to change the law would still not eliminate opportunity for blackmail because homosexuality was socially unacceptable, so that exposure would still incur grave social penalties.

These summaries of the opposing views illustrate the weak position of those who resisted the demand for change. The moral aspect of their case had been badly eroded because the Church of England and some other denominations had accepted the principle that the state should deal with crime but not with sin. It was persuasive to attribute to the law the qualities of a necessary social cement, but

F

this is a general justification for law which cannot provide moral authority for any particular statutory provision. Their medical and psychological assertions were commonly contradicted by expert professional evidence. So the retentionists were forced back into a defensive posture and invoked the fear of freedom – a puritan spectre of society consumed by evil once legal restraints were withdrawn.

A feature of the parliamentary debates on this subject is that the fundamental moral issue was consistently avoided. Why have homosexual acts been regarded as abominable and depraved? For those who resisted change in the law the answer was too obvious and too absolute to require restating: their attitude was based on biblical condemnation and the unnatural character of homosexual behaviour. The idea that 'natural' is the equivalent of 'good' has a powerful attraction, but in modern society we increasingly reject it as a principle of social policy. In any case, homosexual acts are natural for a homosexual. It is more accurate to describe homosexual acts as abnormal rather than unnatural. Why, then, did the scribes of the Old Testament object so violently to this kind of abnormal sexual behaviour? For fundamentalists, who believe every word of the Bible to be divinely inspired, this question has no meaning. To other minds the problem remains valid. It is certain that the thinking of primitive man was dominated by the need for self preservation and the perpetuation of the species. Homosexual acts cannot create new life. If reproduction is regarded as vital, homosexuality must be an unmitigated evil. If homosexuality becomes rife in any group or community, that society is destined for destruction. Further, the mystery of birth gave it supernatural significance, so that any man who obtained sexual satisfaction in a way that avoided the natural, desirable and divine consequences of sexual intercourse came to be treated as a social outcast. In modern times the human condition has changed dramatically: we are faced not with the extinction of the human species but with a population explosion. There are too many of us, not too few. Contraceptive techniques are used and accepted on a scale hitherto unknown. All this has had an effect on attitudes towards the homosexual: he is still 'queer' but is no longer a menace to the continuity of the species. Indeed, by his failure to reproduce he is making a contribution to the future well-being of society.[1]

Clearly, it was not in the interests of the reformers to raise contentious issues of this sort. Their task was to arouse Christian compassion, not Christian controversy. Their tactic was to keep public and parliamentary debate as rational and moderate as possible because of the danger that an upsurge of emotion and prejudice

[1] Desmond Morris, The Naked Ape (Cape, 1967), pp. 100–1.

would ruin their chance of success. There was, however, no national organization trying to whip up opposition to the principles of the reform. Lord Rowallan (a former Chief Scout) condemned the Bill in the Lords, but he was not reflecting the attitude of the Boy Scouts' Association which was concerned only to protect youth from corruption and to secure an adequate definition of privacy. Sir Cyril Black (Con. Wimbledon) stated in the Commons that 'My own church, the Baptist Church, is not in favour';[1] in fact the Baptists were far from unanimous and exercised no tangible influence on the Bill's progress. The one determined lobby against the Bill came from the National Maritime Board and the National Union of Seamen, and this was designed to exclude the Merchant Navy from its provisions. The N.U.S. circulated 63 MPs setting out its attitude; 34 replied to the circular, of whom 4 indicated they opposed the Union's view, 7 were diplomatically non-committal and the remainder, including 5 members of the Government, indicated support. A delegation from the National Maritime Board met Abse on two occasions to press their case. Informal discussions were held with the Home Office and the Board of Trade on the wording of a suitable amendment to the Bill. Faced with this pressure, the sponsors of the Bill yielded, for otherwise the whole Bill would probably have been lost.

This policy of retreat and compromise produced a law which the Homosexual Law Reform Society regards as unsatisfactory. Besides the exclusion of merchant seamen, both the definition of privacy and the age of consent arouse concern. Privacy requires that only two persons shall be present: this leaves an opportunity for blackmail should a third person arrive either by accident or design. To fix the age of consent at twenty-one is to leave a substantial gap between the laws on homosexual and heterosexual conduct, and there is a danger that a man will not know, or will be misled over the age of his partner in a homosexual act. However, the requirement that the consent of the Director of Public Prosecutions is needed before legal proceedings are initiated has restrained police activity.[2]

The opponents of the Society were steadily weakened. They had no coherent organization. Their claim to represent the traditional

---

[1] H.C. Deb., Vol. 724, col. 798. The somewhat doubtful authority for Sir Cyril's statement was a debate in Baptist Union Council in November 1957, which accepted the following resolution: 'While some of us accept these (i.e. the Wolfenden) recommendations, others are impressed by the reservations put forward by Mr James Adair.' An amendment to replace the word 'some' by 'most' was defeated by 94 votes to 34.

[2] It is also anomalous that heterosexual buggery remains a criminal offence, but this is not an issue that affects homosexuals.

moral conscience of the nation was undermined by the attitude of religious bodies. Public opinion was divided. Gallup Poll figures issued in July 1966 gave no great comfort to either side; 44 per cent opposed the Bill, 39 per cent approved, while the 'Don't Knows' were as high as 17 per cent. The House of Lords, formerly a bulwark against change, had led the parliamentary movement for reform. Indeed, it is difficult to overestimate the influence of the Upper House on this issue. The Earl of Arran was himself surprised at the volume of support he won from the peers. As the controversy developed some eminent peers tried to persuade him to drop the Bill, and he was subjected to some highly unpleasant personal vilification. But the support received made the Earl determined to press forward with his attempts to change the law. The attitude of the Lords, combined with that of the churches, made the cause of homosexual law reform much more respectable socially and politically and could not fail to have an impact on MPs previously neutral or uninformed on the subject. In the case of Labour Members, it must have been curiously difficult to oppose a social reform already accepted by the House of Lords. By 1966 the question was no longer whether the law would or should be changed, but *when* it would happen. At this stage, perhaps, many people came to feel that as reform was certain to come, then the sooner the better, as the continuation of controversy would further increase the amount of publicity devoted to homosexuality.

Chapter 5

Abortion

I

Abortion and infanticide were common in primitive societies. The earliest known abortifacient recipe is over 4,600 years old.[1] These forms of population control were accepted as necessary to ensure a reasonable balance between the size of the family or the tribe and the available food supply. Abortion was approved in Greece and Rome. Aristotle considered that abortion must be procured when a couple produced too many children.[2] In Rome the practice was often used for reasons of vanity, as the matrons did not wish for their physical appearance to suffer through pregnancy. Abortion does not raise any great moral issue in a society that does not place a high value on human life. In primitive communities the sense of compassion is weak because it conflicts with the harsh realities of continuing existence. A civilization, like Rome, dominated by its love of gladiatorial combat, could not be concerned with the fate of a foetus in a womb. Later Roman writers regarded abortion as wrong but not as a serious crime.

The development of Christian theology produced a profound change in attitude towards abortion. The Christians taught that every human being had a soul; that in spite of original sin, all were capable of salvation; that baptism was the first step towards salvation. Thus if an infant died before baptism, it suffered eternal damnation. Such a doctrine raised the problem of infants as yet unborn. At what stage did they acquire a soul and so qualify for eternal damnation? The theologians taught that the foetus acquired an immortal being when it achieved animation; so the 'quickening' in the mother's womb gained a new significance. The Christian church thus regarded abortion as a serious crime, not only because it destroyed life but also because it involved the damnation of an immortal soul.[3]

This doctrine was accepted as part of English law. Blackstone

[1] Glanville Williams: *The Sanctity of Life and the Criminal Law* (Faber, 1958), p. 140.
[2] *Politics*, vii.
[3] W. E. H. Lecky: *History of European Morals* (Longmans, 1911), Vol. II, pp. 20–24.

wrote that 'Life begins in contemplation of law as soon as the infant is able to stir in the mother's womb'.[1] The legal authorities disagreed as to whether abortion after quickening should be treated as murder or merely as a misdemeanour. Certainly, whatever the state of the law, it was commonly disregarded and abortion before quickening was not a crime. The stage of quickening was treated as highly important and it aroused interest and comment: Pepys noted in his diary: 'Lady Castlemaine quickened at my Lord Gerard's at dinner.'

Abortion did not become a statutory offence until 1803. The preamble to the Act recorded that 'no adequate means have hitherto been provided for the prevention and punishment of such offences'. Under the 1803 Act, abortion, or an attempt to procure abortion, was a crime whether carried out before or after quickening. However, quickening was still of significance in that if a pregnancy was interfered with after this stage had been reached the penalties were harsher. The statute made no specific reference to the position of a woman who procured her own abortion but presumably it covered such a case since it was designed to make abortion a crime irrespective of the perpetrator or means employed. Abortion was made a capital offence in 1828 but this provision was repealed in 1837. The Offences Against the Person Act, 1837, also made it clear that an attempt to secure an abortion was still an offence even where a woman was not, in fact, pregnant.

The Criminal Law Commissioners, in their review of this part of the criminal law, suggested in 1846 that abortion should not be an offence 'when such act is done in good faith with the intention of saving the life of the mother'.[2] This proposal was not adopted when the law on abortion was re-enacted in 1861, but it was incorporated into the Infant Life (Preservation) Act, 1929, and has had substantial influence on subsequent developments.

Section 58 of the Offences Against the Person Act, 1861, provided the statutory basis of the law on abortion for over a century. 'Every Woman, being with Child, Who, with Intent to procure her own Miscarriage, shall unlawfully administer to herself any Poison or other noxious Thing, or shall unlawfully use any Instrument or other Means whatsoever with like Intent and whosoever, with Intent to procure the Miscarriage of any Woman whether she be or be not with Child, shall unlawfully administer to her or cause to be taken by her any Poison or other noxious Thing, or shall unlawfully use any Instrument or other means whatsoever with the like Intent, shall be guilty of felony.' For the first time it became wholly clear that

[1] *Commentaries* (1769), Vol. i, p. 129.
[2] pp. 41–2; 1846 [709] xxiv.

self-abortion was a crime, but a woman who mistakenly believed herself to be pregnant could not be so convicted.

What may seem to be the unequivocal words of the 1861 Act were subsequently interpreted in such a way as to legitimize abortion in certain conditions. The leading case was *R*. v. *Bourne*[1] which arose from an operation performed by Mr Aleck Bourne to terminate the pregnancy of a fourteen-year-old girl. Bourne was a consultant obstetrician and had performed the operation quite openly at St Mary's Hospital, London. He received no fee for his work and reported to the police what he had done. There was no question of police detection; the matter was a test case to determine the law on therapeutic abortion. The girl had become pregnant having been raped by four soldiers who had enticed her into the Horse Guards' barracks off Whitehall by the promise of showing her a horse with a green tail. Bourne, having learned these circumstances, decided that it was his duty to operate and did so with the consent of the girl's parents. Medical evidence at the trial asserted that had the girl been forced to continue with a pregnancy commenced in such a horrible way, she would have become a mental wreck. Thus there was a strong therapeutic claim for abortion. The alternative claim, that as a matter of equity, the girl should not be required to suffer further for the crime of others, was not put forward by the defence at the trial.

Bourne commanded widespread sympathy, both through support for his action and for his courage in placing his professional career in jeopardy to obtain legal clarification which might help others and which would certainly stimulate public debate of the issues involved. The presiding judge at the trial, Mr Justice Macnaghten, was also sympathetic, and in his summing-up he interpreted the law in a liberal manner which helped to secure Bourne's acquittal. The judge argued that the repeated use of the word 'unlawfully' in Section 58 of the 1861 Act must have meant that Parliament envisaged that there might be circumstances where abortion could be legitimate; that the word 'unlawfully' was not meaningless but represented an essential condition for conviction. The judge then argued that the conditions of lawful abortion as contemplated in 1861 were those set out in the Infant Life (Preservation) Act, 1929, which permitted the destruction of a child when done in good faith to save the life of the mother. So the intentions of Parliament in 1861 were defined by reference to legislation actually passed in 1929. However, the fact

[1] (1938) 3 A.E.R. 615; (1939) I.K.B. 687. For a statement of the evolution of the law see B. M. Dickens: *Abortion and the Law* (MacGibbon and Kee, 1966). Bourne has given his own version of the case in *A Doctor's Creed* (Gollancz, 1962).

that the 1861 Act did not adopt the explicit suggestion of the Criminal Law Commissioners in 1846 to accept this principle must cast the gravest doubt on the judge's interpretation of the statute. The word 'unlawfully' in the 1861 Act was merely repeated from earliest legislation, notably that of 1803, and its use was a consequence of the prolix style of legal draftsmen in the early nineteenth century. The idea that it represented support for therapeutic abortion is fanciful. *R*. v. *Bourne* is a clear example of judge-made law.

There was a second vital piece of statutory interpretation in the judge's summing-up. What meaning was to be attributed to the phrase in the 1929 Act which referred to 'saving the life of the mother'? Did this mean that an operation was permissible only to save her from immediate death or should it also be allowed if the birth was likely to shorten her life substantially? In the *Bourne* case the prosecution accepted the need to save the life of the mother but argued that as there was no threat to the girl's life an offence had been committed. Mr Justice Macnaghten did not accept this view. Instead, he argued that one could not make a clear distinction between a threat to life and a threat to health and that regard must be paid to the quality of life as well as its duration. He noted with apparent approval that Bourne said that he would have refused to perform the operation had the girl been simple-minded or had she had 'a prostitute mind' because in either case a birth after rape would not have such disastrous effects on the health of the patient. The result of this interpretation was again far-reaching, for it meant that abortion was to be justified not by rape but by the physical and mental conditions of the mother.

The judge was careful to distinguish the *Bourne* case from the normal run of back-street abortion cases that come before the criminal courts. He stressed that Bourne was a qualified medical practitioner with specialized experience in this field; that he performed the operation openly and in consequence of his professional judgement; that Bourne had obtained no financial gain from his work; that he had first consulted other medical opinion of high authority. The last condition was important because it helped to demonstrate that the operation was undertaken 'in good faith' as required by the 1929 Act. Thus the Bourne judgement confirmed the criminality of back-street abortions. Yet it did open the way for a professional abortionist provided that he was medically qualified and acted only in consultation with other suitably qualified medical practitioners. Another consequence of the *Bourne* case was that it became immaterial whether the medical opinions on the mental or physical condition of the mother are correct: the abortion was legitimate if based on medical decisions made in good faith. This principle was explicitly upheld in a later case, *R. v. Bergmann and Ferguson* (1948).[1]

A strong argument in favour of abortion law reform was that the *Bourne* case left the law in considerable doubt. In theory, the principles set out by Mr Justice Macnaghten could have been over-turned by the Court of Criminal Appeal or the House of Lords. Yet this possibility was remote because the principles gained much approbation and many medical men were known to act upon them consistently. Another uncertainty was what degree of risk to the physical and mental welfare of the mother justified abortion. So there remained a chance that a prosecution might be initiated to define the degree of risk more closely. The *Bourne* case also limited strictly the right to abort to qualified medical practitioners – but must this be so even in an emergency? Clearly, a person other than a doctor can have an honest belief that a woman's life is in imminent danger, but whether an unqualified person could ever be entitled to act on that belief is another question. If the law were stretched to permit 'emergency' abortions by anyone, there would be a strong possibility of abuse; indeed, the law would tend to become unen-forceable. Finally, there is nothing in the Bourne judgement to justify the termination of pregnancy because of serious deformity of the child unless one attempts to argue that a mother's health would be seriously damaged by caring for deformed offspring. Lord Denning has said that the law on abortion would permit the opera-tion when a mother had German measles, but this comment was made at a medical school not in a formal judgement.[2] The issue became more pressing with the thalidomide tragedies, when seriously deformed babies were born to women who had taken this new drug during pregnancy. There is no record of the prosecution of a doctor for operating on a mother who had taken thalidomide; doubtless no one in authority wished to test the law.

In practice the effect of the 1861 statute on abortion was sub-stantially modified by the pressure of opinion and the growth of medical knowledge. And, inevitably, the law became obscure.

II

There are three basic attitudes towards abortion. That it should never take place. That it should be made available whenever desired by a

---

[1] This case is unreported, but Glanville Williams quotes from the official transcript of the judge's direction to the jury: *The Sanctity of Life and the Criminal Law*, p. 165.

[2] *British Medical Journal* (1956), Vol. II, p. 821.

pregnant woman. That it should be permissible in certain circumstances. The first two views are absolute and rest on fairly simple propositions. The third or intermediate attitude has an almost infinite number of variations and arouses a complex assortment of arguments.

The Catholic condemnation of abortion is unqualified. It rested originally on the need to baptize every living soul to save it from hell fire. This doctrine appears to have been formulated by Origen in the third century and was confirmed by Saint Fulgentius three centuries later: 'Be assured, and doubt not, that even little children that have begun to live in their mother's womb and have there died, or who, having just been born, have passed away from the world without the sacrament of holy baptism, must be punished by the eternal torture of undying fire.'[1] Even this fearsome edict left open the question of when a child had 'begun to live'. It was noted above that the early theologians did not equate the creation of a soul with conception but with quickening. However, the Catholic Church in 1869 pronounced the punishment of excommunication for abortion irrespective of whether the foetus could be regarded as having a soul. An abortion in the early stage of pregnancy was described as anticipated homicide. In 1951 the total prohibition of abortion, even for therapeutic purposes, was restated in a papal encyclical. Thus if there is a straight choice between the life of a mother and that of her unborn baby, a Catholic doctor should not sacrifice the latter to save the former; the mother must die. Non-Catholic women should therefore avoid Catholic doctors. It appears that a Catholic doctor can only act to save the mother when surgery needed to save her life has the indirect effect of killing the foetus, i.e. the extinction of its life must not be anticipated or desired but is an unwanted secondary effect of the operation. (Even this escape clause is not to be used wherever the condition requiring the operation is due to pregnancy.)[2] This is the doctrine of 'indirect effect' by which an action to promote good is permitted if it has secondary and unintended evil consequences. To a very limited extent the Catholic position on abortion is less extreme than other faiths which deny the need for all surgery, because they claim it is either unnecessary or against God's will.

Today Catholics tend to defend their attitude not so much by reference to hell fire but by insisting that a foetus has a natural right to life, a proposition which many non-Catholics accept. Yet if the

---

[1] Quoted by Glanville Williams, p. 181.

[2] By a complex process of reasoning Catholic surgeons are now permitted to remove an ectopic or extra-uterine pregnancy where the death of both mother and child is practically certain if nothing is done.

argument is shifted to the plane of natural rights, the question of the mother's rights must also arise. When there is a stark choice between the life of a mother and that of someone unborn, who has the stronger claim to life? The loss of the mother will cause greater immediate damage to society. On the other hand, it could be urged that the mother has had some opportunity already to enjoy life, that someone unborn has not, so that equity demands the sacrifice of the mother. Either way, the argument is not theological. The importance of the natural rights theory is to provide wider support for a restrictive policy because, as a minimum, it requires that abortion be limited to those cases where it is essential to preserve the mother's life.

At the other end of the spectrum of opinion it is asserted that abortion should be made available on demand. On this view, a woman should have complete control over her body and should be entitled to decide whether an embryo be removed in the same way as she might wish to be rid of a protruding tooth. This implies that a foetus has no right to life. The question then arises – at what stage is an unborn child entitled to the protection of the law? Should legal rights be acquired at the moment of birth? An affirmative answer to this proposition is repugnant to humanitarian principles. Many people would subscribe to what might be termed a common-sense view that the moral position is different when a pregnancy is eight months old from when it has existed for one month. What is invisible and difficult to visualize has a far weaker pull on the emotions than that which is about to emerge as a separate human being. The objection to this approach is that it is difficult to define a stage in time when abortion should become illicit, or to find a rational basis for making such a distinction.

The intermediate position, that abortion is sometimes justifiable, is accepted by much Protestant opinion and the Jewish faith. It raises many issues of when the operation should be permissible, how decisions should be made and what safeguards are necessary. A pamphlet entitled *Abortion: an Ethical Discussion* issued by the Church Assembly Board for Social Responsibility in 1965 was an important attempt to establish an intermediate set of principles, and provided some support for those who wished to liberalize the law. The pamphlet starts with an historical review of attitudes to abortion but is careful to avoid becoming entangled in theological doctrine: instead, it accepts abortion, and the large unsatisfied demand for abortion, as a pressing social problem. The authors agree that society at large has a legitimate interest in individual decisions on abortion both in terms of maintaining an adequate birth rate and of supporting conventional sexual morality, but their emphasis is on the health and well-being of the mother. There is, therefore, a ready acceptance of the Bourne judgement and a disposition to extend it. Apart from cases where the life and health of the mother are endangered, the pamphlet considered three other matters – the risk of giving birth to a deformed child; the effect of an extra child on a family where the mother was already overstrained; pregnancy resulting from illegal sexual intercourse. The pamphlet argued that none of these circumstances *ipso facto* justified abortion but that they might all be taken into consideration when assessing the future well-being of the mother. Thus eugenic and social abortions are ruled out although these factors remain grounds for allowing therapeutic surgery. This compromise can be described as an ingenious way out of the moral difficulties surrounding non-therapeutic abortions, but its practical effect would be to increase the range of discretion of the medical profession. An awkward ethical problem was shovelled on to the doctors. What would happen to a woman wanting abortion would depend on the attitude of her doctor or of any other doctors she could find in time.

The importance of this publication from the Established Church was to mark a major advance of influential opinion from the position reached in the 1930s. This discussion, cut short by the advent of war, had dual origins. The medical profession were uneasy about the obscurity of the legal position, especially before the Bourne judgement; there was also concern at the rate of maternal mortality caused by miscarriages, including those criminally induced. A Departmental Committee established by the Ministry of Health on Maternal Mortality and Morbidity issued an interim report in 1930 and a final report in 1932.[1] The result of further research into maternal mortality was issued by the Ministry of Health in 1937.[2] These investigations convinced Ministers that a full-scale enquiry into abortions was required. From 1932 onwards the problem of abortion had been raised at successive annual conferences of the British Medical Association, and in 1934 the Association formed a special committee to examine the medical aspects of abortion. Two years later this work was completed so that the B.M.A. was fully prepared to present evidence to the official Committee of Enquiry established in 1937 under the chairmanship of Mr Norman Birkett, Q.C. The Committee was required

'To enquire into the prevalence of abortion, and the law relating

[1] These are both non-parliamentary publications.
[2] 1936–37, Cmd. 5422 and 5423, xi.

thereto, and to consider what steps can be taken by more effective enforcement of the law or otherwise, to secure the reduction of maternal mortality and morbidity arising from this cause.'

Their report appeared in March 1939 as a non-parliamentary publication issued by the Ministry of Health and the Home Office. The classification as 'non-parliamentary' is significant. It meant that the report was not automatically issued free to MPs and that it was not included in the bound sets of official publications; in other words the report was not regarded as being of major importance or as being likely to lead to early legislation.[1] Another aspect of this publication is worthy of comment: the price, eleven shillings, was approximately four times that of other publications of similar size issued by the Stationery Office. One can but assume that the high cost to purchasers was deliberately designed to restrict circulation.

No action followed the work of the Birkett Committee, but it furnished a valuable indication of opinion at this period. It distinguished three types of abortion, spontaneous, therapeutic and criminal. Therapeutic abortions were defined as those induced in good faith by a duly qualified medical practitioner when satisfied that continuation of pregnancy would endanger a patient's life or seriously impair her health. The *Bourne* case occurred while the Committee was in being and this definition implied that the Committee fully accepted Mr Justice Macnaghten's interpretation of the law, and recommended that the statutes be amended on the lines of his judgement to make the position unmistakeably clear.[2] Otherwise the conclusions of the Birkett Committee offered no support for reformers. They reviewed the unsatisfactory state of the statistics relating to abortion and concluded that it was unrealistic to expect to be able to gather accurate information either about the total of induced miscarriages or of the maternal mortality arising from them. They examined the law on abortion in various countries abroad; in particular, they noted that the Soviet Union in 1936 had modified its earlier acceptance of abortion by restricting it to medical and eugenic cases because Soviet doctors had found that the operation had undesirable effects on the patient. The Birkett Committee perhaps found it convenient to accept the official Soviet explanation for the change in policy: the disappearance of literature on contraception from Russian bookshops at the same time suggests, however, that the decision was a political one designed to assist population growth

[1] On the classification of parliamentary papers, see P. and G. Ford: *A Guide to Parliamentary Papers* (Blackwell, 1955), esp. pp. 16–17.
[2] Para. 198.

in the face of the menace of Nazi Germany. It is notable that in 1955, after the death of Stalin, the Soviet abortion law was again liberalized.

The Birkett Committee themselves reflected the contemporary concern over the decline in the reproduction rate. It rejected the proposals of the Abortion Law Reform Association for the 'principle of voluntary parenthood' which implied legalization of abortion for social, economic and personal reasons, on three grounds – the destruction of a human embryo; the eventual decline in population; the increase in sexual promiscuity. Nor did the Committee accept that wider knowledge of contraceptive methods would reduce the number of abortions: if contraceptive advice were freely available, those who made use of it and still became pregnant would, in the Committee's view, be even more likely to resort to the back-street abortionist. They recommended, therefore, that contraceptive advice should not be made available through the public health services except to married women whose health was likely to be adversely affected by pregnancy. The Committee accepted that many married women desperately sought abortion from fear of the economic burden of adding another child to the family and suggested the way to ease the problem was through a system of family allowances. Thus the Committee was not merely hostile to abortion on other than strictly therapeutic grounds; it also wished to facilitate the growth of population. 'Any considerable extension of the grounds upon which abortion might be lawfully procured would, we believe, almost inevitably tend to hasten a decline in the size of the population. . . . We should greatly regret the introduction of any measure which would be likely to aggravate the position.'[1] Rape and incest were also not regarded as sufficient grounds for abortion since, were the operation to be done early enough not to be dangerous, it would prejudge a court ruling. Sexual intercourse under the age of legal consent also was insufficient justification since young girls sometimes agreed willingly to copulation. The Committee dealt with – some would say avoided – the problem of eugenic abortions by proposing that it should be treated by sterilization.[2]

The Committee were not wholly unanimous in attitude. Two members were in favour of wider facilities for contraceptive advice. Mrs Thurtle produced a minority report which proposed that the grounds for abortion should be liberalized and that consideration should be given to abortion on demand by any mother who had had four children.

[1] Para. 232.
[2] A Ministry of Health Departmental Committee Report on sterilization had been issued in 1934; 1933–34 Cmd. 4485, xv.

With the pigeon-holing of the Birkett Report the subject of abortion law reform received little public attention for the next twenty years. In 1952 a private member's Bill introduced by Joseph Reeves (Lab. Greenwich) was debated for one minute, but this measure was limited to providing unmistakeable authority for therapeutic abortion.[1] Also in the 1950s occasional parliamentary questions were asked with the aim of urging the Government to clarify the law; these produced a standard reply that Ministers were not convinced of the need for early action upon a very controversial subject.[2] In October 1955 the Magistrates' Association passed a resolution urging reform of the law. By the end of the decade interest in the subject was reviving. In 1958 Glanville Williams' *The Sanctity of Life and the Criminal Law* appeared containing a powerful claim for a more liberal approach. Roy Jenkins (Lab. Stechford) in *The Labour Case*, published before the 1959 Election, referred to the abortion laws as harsh and archaic. The next year Mrs Alice Jenkins in *Law for the Rich* publicized the relative ease with which abortions could be obtained through certain Harley Street specialists in return for a substantial fee, a state of affairs regarded as indefensible both by Catholic opinion and abortion law reformers, and which was highly embarrassing for the official view that nothing needed to be done. At this period the Abortion Law Reform Association, founded in 1936, became more active in organizing meetings and providing speakers. In 1960 the Cambridge Union narrowly defeated, by 146 votes to 137, a motion favouring abortion law reform.

The climate of opinion had become very different from that which had produced the Birkett Report. The demographic position had been reversed dramatically: the worry was not a declining birth rate but a population explosion. Attitudes to contraception had become more favourable, even in the Catholic Church, and artificial family limitation was accepted as a means of improving standards of family life. There was also greater toleration of extra-marital sexual inter-course. The idea that easier abortion would lead to moral decay and sexual licence lost much of its power. Further, the growth of welfare services since 1945 was both a consequence and a cause of the greater attention devoted to the quality of life. If the new levels of minimum social provision were to be maintained, if not improved, there was a clear need to limit the demands made upon them and, therefore, to restrict the numbers of unwanted babies.

In Parliament those who advocated reform tended to ignore these background considerations. Instead, specific issues were pressed. The

[1] H.C. Deb., Vol. 511, col. 2506.
[2] E.g. H.C. Deb., Vol. 544, col. 176 and Vol. 548, col. 47,

uncertainty of the legal position, based as it was on case law, was highly unsatisfactory. Parliament was faced with a situation in which judges had reinterpreted a nineteenth-century statute to bring it more in accord with contemporary thought. The medical profession was still in some doubt about the exact state of the law and a few of its members had been earning high fees while risking prosecution. The moral authority of the abortion law was gravely weakened by the accusation that it provided one rule for the rich and another for the poor. Equally indefensible, although less frequently mentioned, was the fact that the chances of obtaining a legitimate therapeutic abortion varied as between different regions of the country; Aberdeen had the reputation of being liberal while Birmingham was the reverse. A formal restatement of the law was urged on the basis that it would help to even out these inequalities in its application to various income groups and as between different areas. It will be noted that all the arguments in this paragraph could be used without raising the vital issue of whether the grounds for legitimate abortion should be widened.

The grievously deformed thalidomide babies increased sympathy and understanding for eugenic terminations. On the wider topic of social abortions, perhaps the most compelling claim was that a more liberal law would lead to a big reduction in back-street abortions and attempts at self-abortion which could have a most serious effect on a woman's health. There can be little disagreement over the desirability of an operation being carried out by qualified persons in hygienic conditions. A woman will only seek illegal abortion when she is desperate and urgently needs professional advice and aid but, before 1968, the state of the law might deter her from seeing a doctor or might encourage a doctor to avoid a full examination of her condition. And if doctors were somewhat uncertain of their rights in this matter, their women patients were even less well informed. The combination of doubt, secrecy, guilt and fear produced a steady flow of custom for the professional abortionist, and the after-care of illegitimate abortions constituted a substantial burden on the National Health Service. A woman desperate for abortion may suffer grave psychological damage if it is refused. No doubt, only a very small proportion of those who consider or threaten suicide carry out the intention, but any discussion of suicide by a pregnant patient presents a doctor with a complex problem. Finally, there is the general argument for social abortion – that unwanted children should not be brought into the world. This principle can be applied to many situations. Schoolgirls and, indeed, all women can claim to be protected from the full consequences of sexual assault. Single girls may wish to avoid the stigma attached to the unwed mother. Women with large families may want to escape the physical and financial strain of another child. Cases of this type can be extended until the position of abortion on demand has been reached. Probably a majority of those who supported reform in Parliament did not wish to go that far.

Equally, there was no unanimity of view among those who opposed any extension of grounds for abortion. The strict Catholic position, that once a human life has been conceived it must not be extinguished, was put forward in both Houses.[1] On this fundamentalist view, the *Bourne* judgement was unacceptable. However, no serious attempt was made to attack the *status quo* and the arguments advanced against change were essentially practical and limited in scope, emphasizing fears of various unfortunate consequences which might follow from any change in the law. Such tactics were obviously good sense: a theological crusade against abortion was certain to fail in a predominantly non-Catholic legislature.

Much of the case against abortion is medical in character. It is asserted that patients suffer adverse after-effects from the operation; that experience of other countries shows that the liberalization of the law does not eliminate recourse to unqualified back-street abortionists; that a more flexible law would make it easier for unscrupulous members of the medical profession to earn a high income in this way. Within the context of the National Health Service it was argued that there were no spare beds available to deal with a flood of extra women having terminations; that doctors dealing with this class of case might not have appropriate qualifications to make a decision; that doctors and nurses ordered to assist at such operations might have an intolerable conflict between their medical duty and their conscience. It was also suggested that legislation which defines conditions for termination of pregnancy interferes with the freedom of the medical profession: this assertion cuts both ways in that it could be used by advocates of reform to support a claim for having no legislation whatever on abortion. There was also wide agreement for the proposition that a woman distressed over her pregnancy needs social and medical care to relieve anxiety rather than the irreversible act of abortion: again, this argument is not fundamental and can be compatible with acceptance of abortion in certain circumstances. Eugenic abortion was opposed on the grounds that even gravely deformed persons may experience great happiness and give happiness

---

[1] E.g., H.C. Deb., Vol. 732, col. 1086 (W. Wells, Lab. Walsall, N.). *Ibid.*, col. 1123 (K. McNamara, Lab. Hull, N.). *Ibid.*, col. 1155, N. St John Stevas, Con. Chelmsford). Also H.L. Deb., Vol. 270, cols 1207, 1214, 1221.

G

to others. Fear was also expressed that it might provide a bridgehead of justification for the elimination of the unfit. Social abortion was opposed by the claim that life should not be taken merely as a convenience to a pregnant woman, or because of the poverty of an existing family.

The first step in the parliamentary campaign that finally amended the law came in June 1965, when Mrs Renee Short (Lab. Wolverhampton N.E.) introduced a Bill under the Ten-Minute Rule.[1] There was no reply to her speech of introduction, no division, but as always with this type of Bill, there was no opportunity for further progress. Yet the Bill is of interest because of its provisions. It permitted a medical practitioner to terminate pregnancy in good faith on four grounds: to preserve the life of a patient; where giving birth or caring for a child would involve grave risk of serious injury to a woman's physical or mental health; where there was grave risk of a child being born gravely deformed or severely abnormal mentally; where the pregnancy was the result of a sexual offence. Termination under the last three grounds was to require the concurrence of a second medical practitioner and was not to be performed after the thirteenth week of pregnancy. The burden of proof in any prosecution that the operation was not performed in good faith was to rest with the Crown.

In November of the same year Lord Silkin introduced a similar Bill in the Upper House. This measure was more radical in character. Besides the grounds for abortion outlined above, it included what became known as the 'social clause': termination was to be permissible if a medical practitioner believed that a patient's health or social conditions (including those of her existing children) made her unsuitable to assume the legal or moral responsibility for caring for a child or another child. Also, as compared with Mrs Short's Bill, the time restriction on the operation was less narrowly drawn. It was brought forward from the thirteenth week to the sixteenth week and applied solely to terminations under the social clause and those where the justification was a sexual offence. This Bill received a second reading by 67 votes to 8.[2] After extensive discussion and some amendment at the committee stage it passed through the Lords just as Parliament was dissolved for the 1966 General Election.

Meanwhile a private member's Bill in the Commons introduced under the ballot procedure by Wingfield Digby (Con. Dorset, W.) was debated for an hour in February 1966. The Speaker refused to allow the motion for the second reading to be put as the debate had

[1] H.C. Deb., Vol. 714, cols 254–8.
[2] H.L. Deb., Vol. 270, cols 1139–242.

been so brief, and the Bill was talked out by Peter Mahon (Lab. Preston, S.)[1] This measure did not include the social clause but it did contain new provisions requiring the doctor who carried out an abortion to notify the Chief Medical Officer of the Ministry of Health within seven days. The notification procedure was clearly an important safeguards against abuse of the powers conferred by the Bill.

Thus by the 1966 General Election the ground had been well prepared. Lord Silkin's measure had passed the Upper House. A favourable vote in the Commons had been prevented only by deliberate obstruction. Everything depended on whether a sympathetic Member could be found with a favourable place in the sessional ballot. David Steel (Lib. Roxburgh, Selkirk and Peebles), one of the youngest Members and a keen social reformer, obtained third place. Immediately he was approached by the Abortion Law Reform Association, and after some preliminary consultations he decided to promote their cause. For the A.L.R.A. this was a double piece of good fortune. Not only had they a new and able standard-bearer with a good place in the ballot but, because of the timing of the 1966 Election in the spring, the session 1966–67 was to be unusually long, so that the chances of the Bill being lost through lack of time were less than normal. Even so, the Bill nearly did perish for this reason. But the omens at second reading were favourable, for the vote in favour was 223 to 29.[2] The amount of interest in the subject was high; the Speaker made a plea at the start of the day for short speeches as 32 Members had already indicated a desire to enter the debate.[3] Speaking for the Government, Roy Jenkins, the Home Secretary, explained its attitude as one of neutrality but offered drafting assistance for the subsequent stages. Only one Minister, Mrs Shirley Williams, Parliamentary Secretary to the Minister of Labour, voted against the second reading, while 38 members of the Government voted in support.

Steel's Bill was similar, but not identical, with earlier measures. Its original draft provided for therapeutic and eugenic terminations, and the social clause – later rephrased – permitted abortion where a woman's capacity as a mother would be severely overstrained. The clause covering rape was also dropped at the committee stage.

[1] H.C. Deb., Vol. 725, cols 837–56.
[2] H.C. Deb., Vol. 732, cols 1067–1166.
[3] Over half the 32 Members failed to catch the Speaker's eye in the five hour debate but, no doubt, some of these were appointed to the Standing Committee. It is unusual for the Speaker to announce the number of Members who wish to speak.

Concurrence of two registered medical practitioners was required save where an emergency operation was necessary to save a woman's life. All terminations were to be carried out in a National Health Service hospital or other place approved by the Minister of Health, and those not done in hospitals were to be notified.

The later stages of the Bill proved far more difficult than might have been expected from the heavy majority at second reading. A long delay before the Bill reached Standing Committee was due to the extended committee discussion of another private member's Bill which had priority.[1] Yet further obstacles developed as some Members who had abstained on the second reading – or in the case of Leo Abse (Lab. Pontypool) had then given support – became trenchant objectors to particular clauses. So the committee stage was protracted and no less than twelve sittings were needed before the Bill could be returned to the House. Much of this time was consumed by procedural technicalities and irrelevant speeches that can be described only as filibustering. Seventeen divisions took place in committee, but the Bill's sponsors won each of them comfortably, save for Leo Abse's proposal that one of the two doctors concerned in any case should be a consultant gynaecologist. This suggestion appeared to have the support of the Ministry of Health[2] and was defeated by the narrow margin of 13 to 11. Another major controversy grew over the wording of the social clause: the final form accepted that in assessing the risk to a mother's health and well-being, her total environment, actual and potentially foreseeable, should be taken into account and also the well-being of her existing children. An amendment to safeguard the position of those who felt unable for conscientious reasons to assist with abortion operations was agreed unanimously.

Meetings of the Standing Committee lasted from January to April 1967. Not until June did the Bill come before the House on the report stage. One whole Friday of private member's time proved utterly inadequate to deal with the amendments tabled.[3] Inevitably, the Bill must have failed through shortage of time had the Government not agreed to its further consideration at the close of Government business. So on June 29, 1967, the Commons started its discussion of amendments at 10.35 p.m. and continued to do so

[1] This Bill concerned Employment Agencies. It was suggested by the Political Correspondent of *The Observer* (March 12, 1967) that the lengthy arguments on this measures were the start of the filibuster against the Abortion Bill. However, the theory lacks substance since no one who occupied much time on Employment Agencies was opposed to the Abortion Bill.

[2] Later the Ministry's attitude changed: see p. 107 *infra*.

[3] H.C. Deb., Vol. 474, cols 448–536.

for nearly twelve hours. Exactly a fortnight later another marathon session of thirteen hours was needed to complete the passage of the Bill.[1] Twenty-eight divisions were challenged on report, twelve of them on the motion 'that the question be now put'. The arguments were largely a repetition of those heard in committee and there was again some element of deliberate time-wasting. One fresh proposal, defeated by 198 votes to 122, was that the Bill should apply for a trial period only and expire after 1973 unless Parliament decided to the contrary. Other hostile amendments were defeated by similar or sometimes much larger majorities because the Bill's opponents were divided between those who were against abortion on principle, and those who wished the legislation to be more narrowly drafted than Steel's proposals. Among the leading opponents were Norman St John Stevas (Con. Chelmsford), Mrs Jill Knight (Con. Birmingham, Edgbaston) and Michael English (Lab. Nottingham, W.). Their partial success is shown by the third reading vote, 167 to 83, indicating a sharp rise in the opposition as compared with the second reading.

Meanwhile, in the Upper House, Lord Silkin had reintroduced his Bill at the start of the 1966–67 parliamentary session. It passed through second reading and committee but then lapsed as by this time Steel's measure had started its journey through the Commons and the Lords waited for this to come before them.[2] In a formal sense Lord Silkin's efforts were wasted. In political terms they were highly important. They helped to prepare a favourable reception for Steel's Bill in the Upper House and their success had given extra impetus to the cause of reform in the Commons. Even so, the battle in the Lords was not over. Two amendments to Steel's Bill were carried at the committee stage. The requirement that one of the doctors concerned should be a consultant was carried by 116 votes to 67. The other change, carried by one vote, 87 to 86, limited the extent of the social clause by removing the reference to the condition of 'any existing children of the family'. These changes were made in July 1967 just as Parliament adjourned for the summer recess. They immediately raised the prospect of a clash between the two Houses in which the whole Bill would be lost. There was some talk of a constitutional crisis in the relations between the two Houses and a possibility that the old controversy might rekindle about a democratic chamber being thwarted by an hereditary and nominated body. However, this development was avoided. The prestige of the Labour

[1] *Ibid.*, Vol. 749, cols 895–1102; and Vol. 750, cols 1159–1386.
[2] It is virtually unknown for the Commons to find time for a non-Government Bill that originates in the Lords.

Government was not involved since it accepted no responsibility for a private member's Bill. Supporters of abortion law reform had no desire to become involved in constitutional/political arguments that would have divided their own ranks. Then in October the Lords reconsidered the amendments and changed their minds.[1] The House accepted that to insist on the need for a consultant's opinion would, in practice, narrow the operation of the measure in an arbitrary way; the voting was 113 to 79. The original form of the social clause was adopted by 86 votes to 69. It is notable that the swing of opinion was greater on the consultant clause. On second thoughts many peers, including the Archbishop of Canterbury, changed their minds because it was clear the provision created insoluble practical difficulties. So, ultimately, Steel's Bill achieved the Royal Assent but with a new title: an uncontroversial amendment had changed this from the Termination of Pregnancy Bill to the Abortion Bill.

III

The driving force behind the campaign described in this chapter was the Abortion Law Reform Association, originally founded in 1936 at the time of the Birkett Committee. Mrs Dorothy Thurtle, who wrote the dissenting minority report of this Committee, was the wife of a Labour Member and played an active part in the early years of the Association by helping to organize the presentation of its case to sympathetic Members. At the outset support for A.L.R.A. came largely from women members of the Labour and Co-operative movements. The activities of the Association were at a low ebb in the 1940s, strengthened a little in the 1950s and became vigorous after the thalidomide cases in 1962. Membership in 1960 was less than 200; by 1966 it exceeded 1,000. Local branches were established in Birmingham, Manchester and Bristol.[2] Their case was pressed at private and public meetings, parliamentarians were lobbied in person and by correspondence. Much encouragement was gained from a survey of the opinion of doctors engaged in the National Health Service in the London area in 1965: 69 per cent supported the aims of the Association; 84 per cent regarded abortion as a safe operation; 75 per cent thought it should be available through the National Health Service. The sponsors of the Bill in both Houses, David Steel

---

[1] H.L. Deb., Vol. 285, cols 1394–509.
[2] K. Hindell and Madeline Simms: 'How the Abortion Lobby Worked', *Political Quarterly* (1968), Vol. 39, pp. 269–82.

and Lord Silkin, were both persuaded by A.L.R.A. members to espouse their cause. Thanks to a recent questionnaire that A.L.R.A. circulated to its own supporters it is possible to provide a fairly detailed picture of its social composition. Three-fifths of the members were women, two-thirds of whom had some form of higher education. 1 in 3 of the women had required abortion; 1 in 4 had had one, mostly legally but paid for privately. Their husbands tend to be doctors, university lecturers or engineers. Three-quarters of the total membership are agnostics of one kind or another, but there is also significant Christian support. Politically the members are predominantly left-wing and tend to read *The Guardian* or *The Times*. The picture is of a young middle-aged, middle-class, intellectual pressure group, whose strength comes from the quality of its support rather than from its size or financial power.

Members of A.L.R.A. attended all the relevant parliamentary debates and kept in close touch with their leading parliamentary supporters. These included, apart from David Steel, Peter Jackson (Lab. High Peak), Sir George Sinclair (Con. Dorking), Christopher Price (Lab. Birmingham, Perry Barr), Dame Joan Vickers (Con. Plymouth, Devonport) and Mrs Lena Jeger (Lab. Holborn and St Pancras S.). There was less lobbying of the Upper House as peers are not so amenable to such persuasion. Thus the substantial vote in favour of Lord Silkin's Bill in 1965 was in no sense due to careful planning: on the contrary, it came as a surprise, pleasant or unpleasant, to all concerned. As interest in the subject grew in the Upper House, some peers got in touch with A.L.R.A. and were assisted with information and research. One use A.L.R.A. made of peers was to arrange for them to sign sympathetic letters to *The Times* as noble subscription appeared to improve chances of publication. Lady Gaitskell was a Vice-President of the Association. The chairman of its executive committee, Mrs Vera Houghton, was the wife of Douglas Houghton (Lab. Sowerby) a member of the Wilson Cabinet until January 1967, and subsequently the Chairman of the Parliamentary Labour Party. The sponsor of the Bill in the Upper House, Lord Silkin, was the father of the Government Chief Whip, John Silkin (Lab. Deptford). Obviously A.L.R.A. had influential connections and its social composition and attitudes were well in accord with those of the younger Labour Members elected in 1966. But its impact on the Upper House was equally important. A.L.R.A., rather than David Steel and his associates in the Commons, played a vital role in persuading their supporters among the peers, notably Lady Stocks, to undertake the (successful) attempt to reverse the restrictive amendments which the Upper House had adopted at the committee stage.

The opposing pressure group, the Society for the Protection of the Unborn Child, was founded in January 1967 specifically to oppose Steel's Bill. This organization appeared to accept the need for therapeutic abortion strictly defined. Further than that, its policy was unclear. The general tactic followed was to urge the need for further consideration and the appointment of a Royal Commission. It was supported by Catholics, but was not a Catholic organization; indeed, Catholics were specifically excluded from its executive committee. The chairman was Lord Barrington, and there were two bishops on the executive, Exeter and Bath and Wells, as well as three MPs, J. Hiley (Con. Pudsey), A. Mackenzie (Lib. Ross and Cromarty) and G. Oakes (Lab. Bolton W.). No fewer than eleven out of twenty-five members of the executive had medical qualifications. The secretary of the organization worked from a private address in Belgravia. The image created was of a body of wealthy conservative-minded people with a strong medical element. They organized a nation-wide petition that was taken to 10 Downing Street, public meetings were held and MPs and peers were lobbied. A national opinion poll was promoted in which the questions were carefully arranged[1] to encourage the type of answer the S.P.U.C. desired, and the results were published in October 1967, just before the Lords changed its mind on the two crucial amendments. Even more damaging to the cause of the S.P.U.C. was the attempt at shock tactics and the extravagance of language used at some of its meetings. Dr Margaret White was reported as saying: 'Unborn babies have no votes and they are to be sacrificed to placate extreme left-wing members of the party who are restive about the slaughter in Vietnam and the wages freeze. Rather than melt frozen wages too quickly the Government is preparing to allow thousands of unborn children to be burned in incinerators.' The tactical stupidity of a speech of this kind needs no emphasis.

Compared with A.L.R.A., the Society for the Protection of the Unborn Child was very unsuccessful. Yet it did provide a focus of opposition to the Bill and could fairly claim that the struggle was far more extended than at first seemed likely. Equally, it is true that a campaign against the Bill was being organized within Parliament

[1] One question reads as follows: 'Previously the Bill would allow abortions to take place on the agreement of any two doctors. The House of Lords' amendment lays down that one of the two doctors concerned should be of consultant status or be approved by the Ministry of Health for this purpose, with the idea that it might prevent profiteering by unscrupulous doctors. Do you think that the Commons should accept this amendment or put back that the agreement of any two doctors is sufficient'? It will be noted that the question excludes all mention of arguments *against* the amendment.

before the Society was founded. The S.P.U.C. lacked the political skill of A.L.R.A. In a controversy over the content of legislation, medical expertise is no substitute for political influence, especially if the experts can be accused of trying to defend the rights of their profession.

Many other public bodies have expressed opinions on abortion law reform. Their attitudes defy easy analysis because those which favour change want particular types of change: thus acceptance of the need for reform by no means produced agreement with the precise wording of Steel's Bill. In 1959 the National Council of Women passed a resolution in favour of abortion where pregnancy resulted from rape or other criminal assault. In 1965 a further resolution favoured abortion for therapeutic reasons and where there was grave risk of a seriously defective child being born. (7 of the 90 organizations affiliated to the N.C.W. disassociated themselves from this view – they were the Mothers' Union, the Salvation Army and a variety of Catholic bodies.) Steel's Bill was therefore both too restrictive and too permissive for the N.C.W. policy. It contained no specific authority to terminate in cases of rape or incest: on the other hand, the 'social clause' with the reference to the well-being of other children in the family goes far beyond the N.C.W. definition of therapeutic termination.

Christian opinion, Roman Catholics excepted, was generally in favour of some liberalization of the law. In 1966 the Free Church Federal Council and the Methodist Conference both supported the cause of reform; Lord Soper played an active part in the Conference debate. Also in 1966 the General Assembly of the Church of England welcomed the report, *Abortion – an Ethical Discussion*, described above,[1] although there was also a general feeling in favour of delay to allow time for further examination of the problems involved. Opposition to the form of Steel's Bill was expressed by the Archbishops of Canterbury and York and the Bishops of London and Durham in a letter to *The Times* published on May 24, 1967. They had two objections. Eugenic abortion was based on statistical risk of deformity and this implied that many healthy foetuses would be destroyed. Exception was also taken to the form of the 'social clause' which allowed the well-being of existing children in a family to be taken into consideration. However, these objections are less fundamental than they may seem. The letter accepted that the risk of deformity could be dealt with by reference to risk to the mother: in other words, if the health of the mother was gravely affected by the fear of producing a defective child – then abortion should be per-

[1] pp. 91–2, *supra*.

mitted. On the second objection, the draft Bill on abortion proposed in the Church's report mentioned above, itself included what must be described as a social clause: 'In determining whether or not there is grave risk of serious injury to health or physical or mental well-being, account may be taken of the patient's total environment, actual or reasonably foreseeable.' Since a mother's total environment must be affected by her economic circumstances and her responsibility for existing children, the difference between this report and the Bill amounts to a shade of emphasis rather than a matter of principle. The attitude of the ecclesiastical members of the Upper House in the debates on the Abortion Bill, in the end, was one of acceptance rather than opposition.

To the Bill's sponsors, the attitude of the medical profession caused far more difficulty than that of the church. Both the British Medical Association and the Royal College of Obstetricians and Gynaecologists objected to some of its provisions. The views of the two bodies were not completely identical as the B.M.A. was more liberal than the R.C.O.G. There were also divergencies of view within each organization: some doctors sympathized with A.L.R.A. while some gynaecologists supported S.P.U.C. A statement issued in November 1966 summarized the official views of the two medical organizations and showed some differences between them. The R.C.O.G. felt that termination should be permitted where there was 'substantial risk of serious abnormality of the foetus'; the B.M.A. agreed that the risk should be 'substantial' but felt that this word should be omitted from actual legislation. A much more important difference arose over the view of the R.C.O.G. that any termination should be carried out by, or under the supervision of, a consultant in gynaecology; the B.M.A. felt that this limitation was too severe and that other types of consultant should be included. The R.C.O.G. subsequently modified its position and a joint letter to *The Times* published on May 29, 1967, from the R.C.O.G. and the B.M.A., proposed that termination might be carried out 'by a consultant in the National Health Service or by a registered medical practitioner approved for this purpose by the Minister'. Argument over the 'consultant clause' consumed many hours of parliamentary time. Initially, the Ministry of Health appeared to accept it as a reasonable safeguard.[1] The Minister, Kenneth Robinson, tried to get David Steel to accept the clause in return for a promise of extra parliamentary time if this should be necessary to get the Bill through. Steel felt himself in a strong enough position to refuse this offer. Obviously the Ministry was under heavy

[1] Cf. comments by Julian Snow, Parliamentary Secretary to the Ministry of Health, Standing Committee F, March 8, 1967, col. 401.

pressure from the medical profession, but the official attitude changed subsequently as the administrative difficulties inherent in the clause came to be fully appreciated and it became clear that medical opinion was far from unanimous. Lord Kennet, speaking for the Ministry in the Lords at the final debate on the clause, commented: 'The point here is that no Minister of Health has ever arrogated to himself the right to say "This class of doctor shall carry out a surgical operation and that class of doctor shall not" and the present Minister of Health is unwilling to be the first to arrogate to himself that right.'[1] This statement, combined with the manifest difficulties of limiting the clause to consultant gynaecologists, no doubt helped to produce the ultimate rejection of the clause in the Lords. But this had been a difficult fight for the Bill's sponsors and their victory had been narrow, for the consultant clause had been rejected by the Commons' Standing Committee by a majority of two and had, at one stage, been accepted by the Upper House.

The medical profession was also opposed to the concept of social abortion. It accepted that termination should be permissible on medical grounds, and followed the Church of England phraseology that this should be assessed in the light of a patient's total environment. The crucial difference was that doctors objected to the assessment of 'well-being' as well as of health. After the Bill became law the B.M.A. advised its members against social abortion, but this advice has no statutory force and the B.M.A. cannot command the conscience of its individual members.

Opponents of the Abortion Bill made full use of the ammunition provided for them by the doctors. A popular defence of the consultant clause was that it insisted on the highest standard of medical care. Another persuasive argument was that doctors should not be expected to undertake an operation which they found deeply repugnant for non-medical reasons: the basic task of the medical profession is to save life, not destroy it. The social clause also required doctors to consider non-medical matters when making an important decision and, until the pattern of medical education is changed, one may claim that doctors have no professional competence to judge social conditions. These objections would have made an even bigger impact had medical opinion been clear-cut and united. But the medical world accepted abortion and the need for reform, if only to safeguard professional freedom. An opinion survey of doctors carried out through A.L.R.A. in 1965 showed much support for Mrs Short's Bill which did not contain a social clause.[2]

[1] H.L. Deb., Vol. 285, col. 1419.
[2] See p. 102, *supra*.

Supporters of reform obtained much encouragement from opinion surveys. According to a study in 1965 by the National Opinion Poll, 72 per cent of the sample were in favour of reform. 60 per cent of Catholics questioned were also in favour. Naturally the extent of support varied between different social groups, between categories of abortion and also geographically. Strongest opposition came from old people (the least concerned), Catholics, the lower-income groups and Scotland and northern England. A majority supported abortion where mental and physical health were endangered and where pregnancy was caused by sexual assault. But there was no majority for termination merely because of a prospect of illegitimacy, financial hardship or because the expectant mother was under sixteen.

The Times, with a Catholic editor, was less progressive on abortion than on other social issues. On the last day of 1966 a strong leader called for an end to Government neutrality. By going beyond medical matters 'the present Bill opens the way to the establishment of abortion as a form of social eugenics, the prenatal destruction of "unwanted" children thought likely to be a burden to their mothers and so possibly to society. That is a very serious step to take and it is not one to which the Government can be indifferent.' However, both the Government and the Opposition remained resolutely uncommitted. The struggle in Parliament continued between groups organized on a non-party basis. Peter Jackson (Lab. High Peak) and Sir George Sinclair (Con. Dorking) organized support for the Bill, while James Dunn (Lab. Liverpool, Kirkdale) played a leading part in rallying the opponents. As public interest increased, stimulated by controversy in the mass media, some Members received a significant amount of correspondence on the subject.[1] The amount of this correspondence varied considerably as between individual Members: the size of flow depended mainly on the social characteristics of their constituencies. Naturally, the greater volume of anti-Bill protest tended to come from areas with a large Roman Catholic community, but even here the quantity of protest varied substantially. Some Roman Catholic bishops were more energetic in their opposition than others; partly, no doubt, because of variations in encouragement from the hierarchy, the attitude of priests was not uniform. There is no evidence that Members were much affected by this correspondence, as can be seen from the following selection of their comments about it. 'Not a lot: some normal R.C. stuff only' (Con-

---

[1] This paragraph is based on interviews with MPs conducted by Antony Barker and Michael Rush when preparing their book, *Information for Parliament* (Allen & Unwin, 1970). I am grateful to these authors for permission to quote their interview material.

servative, Southern England). 'I have an actively anti-Bill Roman Catholic priest which leads to letters arriving from his flock. An interesting current comparison is with the anti-hare coursing Bill on which there is an urban-rural disagreement in my constituency' (Conservative, Northern England). 'On abortion only two letters from my constituency, one on each side. My local Catholic priest is very liberal: I'm pro-Bill' (Labour, Wales). 'I got a wave of stereo-typed letters against the Bill plus a 1,500-strong petition: then about 30 pro-Bill letters' (Labour, Northern England). 'I got about 60–70 letters against the Bill and about 20 for it. I answered fully and personally all non-stereotyped letters as I do on all other issues' (Labour, Midlands). 'Very little on abortion: 38 individual letters against the Bill and two pro-Bill' (Conservative, Midlands). 'Not a lot from the constituency on abortion and about 50–50 split on what there is. All my letters from elsewhere have been pro-Bill: Abortion law reform people. My own line has been moderate, neutral' (Conservative, Southern England). 'My public support for the Society for the Protection of Unborn Children led to a lot of support from the public. I got 150 letters from the constituency and 250 from outside, mostly anti-Bill' (Labour, Northern England). 'A lot on abortion: the first R.C. wave was stereotyped. The local priest was active against the Bill: later the pro-Bill stuff came in and was of higher quality. I am pro-Bill, although I don't think local knowledge of this led to fewer pro-Bill letters arriving' (Labour, London). 'I've had six or seven constituency letters pro-Bill, and one petition from 150 R.C.s and 5 to 6 letters against the Bill. The printed circulars on abortion were badly timed and were typical of the shocking quality and timing of all such material. It comes in at the last minute, e.g. the anti-abortion pressure all came after the second reading decision' (Liberal).

Yet a comparison of the votes on second and third reading does show partial success for the campaign against the Abortion Bill. It should be recalled that the interval between these two votes was almost a year.

	Second Reading[1]	Third Reading[1]
Ayes	225	169
Noes	31	85

Those voting on the second reading behaved as follows on the third reading:

[1] The figures in this table differ slightly from those given earlier in the text because they include the two tellers on each side.

	Second Reading	
	Ayes	Noes
Third Reading Aye	116	—
Third Reading No	10[1]	19
Not voting	99	12
	225	31

The behaviour of Ministers is shown below:

	Second Reading	Third Reading
Aye	38	33
No	1	7[2]
Not voting	51	49

The category 'not voting' includes Members who are present in the House but deliberately abstain, and those who are absent for a variety of reasons which are more or less compelling. Whipping on a private member's Bill lacks the authority of formal party whipping so attendance is lower and there is less certainty that convinced supporters or opponents of a measure will actually appear when the division bells ring. Viewed in this light the high number of 99 second reading supporters who were absent from the third reading is less remarkable: the proportion of second reading opponents who were away from the third reading is not very different. But the success of the objectors has two facets. First, ten Members changed from support to opposition while no one moved in the reverse direction. However, it does not *necessarily* follow that these Members altered their attitude. Support for a Bill at second reading may be conditional on certain amendments being made at the committee stage: if such amendments are not made, there is no inconsistency in opposing the third reading. Far more significant was the ability of the objectors to recruit fresh adherents for the vote on the third reading: including the ten listed above, they gathered 66 Members not in their camp

[1] They were James Allason (Con. Hemel Hempstead), Bernard Braine (Con. Essex S.E.), Sir Edward Brown (Con. Bath), Tim Fortescue (Con. Liverpool, Garston), Mrs Anne Kerr (Lab. Rochester and Chatham,) James MacColl (Lab. Widnes), David Mitchell (Con. Basingstoke), R. Bonner Pink (Con. Portsmouth S.), Sir Ronald Russell (Con. Wembley S.) and Duncan Sandys (Con. Streatham).

[2] They were A. Greenwood (Rossendale), J. D. Mabon (Greenock), N. McBride (Swansea, E.), J. MacColl (Widnes), R. Mellish, (Bermondsey), B. O'Malley (Rotherham) and Mrs Shirley Williams, (Hitchin), who also vote against the second reading.

at the second reading. The Bill's sponsors recruited 53 such Members, a lower figure in absolute terms and much lower as a proportion of their initial support. Even so, the progress made by the anti-abortion lobby was insufficient. At the end of the road there was still a majority to 2 to 1 against them in the Commons.

There can be no doubt that the success of the Abortion Bill was due in great measure to the benevolence of Ministers. Their assistance was especially valuable in preserving the measure from shipwreck in the dangerous seas of the parliamentary timetable. When the Standing Committee dealing with private members' Bills was slowed down by the Employment Agencies Bill, arrangements were made to move the Abortion Bill to another committee and so avoid the log-jam. Again, when the filibuster developed at the report stage, David Steel was able to persuade Ministers to find extra time. It must be significant that the Chief Whip was the son of the Bill's sponsor in the Lords. The Leader of the House at this period, R. H. S. Crossman, was both a keen social reformer and devoted to the modernization of parliamentary procedure; he could be expected to resist the prospect of a measure supported by a clear parliamentary majority being defeated merely by the technicalities of a legislative timetable.

Thus the Abortion Bill enjoyed an exceptional amount of good fortune. Perhaps another reason for success was that it did not involve – as compared with homosexuality legislation – the reversal of an established principle of social policy. Abortion was an accepted practice, legitimized by case law. Few rejected the need for it where medical reasons were compelling. No one disputed the prevalence of back-street abortions and the desirability of reducing them. Thus the *status quo* was unsatisfactory to all and the basic principle was scarcely in question. The issues became how far should an existing practice be permitted and what safeguards were needed to prevent abuse. So the parliamentary controversy centred on the more important details, the qualifications of doctors and the inclusion or precise wording of the social clause. Such matters were vital to the character of the Bill but they had insufficient public impact to cause the flood of emotion needed for the success of the S.P U C.

In passing the Abortion Bill, Parliament may be regarded as having promoted the policies of the social welfare state or the attitudes of a permissive society. Alternatively, it can be considered as a contribution to women's rights. Yet the main outcome of the Bill, welcomed by the sponsors and hated by the opponents, is to give abortion a degree of respectability it lacked before. No longer is it largely hush-hush, back street or Harley Street. Instead it is authorized by statute, subject to conditions that are not unduly restrictive.

IV

Since the Abortion Act was passed, two attempts have been made to amend it by inserting the 'consultant' clause described above.[1] Norman St John Stevas introduced a Ten-Minute Rule Bill on these lines in July 1969, which was narrowly defeated. The second Bill introduced under the ballot was sponsored by Godman Irvine (Con. Rye): it was the second Bill due for debate on February 13, 1970, but little more than two hours was available for its consideration and no decision was reached.

[1] See pp. 101–2, 106–7.

Chapter 6

Censorship of the Theatre

I

Censorship may be formal or informal; it may be prospective or retroactive. Formal censorship depends on rules of conduct imposed by authority while informal regulation stems from social taboos. Prospective censorship operates on material before it is publicly available so that the censor's decision may not become public knowledge, while retroactive censorship suppresses matter already published. Pre-publication control is more effective and convenient for a censor because the alternative invites widespread comment on his decisions. British theatre censorship has been formal and prospective. Discussion on its operation was further hindered by the person of the censor, the Lord Chamberlain, being an officer of the Royal Household whose actions were protected by the Royal Prerogative from challenge in Parliament.

The incentives for censorship are political and moral; they often join together when it is feared that moral argument may have political repercussions. British experience of stage censorship provides abundant evidence to support this generalization.

The history opens in 1543 when an Act was passed 'for the advancement of true religion and the abolishment of the contrary'. Any plays, together with ballads and other material which challenged authorized religion, were 'abolished, extinguished and forbidden'. The date of the Act is significant for, coming four years after the dissolution of the monasteries, it was clearly an attempt to reinforce the religious authority of the King after the quarrel between Henry VIII and the Pope. The legislation was subject to many changes and no attempt will be made here to describe them fully.[1] The first official to exercise the duties of censor was the Master of the Revels. In 1581 both the Church of England and the City of London endeavoured to send representatives to form a team of censors, but the Master of the Revels managed to evade their assistance and to earn a good income, in addition to his court salary, from the licence fees obtained from playwrights. At this period the censor was con-

[1] For an excellent account see R. Findlater: *Theatrical Censorship in Britain* (MacGibbon & Kee, 1967).

H

cerned with the preservation of political authority judged in terms of divinity and the state, rather than with the moral effect of plays. There is no evidence that Shakespeare suffered seriously from censorship and the licentious character of seventeenth-century drama aroused deep Puritan hostility to the theatre. Under the Commonwealth, theatres were closed. With the Restoration the theatre again became an important part of the London scene and by the end of the century the Lord Chamberlain began to replace the Master of the Revels as the censor. The Lord Chamberlain attempted to raise the moral tone of drama but his authority was not infrequently disregarded.

In 1735 an attempt in the Commons to strengthen control over public entertainments failed because the sponsor of the measure, Sir John Barnard, had second thoughts when he realized that the legislation would give wider powers to a court official. At this time the Cabinet, in particular the Prime Minister Sir Robert Walpole, became enraged by the political attacks upon them in the current popular dramatic productions. Fielding's commentary on corruption and immorality in high places caused great offence. The *Historical Register for 1736*, produced at the Haymarket Theatre in 1737, stimulated the Prime Minister to action. To avoid the charge of political censorship, he produced a *moral* case for imposing a fresh curb on the stage. Walpole announced that a theatre manager named Giffard had submitted an anonymous farce to him entitled *The Golden Rump*, which was so indecent as to require fresh restraints on theatrical liberty. Whether *The Golden Rump* ever existed is not clear; if it did, perhaps one of Walpole's *aides* wrote it. Certainly Giffard was paid the huge sum of £1,000 for sending it to the Prime Minister. The Licensing Act of 1737 re-established firmly the Lord Chamberlain as the censor of plays and in future he was to have full-time salaried assistants to help with this task. The Act was passed hurriedly at the end of the parliamentary session but not without a notable protest from Lord Chesterfield, which foreshadowed many of the arguments used 230 years later. 'Our laws are sufficient for punishing any man that shall dare to represent upon the stage what may appear, either by words or by representation, to be blasphemous, seditious or immoral . . . if the stage becomes at any time licentious, if a play appears to be a libel upon the Government or upon any particular man, the King's courts are open.'[1]

In spite of some protest, the Bill became law. Effective censorship of plays remained until 1968. The 1737 Act also restricted the com-

[1] Cobbett's *Parliamentary History*, Vol. 10, cols 330–1.

mercial presentation of 'straight' plays to licensed 'patent' theatres. This aspect of control, however, was often evaded. Audiences were sometimes admitted free in return for paying an extortionate price for a cup of chocolate. Since the restriction on premises was limited to 'straight' drama, unlicensed theatres would present shows with a musical element, or even a straight play with a piano tinkling in the background to keep the theatre manager possibly on the right side of the law. Alternatively, the law was simply ignored and the Lord Chamberlain often took no action provided he thought the entertainment to be unobjectionable. But while the control of premises stayed flexible, the censorship of play scripts remained firm and vigorous. In the age of Bowdler the censors exerted themselves ever more strongly to protect the morals of the populace. Indeed, with the revival of Puritan values, audiences themselves became highly critical of any hint of immodesty and so reinforced the censors.

The Theatres Act, 1843, produced some element of liberalism in that the monopoly of the 'patent' theatres over the drama was ended. The Lord Chamberlain was authorized to license theatres in the Cities of London and Westminster, Windsor and the neighbourhoods of other royal residences. Elsewhere theatres were to be licensed by magistrates.[1] The censorship of the Lord Chamberlain was confirmed in the 1843 Act, although one limiting clause was attached to the exercise of his jurisdiction. A stage play could be banned, in whole or in part, whenever the Lord Chamberlain was of opinion that the prohibition 'is fitting for the preservation of good manners, decorum or of the public peace'. The definition of stage play was comprehensive: it included 'every Tragedy, Comedy, Farce, Opera, Burletta, Interlude, Melodrama, Pantomime or other Entertainment of the Stage, or any Part thereof'. No loopholes appeared for playwrights until the closing years of the nineteenth century when the growth of interest in serious drama led to growing complaints about the operation of the censorship. When a play was rejected by the Chamberlain's office, the practice developed of putting on private performances. In the inter-war period these arrangements developed into theatre clubs which ignored the Lord Chamberlain. With a few exceptions, the Lord Chamberlain took no legal action against theatre clubs. There are a number of instances where the Chamberlain, having seen a private production of a banned play, changed his mind and granted a license for public performance; three examples are

[1] The powers of magistrates were transferred to county councils and county boroughs by the Local Government Act, 1888. They were also capable of delegation: for the present confusing position in county areas see Peter G. Richards: *Delegation in Local Government* (Allen & Unwin, 1956), p. 133.

Tolstoy's *The Power of Darkness*, Oscar Wilde's *Salome* and John van Druten's *Young Woodley*.

Two factors have affected the degree of tension between the censorship and the playwrights and theatre managers – the liberalism (or otherwise) of the Lord Chamberlain's office and the social climate which determines how far theatre audiences welcome plays which raise serious moral, religious or political issues. The Edwardian era was one period of major conflict, another was the decade after 1958: on the former occasion the censorship stood its ground and rarely relented; in the latter period the censorship was steadily in retreat.

Edwardian discontent led to the establishment in 1909 of a Joint Select Committee of both Houses of Parliament to enquire into stage censorship.[1] The background to this development can best be summarized by a list of just some of the plays rejected by the Lord Chamberlain. The second column in the table gives the date when they were accepted for public performance.

Playwright	Play	Licence refused	Licence granted
Shelley	*The Cenci*	1886	1922
Wilde	*Salome*	1891	1929
Ibsen	*Ghosts*	1892	1914
Shaw	*Mrs Warren's Profession*	1894	1925
Housman	*Bethlehem*	1902	1912
Maeterlinck	*Monna Vanna*	1902	1914
Brieux	*Damaged Goods*	1902	1914
Brieux	*Les Trois Filles de Mme Dupont*	1906	1917
Brieux	*Maternite*	1907	1932
Gilbert and Sullivan	*The Mikado*	1907[2]	1908
Granville Barker	*Waste*	1907	1920
Shaw	*The Shewing Up of Blanco Posnet*	1907	1921[3]

Sometimes a play was reprieved after a few minor changes: on other occasions the censor accepted the original version in full. *Waste* was completely rewritten for the 1920 production, but the issue it raised, abortion, remained unchanged. The plays listed above – and others –

[1] Earlier enquiries in 1853, 1866 and 1892 had each approved the working of the censorship: cf. 1852–53 (855), xxxvi, 1866 (373), xvi, 1892, Sess. 1 (240), xviii.

[2] First licensed in 1887, the ban was imposed in 1907 because of the visit of the Japanese Crown Prince to London.

[3] A modified version was passed in 1916.

managed to outlive the censor's ban because of the international reputation of their authors. Other rejected scripts, perhaps including unrecognized masterpieces, were heard of no more.

There were two principal causes of dispute with the censorship: it was determined to protect the Bible and it refused to permit serious discussion of social problems which were sexual in origin. Thus Rostand's *La Samaritaine* was banned, although it was revived regularly in Paris. French theatre censorship ended in 1905 and, inevitably, English dramatists longed for continental freedom. Meanwhile, the Lord Chamberlain's veto on sexual themes caused constant friction. Shaw's discussion of prostitution in *Mrs Warren's Profession* might have been unacceptable to Victorian audiences, but the Edwardian censor was beginning to fall behind the times in avoiding discussion of venereal disease (*Damaged Goods*), abortion (*Waste*) and birth control (*Maternite* and *Les Trois Filles de Madame Dupont*). Objections to this repressive policy were expressed in a letter to *The Times* on October 29, 1907, signed by 71 leading dramatists, which announced that the Prime Minister had agreed to receive a deputation on the subject. On the same day a sympathetic article appeared which argued that 'If you cut off the dramatist from all religious subjects and from a very large class of the most serious subjects, you keep out of the theatre that class of audience which is interested in those subjects and leave it to cater for baser tastes'. A further letter to *The Times*[1] signed by 72 persons including Hilaire Belloc, Winston S. Churchill, Bertrand Russell and Sidney and Beatrice Webb: 'We are all anxious that the moral and educational influence of the drama should be for good; but we agree that the present method of supervision has failed to achieve this object; and we should be glad to see the necessary public control secured by other means.' The Home Secretary, Herbert Gladstone, told a deputation to the Home Office that he would suggest to the Prime Minister that decisions of the censor should be subject to a right of appeal to some tribunal.[2]

It was this pressure which forced the Government to appoint a Joint Select Committee to re-examine theatre censorship. The Lord Chamberlain himself avoided coming before the Committee. All the orthodox arguments for and against censorship were ventilated in evidence heard by the Committee; the discussion centred on issues of morality, education and administration, save for the submission of the West End Theatre Managers who favoured censorship because it reduced the commercial risks of their business. The Committee

[1] February 24, 1908.
[2] *The Times*, February 26, 1908.

found itself torn between incompatible ends. The constitutional position of the censor was unsatisfactory and some of his decisions had become highly controversial; on the other hand, there was fear of the consequences if his restraining influence were to be removed. So the Committee proposed a compromise. It recommended that the Lord Chamberlain should retain the power to license plays submitted to him but submission should become *optional*. To perform an unlicensed play would become legal whether it had been submitted or not. This new freedom was to be subject to two safeguards. First, the Attorney-General could stop further performances of a play held to be objectionable on any of the grounds on which a Lord Chamberlain's licence might be refused. Second, the Director of Public Prosecutions should be able to bring an action against the theatre manager and the author of an unlicensed play he thought indecent. In essence, post-production censorship was to be substituted for pre-production censorship: this offered the advantage that public opinion could have an effect on censorship decisions. However, for theatre managers the production of an unlicensed play involved such great financial risk that it seemed improbable that the proposed option would ever be exercised. So the Joint Committee's scheme met stern criticism both from those who favoured censorship and from those who opposed it. No action was taken on the report.[1]

As can be seen from the table above, from 1914 onwards the censorship slowly began to take a more liberal view. Indeed, in 1917 the Stage Society decided, very prematurely, that there were no battles left to fight with the censor. Lord Cromer, who held the office of Lord Chamberlain from 1922 to 1938,[2] was relatively deaf to cries of moral outrage. Many plays banned before 1909 were pronounced acceptable. Some new plays, e.g. Coward's *The Vortex*, which caused public protest, were left alone. By the 1930s girls were permitted to pose in the nude, provided they were immobile and the lighting was sufficiently subdued. In the inter-war years the difficulties were chiefly political. References to the Royal Family, seemingly

[1] A scintillating account of the conflict between the Select Committee and George Bernard Shaw is given by Shaw in his Preface to *The Shewing-up of Blanco Posnet*. This Preface also contains a Shavian critique of censorship. For another account of the work of the Committee see Dorothy Knowles: *The Censor, the Drama and the Film* (Allen & Unwin, 1934) Ch. II. The report itself is 1909 (303) viii.

[2] In 1924 with the advent of the first Labour Government, it was agreed between King George V and the Party leaders that certain offices in the Royal Household, including the Lord Chamberlain, should become non-political. Thus the Lord Chamberlain achieved greater security and independence as he no longer vacated office each change of government. See: H. Nicolson, *King George V* (Constable, 1952), pp. 390–1.

innocuous, aroused the censor's ire; plays which referred to recent and not-so-recent political controversies were banned; leaders of foreign countries, other than the Soviet Union, were fully protected by the censor. Critical commentary on the policy of fascist states was prohibited in order not to damage international relations. However, an element of freedom was provided by theatre clubs which began to give regular performances of unlicensed plays instead of one or two private showings. The censor clearly regarded the clubs as a useful venue for experiment and as a safety valve for protest. Indeed, during the inter-war period the censorship never became a major public issue. After 1939 the political sensitivity of the Lord Chamberlain's Office was greatly weakened and the main problem was the moral tone of many of the shows presented to entertain wartime London. The Public Morality Council, which over the years had urged the Lord Chamberlain to make fuller use of his powers, now urged stern action to restrain nudity on the stage.

In 1949 a private member's Bill proposed the abolition of theatre censorship and added the further safeguard for liberty that no prosecution of a play could be initiated without the consent of a judge in chambers. The Bill was introduced by E. P. Smith (Con. Ashford) and supported by playwright Benn Levy (Lab. Eton and Slough). A British Theatre Conference composed of representatives from various groups of workers in the theatre from Equity to the League of Dramatists had given approval to the terms of the Bill. However, the *status quo* was sternly defended by a Theatres' National Committee representing the Society of West End Theatre Managers, the Theatrical Managers' Association, the Entertainments Protection Association, the Provincial Entertainments Proprietors and Managers Association and the Association of Touring and Producing Managers.[1] Clearly, the entrepreneurs of the stage were afraid of freedom. In the Commons the Bill was opposed both by A. P. Herbert (Ind. Oxford University) and T. O'Brien (Lab. Nottingham, West) the President of the Federation of Theatre Unions. Yet in spite of opposition the second reading was carried by 76 votes to 37,[2] but due to lack of parliamentary time the Bill made no further progress.

Since the war the censorship has been in steady retreat. Many attempts to exercise control have led to defeat and ridicule which further undermined the Lord Chamberlain's authority. In 1949 a licence for *Pick-Up Girl* was made conditional upon certain changes in the script: the play was presented at the New Lindsay Theatre Club with an unchanged script: Queen Mary saw the play at the Club

[1] Letter in *The Times*, March 31, 1949.
[2] H. C. Deb., Vol. 463, cols 713–798.

on her seventy-ninth birthday: the play was subsequently licensed. Samuel Becket's *Endgame* was accepted in 1957 in French; next year an English version was rejected as blasphemous. This incident offered an opportunity for a wide range of speculation; that the Lord Chamberlain did not understand French, that he thought that God did not understand French or that he thought that Englishmen who understood French were already so corrupted as to be beyond salvation. Also in 1958 the Theatre Workshop was successfully prosecuted for introducing material which had not been submitted to the censor into a play which had received a licence. The material in question concerned an incident where a character in the play began to imitate Winston Churchill and made a Churchillian speech in opening a public convenience. This may possibly be considered vulgar but no one could condemn it as obscene. Four years later another action over unlicensed material was brought against an American revue *The Promise* four months after the show, advertised as using improvised material, had opened. In spite of the successful prosecution the company announced that they would continue as heretofore and the Lord Chamberlain took no further action.

On all fronts the censor – and his four part-time assistants – withdrew. An increasing range and frequency of swear-words was permitted. The Lord Chamberlain adjusted slowly to the growing frankness of sexual discussion, and in 1958 a statement from his office announced that, subject to certain safeguards, plays incorporating homosexual themes could be accepted; this decision was almost certainly the result of the favourable reception of certain plays performed at the New Watergate Theatre Club. The ban on the representation of living persons was broken by Peter Cook's imitation of Harold Macmillan in *Beyond the Fringe*. Restrictions were placed on *Mrs Wilson's Diary* to protect the Queen and President Johnson, but Harold Wilson and George Brown were subjected to sustained ridicule.

The censor has always been kinder to comedy and farce than to serious dramatic productions. Thus Hochhuth's *Soldiers* was refused a licence unless permission to perform it was obtained from all the surviving relatives of all the characters. This was impossible because the Churchill family objected on the grounds that the play implied that Winston Churchill had some foreknowledge of the death of General Sikorski. In fact the Sikorski theme was of secondary importance; *Soldiers* is essentially concerned with questions about the morality of war.[1] Hochhuth's earlier play *The Representative* also

---

[1] *Soldiers* was produced at the New Theatre without incident four months after the Lord Chamberlain's powers were withdrawn.

caused difficulty with the Lord Chamberlain as it criticized Pope Pius X for his failure to intercede with Hitler on behalf of the Jews. Ultimately the Royal Shakespeare Company obtained a licence for the play on the condition that the programme contained a Roman Catholic 'answer' to the case presented by the dramatist. This attempt to enforce 'balance' when political issues were raised on the stage immediately invited comparison with the freedom of the press in political matters. Increasingly, political prohibitions became untenable. *U.S.*, the Royal Shakespeare Company's semi-documentary about the Vietnam war, was declared wholly unacceptable: ultimately *U.S.* was given a licence. In 1966 Christ was allowed to appear on the stage in a Passion play *A Man Dies*, a play already presented on television which had then earned the approval of religious organizations.[1]

Theatre clubs flourished in the post-war period both in size and influence. They also ran into legal difficulties. Under the Theatres Act, 1843, it was an offence to present a play in an unlicensed theatre or to present a play that had not been accepted by the Lord Chamberlain. Two exceptions developed to this control. The Lord Chamberlain defined 'play' to exclude dancing, ballet and cross-talk acts between music-hall comedians. The other loophole, theatre clubs had no legal claim for privileged treatment. The censor tolerated them because he felt it useful to have an outlet for experimental and unconventional drama, so long as it was provided on a small scale for audiences who had personally indicated their interest in such entertainment by joining a 'club'. A convention developed that application for membership had to be made 48 hours before admission to a performance; this gave verisimilitude to the club, but it had no legal significance whatever. In 1951 the Unity Theatre was successfully prosecuted for staging an unlicensed play. It seems that this action was taken not because of the left-wing character of Unity but because it had extended club membership to associations and so had acquired a nominal membership of millions. Five years later a 'club' took over an ordinary commercial theatre, the Comedy, and presented three American plays concerned with homosexuality. In 1958 the Comedy Theatre reverted to normal operation but, as noted above, the Lord Chamberlain revised his policy on homosexuality. The club device was finally shown to confer no protection by the prosecution of the Royal Court Theatre over the production of *Saved* in 1966. This play had aroused hostile comment in the press. It seems that the decision to prosecute was caused not by the nature of the

[1] E. G. Wedell: *Broadcasting and Public Policy* (Michael Joseph, 1968), pp. 38-9.

play but through doubt whether the Royal Court was a genuine club theatre as it interspersed club performances with public performances of licensed plays. The magistrate ruled that the club at the Royal Court was a genuine club but that, even so, the theatre had contravened the law because the club arrangement did not provide exemption from the Lord Chamberlain's surveillance. After this case theatre clubs continued to operate but without any security. It was paradoxical that the full rigour of early Victorian law should be restated at a time when greater permissiveness in society was widely accepted. The gap between law and opinion had become impossibly wide.

II

Arguments over stage censorship fall naturally into two classes, those concerned with censorship in general and those which have a particular application to the theatre. The case against control of any form of public expression is familiar. It hinders the search for truth and the public understanding of every kind of problem. It can be – and usually is – used for political purposes, to uphold the authority of an existing regime. It tends to impede every kind of intellectual initiative and produces a strong tendency towards cultural and moral stagnation. The social history of totalitarian states bears eloquent witness to these generalizations. A censor, by the very nature of his task, must exercise a discretion much wider than other public officials designated to apply the law. To quote Bernard Shaw: 'A magistrate has laws to administer: a censor has nothing but his own opinion. A judge leaves the question of guilt to the jury: the censor is jury and judge as well as law-giver.' In a country where the courts of law are held in high respect and where the concept of the rule of law (however muddled this may be) is held in high esteem, a censor appears as an element of arbitrary rule difficult to defend. The lack of any appeal procedure emphasized the difference from normal judicial proceedings.

The peculiar situation of the Lord Chamberlain opened up other lines of attack. Censorship is gravely weakened if it is partial. What was prohibited for the stage could be published: the publication of censored material gave a wide public the opportunity to judge the censor's decisions for themselves. More recently radio and television have provided new opportunities to by-pass the censor. Again, his writ did not run to plays written before 1737. Could the censor have passed *Hamlet* or many of the restoration comedies? It is true – and this is another ground for criticism – that the censor was much kinder to slightly naughty farce than he was to serious discussions of social problems. The fact that the Lord Chamberlain sometimes changed his mind could be interpreted as a sign of liberality and flexibility, but it was also an admission that his decisions were less than perfect. This raised the question if there is to be censorship, what qualifications should the censor have? Did a court official necessarily have these qualifications? Indeed, was not the Lord Chamberlain curiously unsuitable for this task in that his licence could imply a seal of Royal approval on controversial matter, an approval which could be acutely embarrassing for the Foreign Office and perhaps the Monarch in the case of a play which commented on political and social questions in other countries? The Lord Chamberlain's powers were also harsh in that they were exercised pre-publication. Those who urged the abolition of his powers could claim that this would not provide unfettered freedom for the stage since the laws of slander and of obscenity would still apply. They could also point to the fact that many other countries, notably Ireland and France, managed to avoid censorship of drama without evil consequences.

The case for censorship can be stated more briefly. Its cornerstone is the fear that to remove control will be to lower standards of public entertainment and to encourage indecency and vice. The argument for the Lord Chamberlain was another example of the fear of freedom – that if restraints are removed, then the evil tendencies in human nature will obtain wider opportunities for expression. The theatre was said to need firmer control than the printed word because the intellectual and emotional impact of the stage is far greater than that experienced in reading a book. The censor could safeguard the reputation of persons unable or unwilling to institute legal proceedings for defamation of character; this applies particularly to the Royal Family and the dead. Another rather different fear was the prospect that if the Lord Chamberlain lost his powers he would then be replaced by a fresh, worse form of censorship. The new censors could be the local authorities or magistrates who have the power to license theatres. Their decisions might well be more puritanical in character than those of the Lord Chamberlain. No doubt they could vary between different areas. The risks of putting on some theatrical productions would become incalculable, especially on a provincial tour. Theatrical management would lose the security of the cheap insurance policy provided by the Lord Chamberlain's licence, and instead could suffer from costly and penal legal processes. These dangers of local intolerance were very real and any satisfactory reform proposals had to take account of them. But the original reason for the 1737 Act, to suppress political comment, is intolerable in a modern democracy. What had kept the Lord Chamberlain in business until 1968 was the puritan fear of the theatre as a potential temple of vice.

III

The successful campaign to free the stage of the supervision of the Lord Chamberlain may be said to start in 1958 when the Theatre Censorship Reform Committee was formed. Its members included Noel Annan, Roy Jenkins and representatives of the League of Dramatists and Equity. Meetings were held at the house of Wayland Young. The Committee communicated with the Lord Chamberlain to try and obtain further information on how his powers were exercised, but he replied that it would not be proper for him to enter into correspondence with an unofficial body. The Committee then turned to drafting a parliamentary Bill to reform the law, but subsequently decided to take no immediate action to promote the Bill as the censor appeared to be moving towards a more liberal policy, especially in relation to homosexuality.[1] Dingle Foot (Lab. Ipswich) proposed a Bill under the Ten-Minute Rule in December 1962, which sought to make optional the submission of a play to the Lord Chamberlain: this was rejected by 134 votes to 77.[2] The advent of a Labour Government reflected and reinforced a change of parliamentary mood. In reply to a question from William Hamling (Lab. Woolwich, West) in July 1965, Prime Minister Harold Wilson explained that the Government had no immediate proposals for legislation, but he added: 'I am well aware of the strong feeling that exists on this question, and to the extent that this aspect of our national life needs some degree of modernization. . . . How it is to be done is a matter we need to think further about.'[3] By 1966 when the final assault began, the leading personalities of the Theatre Censorship Reform Committee had acquired positions of authority: Roy Jenkins was Home Secretary and Noel Annan and Wayland Young were members of the House of Lords. Roy Jenkins suggested to Lord Annan that he move a motion in the Lords calling for a Joint Committee of both Houses to review the law and practice relating to the censorship of stage plays. Annan discussed the position with the Lord Chamberlain and found that he was far from happy about

[1] Cf. Speech in the Lords by Lord Kennet (Wayland Young) on Feb. 17, 1966: H. L. Deb., Vol. 272, col. 1218 *et seq.*

[2] H. C. Deb., Vol. 668, cols 1321–34.

[3] H. C. Deb., Vol. 716, cols 1335–6.

the existing situation. Annan then put down his motion for discussion and asked various peers to support him in debate. The Lords time-table is not congested, at least in the early part of the session, and the debate was arranged for February 17th. The motion was accepted without a division. There was almost a full consensus that the position demanded re-examination. Both the Lord Chamberlain, Lord Cobbold, and a former Lord Chamberlain, the Earl of Scarborough, supported the motion. A General Election intervened before the matter could be considered by the Commons[1] but early in the new Parliament they accepted the Lords' proposal without debate.[2]

Particularly in this instance, the membership of the Committee was most important in relation to the recommendations it was likely to produce. But if a committee is to command respect it must not be obviously 'packed': a diversity of backgrounds and interests gives strength to a committee. Equally, it was important for the reformers that the Committee should produce a unanimous report. The per-sonnel of the Committee is therefore of particular interest. It was selected through the 'usual channels', the whips' office in both Houses and, while the membership was suitably diverse, there were no committed advocates of the need for theatre censorship.[3] The Lords' representatives were:

The Earl of Scarborough, ex-Lord Chamberlain
The Earl of Kilmuir (Conservative ex-Lord Chancellor who died
    while the Committee was sitting) replaced by Lord Brooke,
    Conservative ex-Home Secretary
Viscount Norwich
Lord Tweedsmuir
Baroness Gaitskell
Lord Lloyd of Hampstead
Lord Annan
Lord Goodman, Chairman Arts Council

The representatives of the Commons were:

A. Faulds (Lab. Smethwick) ex-actor
M. Foot (Lab. Ebbw Vale)

[1] Just before Parliament was dissolved the Commons gave an unopposed first reading to a Ten-Minute Rule Bill to abolish stage censorship. This initiative by Michael Foot (Lab. Ebbw Vale) could have no practical effect because of the imminence of the Election: H. C. Deb., Vol. 725, cols 2053–60.
[2] H. C. Deb., Vol. 729, col. 419.
[3] The Member who has opposed Michael Foot's Bill, William Shepherd (Con. Cheadle), had been narrowly defeated at the General Election and so was not eligible.

E. Hooson (Lib. Montgomery)
H. Jenkins (Lab. Putney) ex-officer of Equity
Sir D. Renton (Con. Nat. Lib. Huntingdonshire) ex-Under-
Secretary, Home Office
N. St John Stevas (Con. Chelmsford)[1]
G. Strauss (Lab. Vauxhall) Minister of Supply 1947–51
W. Wilson (Lab. Coventry S.)[2]

The Committee received a wide range of evidence. The main case
for reform was presented by the League of Dramatists. In particular,
the League complained that the Lord Chamberlain interfered with
the expression of political and religious ideas in the theatre, and
quoted the cases of *Green Pastures* and *The Representative*. Another
play banned by the Lord Chamberlain, *Saved*, had been supported
by a government bursary of £1,000 received by way of the Arts
Council; the ludicrous position had been reached that a public
official had prohibited a dramatic production deemed worthy of a
subsidy from public funds. The League summarized its argument in
this way: 'We feel that this is a *moral* issue, and are deeply resentful
of the way in which we have been treated by arbitrary regulation by
a court official. We only wish to be subject to the same controls as
our fellow writers and citizens.' John Mortimer and John Osborne
both criticized the banning of Osborne's play *A Patriot for Me*. A
memorandum submitted by the directors of the Royal Shakespeare
Company complained that the Lord Chamberlain took comments
and quotes out of context to make them obscene, and told how he
had tried to block the production of *U.S.* The Archbishop of
Canterbury's attitude was equivocal: 'The positive reasons for freeing
stage plays from censorship . . . are all ones to which the Church can
subscribe provided that restrictions can be relaxed without encouraging lower moral standards or a lessened sensitivity to other people's
feelings on what is seemly and reverent in matters of religion.'
Evidence favouring censorship came from the Roman Catholic
Church which urged that 'some form of censorship is necessary and
desirable in order to protect Christian people from the dissemination
of ideas which could hinder them or turn them aside from the
attainment of their goals': this memorandum, however, did not urge
the retention of the Lord Chamberlain but envisaged a system such
as that used for films with greater powers for local authorities. The
Lord Chamberlain himself, Lord Cobbold, also felt that there should

[1] Catholic noted for his liberal views: keen supporter of Roy Jenkins'
Obscene Publications Act, 1959.
[2] Sponsor of Divorce Reform Bill, session 1967–68.

be some supervision over the theatre and suggested that these powers should be given to the Arts Council. Lord Goodman stressed that the task of censorship would be incompatible with the Arts Council function of promoting the interests of artists. The Secretary of West End Theatre Managers remained to champion the cause of the Lord Chamberlain. However, the Society was not wholly in favour of the *status quo* since it urged that plays, like films, might be graded 'A' or 'U'; one of the Society's spokesmen, Peter Saunders, went further by proposing an 'X' certificate for plays.[1]

The Committee produced a unanimous report in favour of reform. It viewed the political aspect of censorship with distaste. The Committee was careful to say that when exercising political censorship the Lord Chamberlain had not, in fact, exceeded the powers given to him by Parliament: however, it considered that these powers were inappropriate in a modern democratic society. A coincidence of factors swept the Committee along to an almost inevitable conclusion. The Lord Chamberlain did not want to continue to be a stage censor; no acceptable alternative to the Lord Chamberlain had emerged; there were powerful considerations in favour of the abolition of censorship. Accordingly the report proposed that the censorship powers of the Lord Chamberlain should be abolished as soon as possible. It argued that the very nature of the theatre, relatively expensive and supported by a minority, made special provision for the protection of children unnecessary. Other dangers were adequately covered by the safeguards of the existing law. New legislation governing the theatre should have regard to the following considerations: prevention of frivolous prosecutions; right of trial by jury; advisability of expert evidence; effective treatment of obscene plays; uniform application of the law. In essence, these criteria could be met by making the Obscene Publications Act, 1959, applicable to the stage, plus the proviso that any prosecution should require the consent of the Attorney-General. Thus the theatre would achieve freedom of speech, subject to the overriding requirements of the criminal law, and political censorship would cease. The Committee rejected the idea that there was any need to protect the Sovereign or her family in the theatre when no such special protection existed in relation to other forms of communication. Finally, the Committee recommended that the duties of the Lord Chamberlain in licensing theatres should be transferred to local authorities.

From the press came a general welcome for the ending of theatre censorship. Papers as diverse as the *Daily Express* and the *Morning*

[1] All the written and oral evidence was published with the report of the Committee: H. C. 503 or H. L. 255 (1966–67).

Star approved the proposal. A leading article in the *Daily Telegraph* argued[1] 'it is ridiculous that the theatre should be subject to restraints which do not apply to any other form of entertainment or artistic expression'. *The Times* alone had doubts: its leader – 'The Last of the Blue Pencils'[2] – observed: 'The Lord Chamberlain's jurisdiction in the licensing of plays may be indefensible, but it is not as indefensible as all that. . . . It is a fair guess that the general effect of the proposed change would be to relieve the artistic consciences of playwrights and producers, to stimulate dramatic controversy and political bite, and to make the English stage perceptibly more scurrilous and licentious – in which latter respect it would match the manners of the age.'

The Government's view was expressed in a written answer from the Home Secretary to a parliamentary question from George Strauss: 'The Government intend at a suitable opportunity to introduce legislation to give effect to the general principle of the Joint Select Committee's recommendations.'[3] This was a muted promise of action, but shortage of parliamentary time remained a serious obstacle. Due to the heavy programme of government legislation, Ministers could find no space to devote to the theatre. A solution was found in the luck of the draw. George Strauss, who had been Chairman of the Joint Select Committee, won tenth place in the ballot for private members' Bills. He approached the Home Office for help in drafting a Bill to embody the proposals of the Joint Select Committee; after some delay, this assistance was forthcoming. The aid of official draftsmen was needed especially in connexion with the complex provisions which transferred the licensing powers of the Lord Chamberlain to local authorities. In content the Bill was based squarely on the recommendations of the Joint Select Committee, and all the Commons' representatives on the Committee joined together to sponsor the Bill. The date chosen for the second reading was February 23, 1968, but as Strauss had won but tenth place in the ballot his Bill was the second measure to be debated on this day. It could, therefore, have failed through lack of time and would have been an easy victim of a filibuster. However, the first Bill of the day, the Adoption Bill, proved uncontroversial and was quickly accepted. The debate on the Theatres Bill was almost as uncontroversial and the second reading was achieved at 2.20 p.m. without a division, well inside the 4 p.m. deadline.[4] Only 2 of the 11 speeches were basically

[1] June 22 1967.
[2] June 22, 1967.
[3] H. C. Deb., Vol. 751, col. *215*.
[4] H. C. Deb., Vol. 759, cols 825–74.

hostile. The sponsors were surprised at their easy success: as George Strauss wrote in a *Times*[1] article: 'none of the troglodytes turned up'. The efforts made by the sponsors of the Bill to marshal the attendance of sympathetic Members proved to be unnecessary. Just one division occurred at the committee stage when a new clause proposed by Norman St John Stevas to safeguard the Royal Family was rejected by 9 votes to 2: there was no reason to believe that this amendment had any support in the Palace because the Lord Chamberlain had advised the Select Committee that it would be difficult to make special provision for members of the Royal Family and no one else. The Bill then passed the Commons and went on to the Lords, where again the second reading showed almost unanimous approval for the main principle.[2] Both the committee and report stages occupied some time on points of detail. Lord Goodman argued that the Attorney-General should not normally institute proceedings against a play without first considering the views of an advisory committee to be established for this purpose. This amendment was withdrawn 'reluctantly'.[3] The other main issue was the need to protect the reputation of those recently dead; ultimately their Lordships were not convinced that special rules should apply to the stage that did not apply to other forms of mass communication – but only by the fairly narrow margin of 41 votes to 24.[4] These hurdles overcome, the Bill went forward for the Royal Assent.

Thus, in many respects, the story of the Theatres Bill, 1968, differs substantially from the other case-studies of private members' legislation included in this volume. It is the sole example of a major social change becoming law without a challenge to the principle of the reform being made in the division lobbies. Granted the social climate of 1968, it is not surprising that the law of theatre censorship was altered: that this was achieved virtually without opposition does require explanation. The explanation can proceed at three different levels. There were a number of fortuitous or personal factors; the prevailing mood was favourable to this type of reform; those who guided the campaign did so with considerable political skill.

To commence with the personal and fortuitous items, it was an immense benefit to those who wished to free the stage from the manacles of the Lord Chamberlain that Roy Jenkins was appointed Home Secretary. His part in public discussions was negligible; in private his influence was great. Indeed, his transfer to the Treasury

[1] September 24, 1968.
[2] H. L. Deb., Vol. 292, cols 1044–1104.
[3] *Ibid.*, Vol. 293, cols 960–74.
[4] *Ibid.*, Vol. 295, cols 594–624.

I

could have been a major threat to the Bill's progress because his successor at the Home Office, James Callaghan, was not thought to have such clear views on the need for freedom of artistic expression. It was also fortunate for the reformers that Lord Cobbold and his predecessor, the Earl of Scarborough, agreed that the Lord Chamberlain's office should lose the censorship function. The wish to protect the Royal Household from controversy was most acceptable to that brand of Conservative opinion that might otherwise have wished to retain the censorship. And no alternative censors were visible, let alone acceptable. The Arts Council was unwilling to serve. No analogous body to the British Board of Film Censors was practicable because of widespread opposition in the theatre to any form of censorship. To give such powers to local authorities or magistrates would be to invite conflicting decisions which would immediately bring censorship into disrepute. So potential objectors to the Theatres Bill found it difficult to support the *status quo* and even more difficult to propose alternative institutions. The timing was also against them. The forces of social conservatism had suffered heavy defeats in Parliament during 1967 on abortion and homosexuality: support for the Theatres Bill was more firmly based than support for these earlier measures; to proclaim the need for stage censorship seemed to invite another certain defeat.

The chain of causation has led to the second level of explanation, the climate of social opinion. No voice was raised in favour of the Lord Chamberlain's attempts to suppress political comment. On questions of morality or taste he had lagged too far behind the conventions of the day, especially the conventions accepted by those who attend London theatres. The concern with four-letter words became absurd as these were increasingly used in popular literature. Whether a representation of Christ or God should be allowed to appear on the stage ceased to be an important issue in society either indifferent to, or more sophisticated in, its religious beliefs. The churches made no real attempt to preserve censorship. Puritanism was in retreat. On sexual matters, frankness was in fashion. In this atmosphere any censor was liable to perish.

Even so, the task facing the reformers was still one of great delicacy. In British politics anything that touches upon the Monarchy must be handled with care. There was always a slim chance that any reduction in the functions of the Royal Household could be interpreted as an attack upon the Monarchy itself, an interpretation that could produce floods of unreason. Such a possibility was frustrated by judicious preparation for the reform, in particular by the appointment of the Joint Select Committee representing all parties and both

Houses. The careful selection of the members of this Committee was noted above. Its unanimous report in favour of radical change created a firm basis for legislative action. None of the other Bills discussed in this book had this quality of support. The fact that the Government accepted the report's recommendations was also important. Again, from the Government's viewpoint, this move was scarcely controversial for Ministers could claim that they were merely following an initiative that had come from the legislature. Thus Ministers were in favour, but Ministers were not responsible. At every stage the reformers pitched their speeches in low key. No great publicity was sought. So tempers were not aroused and if some guardians of virtue were asleep – then their slumbers were undisturbed. Judged in terms of political craftsmanship, the campaign for the Theatres Act, 1968, was surely a masterpiece.

Chapter 7

Divorce

I

In 1697 Parliament agreed to pass a Private Bill which gave the Earl of Macclesfield an absolute divorce from the Countess: the Earl had previously failed to obtain a divorce *a mensa et thoro* (in essence, a judicial separation) from the ecclesiastical court. This measure established the authority of Parliament in the matter of divorce, and thus removed it from the prerogative of the church.

Church policy had varied before 1697. Prior to the Reformation the doctrine of the Roman Church had been supreme. Marriage came to be regarded as a sacrament which could not, therefore, be broken by human agency. Divorce was impossible. The only way to part husband and wife was to declare the marriage a nullity, i.e. that it never had been a marriage because a basic impediment existed at the time when the supposed marriage took place. If such an impediment could be discovered, the facts that the marriage had lasted *de facto* for many years and had produced many children were ignored as irrelevant. The barriers to a valid marriage were complex. At the beginning of the thirteenth century marriages were barred between persons within the fourth degree of consanguinity. But blood relationships were not the only bar. Extra-marital sexual relationships were treated for this purpose in the same way as legitimate copulations. Thus a man could not contract a valid marriage with a distant relation of his mistress. The church also ruled that baptism created a spiritual relationship which inhibited marriage equally as carnal connexion, and so relations to godparents could be excluded from marriage to the godchild. In this situation it was often not too difficult for a husband to find a reason to show that he had never properly been married; especially was this true in Scotland where intermarriage within the land-owning class produced a sexual network which commonly violated the law of the church.

After the Reformation the position changed. Calvin followed Luther in accepting adultery as a ground for divorce. Scottish practice became more liberal than that south of the Border. (This chapter is concerned with divorce law reform in England and Wales: Scotland is excluded). In England the position was more confused.

The early Protestants rejected the idea of marriage as a sacrament, and divorce was not unknown in the Elizabethan period. But at the beginning of the seventeenth century the Church of England re-affirmed its belief in the indissolubility of marriage, and its courts would grant only decrees *a mensa et thoro* which recognized separation but did not permit remarriage. Since the loopholes provided by the Roman technique of nullity were also ended, the Reformation in England had the effect of strengthening, rather than weakening, the marriage tie.

Three years after the Earl of Macclesfield's divorce, a similar privilege was granted to the Duke of Norfolk. The precedent was then established and wealthy husbands could be certain of securing a divorce if it could be shown that a wife had committed adultery. Before 1775 these Private Bills for divorce averaged one a year; subsequently the average went up to three. In 1798 the House of Lords created Standing Orders to deal with divorce Bills. One requirement of Standing Orders was that the petitioner must first have obtained a divorce *a mensa et thoro* from the ecclesiastical court: this was an extraordinary provision because a decree *a mensa et thoro* was, in essence, no more than a separation which required a pledge from a petitioner that he would not marry again during the lifetime of the spouse from whom he was formally separated.[1] The pledge, however, did not diminish the flow of divorce legislation and its disregard served to illustrate the diminishing authority of the church.

Parliament carried through a full-scale revision of the marriage law in 1753, but it was not until 1836 that marriages could be celebrated in non-conformist chapels. Also in 1836 a civil ceremony was permitted. Steadily the position of the church was eroded and in 1857 the divorce work of the ecclesiastical courts passed on to a new state Court for Divorce and Matrimonial Causes established by the Matrimonial Causes Act of that year.

The legislation of 1857 followed the recommendations of the Royal Commission on the Law of Divorce.[2] The ecclesiastical divorce *a mensa et thoro* was replaced by a decree of judicial separation. Absolute divorce – divorce *a vinculo matrimonii* – was to be granted on the same basis as had applied in the private divorce legislation, i.e. adultery by a wife and aggravated adultery by a husband. Thus the principles of the divorce law were not changed. All that was done, as with local government legislation, was to

---

[1] O. R. McGregor: *Divorce in England* (Methuen, 1957), p. 11. The second marriage had to be celebrated in church because in 1798 civil marriage was unknown.

[2] 1852–53 [1604], xl.

include in the public statutes what had been permitted already in private legislation. The procedure was simplified; divorce became cheaper and, therefore, more frequent. The main complaint about the legislation made by *The Times*[1] was that it gave lesser rights to wives than to husbands.

With the extension of the franchise, Parliament was made more aware of the matrimonial problems of poorer people. It was accepted that working-class wives and their children required protection from the cruelty that could be inflicted by husbands and fathers. The Matrimonial Causes Act, 1878, enabled a wife to apply to the magistrates for a separation order and a maintenance order where the husband had been found guilty of aggravated assault upon her. Subsequent legislation widened the grounds on which separation could be granted to include cruelty, desertion and drunkenness. Thus a class differential developed. By the end of the nineteenth century the wealthy could seek relief in the divorce court while the working-class wife went to the local magistrates.

In the Edwardian period there was a marked rise in controversy over divorce. The Divorce Law Reform Union was established in 1906 by the amalgamation of two earlier organizations with parallel aims. On the other hand, resistance to divorce in the Established Church hardened. The 1908 Lambeth Conference resolved that the Church could not sanction the remarriage of a divorcee during the lifetime of the spouse;[2] the majority was negligible, 87 to 84, but this still represented a great change from the practice of the church a century earlier. A cynic could claim that the Church was prepared to countenance an occasional remarriage by a landowner but not a regular pattern of remarriage by professional people and tradesmen. In 1910 the Convocation of Canterbury carried by a clear majority a resolution that it would be desirable to repeal the Act of 1857.[3]

The Asquith Government established a Royal Commission under the chairmanship of Lord Gorell to examine the problem. The Commission deliberated for three years 1909–12, and their report[4] is an effective statement of the diverse considerations involved and of the opposing points of view. The report was not unanimous and the outbreak of war in 1914 eliminated any possibility there may have been of early legislation. Nevertheless, it made a useful contribution to public understanding of the issues.

On some matters the Commissioners were unanimous. They

---

[1] Leading articles, June 18, 1854, and May 22, 1856.
[2] *The Times*, August 8, 1908.
[3] *Ibid.*, April 29, 1910.
[4] 1912–13, Cd. 6478, xviii.

agreed that sex inequality should be eliminated, that a wife should be able to obtain divorce on the same grounds as a husband. They agreed also that extra reasons for declaring a marriage to be a nullity should be permitted. These included wilful refusal to consummate the marriage and the existence of certain defects at the time of marriage of which the other party was ignorant, i.e. unsoundness of mind, venereal disease and pregnancy caused by a third party. Where the Commissioners failed to agree was on whether the grounds for divorce should be expanded. The Majority Report argued that the grounds for divorce should be not only adultery but also desertion for more than three years, cruelty, incurable insanity after five years' confinement, habitual drunkenness found to be incurable three years after an initial separation order and imprisonment under a commuted death sentence. The minority of three, including the Archbishop of York, rejected these proposals, arguing that they would serve to undermine the stability of marriage. *The Times* supported the minority view and reprinted the dissenting report in full.[1] The 1913 Labour Party Conference adopted a resolution supporting the Majority Report: no doubt Labour was especially attracted by the Commission's further proposal to decentralize divorce hearings in order to reduce costs.

After the war minor reforms were made. In spite of the wish of divorce lawyers to retain their centralized and lucrative monopoly, from 1920 some Assizes began to hear poor persons' divorce suits and undefended cases.[2] The grant of votes to women meant that unequal operation of the divorce law as between the sexes became a political impossibility: in 1923 women were allowed to claim divorce on the same grounds as men, i.e. adultery. But nothing was done to implement the majority proposals of the Gorell Commission until A. P. Herbert's crusade in the 1930s. His Divorce Bill, which became law in 1937, followed closely the lines of the Majority Report which thus became effective after a delay of exactly a quarter of a century.[3] This Bill was passed under the private members' ballot procedure and, in a sense, was a trail-blazer for the other private members' Bills discussed in this book. The Established Church was divided over its attitude to reform. The Convocation of Canterbury opposed Herbert's Bill but liberal churchmen argued that the existing law

[1] November 12, 1912.

[2] For further details, R. M. Jackson: *Machinery of Justice in England* (Cambridge U.P., 3rd edn, 1961), pp. 50, 280.

[3] A. P. Herbert, in inimitable style, wrote his own account of the passage of the Bill in *The Ayes Have It* (Methuen, 1937). The formal promoter of the Bill was a Conservative Member, Rupert de la Bere, who had been more fortunate than Herbert in the ballot.

forced those seeking divorce into immoral conduct since they had to choose between adultery and perjury. Compared with more recent legislation the Herbert Bill had a smooth passage through Parliament. The second reading was carried by 78 to 12 – only one speech was hostile to the measure. Many more Members attended the third reading but the majority was equally overwhelming, 190 to 37. Sir Donald Somervell, the Attorney-General, left an impression that the Government attitude was one of benevolent neutrality.

To maintain morale in the armed forces during the Second World War it was thought essential to deal sympathetically with the matrimonial difficulties of servicemen. A Services Divorce Department financed by the Government was set up by the Law Society. The earlier poor persons' procedure was manifestly inadequate; acting upon the report of the Rushcliffe Committee,[1] the Legal Aid and Advice Act, 1949, provided assistance, subject to a means test, with divorce and other legal problems. The rush of post-war divorces also created acute administrative difficulties, and following the report[2] of the Denning Committee on Procedure in Matrimonial Causes, special commissioners were recruited largely from the ranks of county court judges to hear divorce suits in provincial towns.

The forerunner of the contemporary debate on divorce-law reform was the Bill promoted by Mrs Eirene White (Lab. East Flint) in the 1950–51 parliamentary session. Her measure sought to allow divorce in cases where a couple had lived apart for seven years, even where one party to the marriage objected. Wholly new principles were involved. No longer would the concept of a matrimonial offence be the basic theme of divorce. (It is true that the inclusion of insanity in the Herbert Act was a breach in the principle, but it was a breach which applied solely to involuntary action.) Instead, the concept of breakdown of marriage was introduced: if it was clear that a marriage was dead, then society was asked to accept the fact without seeking to classify the spouses into guilty and innocent parties. The Labour Government at this stage had but a negligible majority in the Commons and decided to avoid the issue by the traditional delaying device of a Royal Commission. However, the second reading was carried by a clear majority, 131 votes to 60; the motion that the question be now put was previously carried by 102 votes to 99. For the Government the Attorney-General, Sir Hartley Shawcross, argued to take a vote on the Bill would gravely prejudice the subsequent enquiry. No doubt his speech accounted for the difference in the two divisions.[3] In view of the Government attitude there was

[1] 1944–45, Cmd. 6641, v.   [2] 1946–47, Cmd. 7024, xiii.
[3] H. C. Deb., Vol. 485, cols 1017–20.

little hope of the Bill becoming law, so Mrs White withdrew her Bill in return for the promise of the Royal Commission.

The ensuing Commission, headed by Lord Morton, laboured for four years. There was a strong legal element on the Commission, but the churches were not directly represented. The report[1] is an undistinguished document. Not merely did the Commissioners fail to agree but they took no steps to initiate research into their problem. For them the collection of evidence meant the collection of opinions. Their method of proceeding was wholly that of the nineteenth century. Either the Commission knew nothing of social science or they believed it had nothing to offer them.[2]

Neither the advocates of divorce reform not its opponents could derive much comfort from the Commission's recommendations. Only one of the nineteen members, Lord Walker, felt that the doctrine of the matrimonial offence should be replaced. On the other hand, nine members were prepared to accept seven years' separation as evidence of the complete breakdown of a marriage and for one spouse then to obtain a divorce providing that the other spouse did not object. This was less radical than Mrs White's Bill, which would have allowed divorce even against the objections of the other partner of the marriage. Four of the nine went some way towards Mrs White's position by suggesting that divorce be allowed, notwithstanding the objection of the other spouse, where the petitioner could satisfy the court that the separation was at least partly due to the unreasonable behaviour of the objector – a curious blend of the breakdown of marriage principle with a modified version of a matrimonial offence. Fourteen members of the Commission also suggested that an estranged couple should be able to live together for a while in an attempt at reconciliation without thereby barring the innocent spouse from the remedy of divorce. Apart from this last item the report had no influence. It was less progressive than the House of Commons had been in 1951. The one conclusion on which it was virtually unanimous, the retention of the doctrine of the matrimonial offence, was to be decisively rejected in the next decade.

Eight years passed before any action was taken. Then in 1963 Leo Abse (Lab. Pontypool) introduced a Bill under the ballot procedure which sought to facilitate reconciliation between estranged couples and also authorized divorce after seven years' separation. The Bill enjoyed a second reading without a division:[3] the 'kiss and make up'

---

[1] 1955–56, Cmd. 9678 xxiii.

[2] For detailed criticism of the Commission's work, see O. R. McGregor: *Divorce in England*.

[3] H. C. Deb., Vol. 671, cols 806–84.

provisions were generally welcomed, but some Members objected to any extension of the grounds for divorce. Strong religious opposition developed to the separation clause which culminated in a joint statement criticizing the clause from the Church of England, the Church in Wales, the Roman Catholic Church and the Free Church Federal Council.[1] Faced with the certainty of obstruction in the Commons, Abse felt obliged to withdraw the separation clause in order to secure the passage of the uncontroversial reconciliation provisions.[2] No vote was taken on his measure so there is no evidence of the state of parliamentary opinion at this stage.[3] However, there is no doubt that Abse's measure and the Ten-Minute Rule Bills introduced by John Parker (Lab. Dagenham) helped to reactivate discussion of the issue.

Following upon discussions with the Home Secretary and the Lord Chancellor, the Archbishop of Canterbury, Dr Ramsay, appointed in January 1964 a group to 'review the law of England concerning divorce'. Only three of the thirteen members were clerical. The legal profession was heavily represented;[4] it included also a professor of sociology, a consultant psychiatrist and the President of the National Council for the Unmarried Mother and her Child. The Chairman was Dr Mortimer, Bishop of Exeter. The terms of reference for the group explicitly recognized the difference in attitude between church and state: in their report, *Putting Asunder*, issued in July 1966, the group noted that it would amount to tyranny for the Christian minority to impose upon the secular majority. *Putting Asunder* was a powerful document, perhaps because it was almost free of theological argument. It proposed that breakdown of marriage should replace the matrimonial offence as the basis for divorce, thus upholding the minority of one on the Morton Commission. The reasoning of the group will be examined in the following section of this chapter, but the effect was to side-step much of the controversy aroused over Abse's Bill. An entirely new framework was suggested. There would be no accusatory procedure, no guilty party and no innocent party. A divorce would be granted if a court was satisfied that a marriage was truly at an end, that no reconciliation was possible, that adequate financial provision had been made for

---

[1] *The Times*, April 3, 1963.

[2] H. C. Deb., Vol. 676, cols 1555–83.

[3] When the House of Lords came to debate the Bill, Black Rod refused admission to several young people in order that their lordships should not feel inhibited by the presence of children in the gallery. *The Times*, July 13, 1963.

[4] Lord Devlin was one of the lawyers. Owing to the pressure of other duties he was able to attend only one meeting of the group. However, he assisted the group by commenting on the draft report.

the dependent spouse and the children, and that there was nothing in the conduct of the petitioner that would make it contrary to the public interest to grant a divorce. A court hearing into a divorce application would become an inquest. Thus a revolution was demanded in the *modus operandi* of judges and lawyers. These challenging ideas earned the sympathy of *The Times*: 'It is doubtful whether there has been published in recent times a more persuasive, thoughtful or constructive plea on behalf of the breakdown of marriage doctrine or a more effective condemnation of the present method of divorce.'[1]

Meanwhile, pressure for reform was growing. In April 1966 the Divorce Law Reform Union issued a statement that over a hundred members of the House of Lords would support *de facto* separation for five years as an additional ground for divorce: seven peers were prepared to introduce a Bill on these lines. So the publication of *Putting Asunder* was well received. It was immediately referred by the Lord Chancellor, Lord Gardiner, to the Law Commission for their advice. The Law Commissioners worked with commendable speed and produced a wide-ranging commentary, *The Field of Choice*, in less than four months.[2] They rejected the proposals in *Putting Asunder* as impracticable. An impossible extra burden of work could be placed upon the courts. 93 per cent of divorce suits were undefended, so that if a full inquest had to be held into each divorce application the extra time involved in court hearings would be enormous. Divorce would become more expensive. Extra staff would have to be employed, especially in the Queen's Proctor's Office, to check the accuracy of statements. Further, breakdown of marriage was not easily triable and it was proposed to try it through a procedure unfamiliar to the courts; the 'result would be varying and unpredictable conclusions' and solicitors would find it difficult, especially at first, to advise their clients.

The Commissioners themselves put forward three alternative patterns for the legislature to consider. These were divorce by consent, divorce based upon separation, and the breakdown of marriage principle without the detailed inquest by a court. They recognized that mutual consent might not be acceptable, and suggested that breakdown without inquest might be linked with the separation principle. Where both parties wished for divorce a shorter period of separation could be appropriate than where one objected.

All these ideas were considered in a House of Lords debate in November 1966.[3] The Archbishop of Canterbury supported the

[1] Leading article, July 29, 1966. [2] 1966–67, Cmnd. 3123.
[3] H. L. Deb., Vol. 278, cols 239–348.

breakdown of marriage basis for divorce. Lord Soper, on behalf of the Free Churches, agreed with the Archbishop. The Earl of Iddesleigh, a Roman Catholic, recognized the need for divorce in society, although not for himself. The Bishop of Exeter, Chairman of the group which produced *Putting Asunder*, argued that the 'time has come to move away from our present marriage system, with all the bitterness it unnecessarily engenders, in the direction of something more civilized and more enlightened'. He also stressed the need for further discussion to try to remove differences of view between his group and the Law Commission. The Spring Session of the 1967 Church Assembly expressed approval of *Putting Asunder*: so did the Chairman of the Divorce Law Reform Union at the Union's annual meeting. A quite remarkable consensus appeared to have been reached on the broad lines for reform: the difficulties arose when precise proposals were formulated. However, the Lord Chancellor, Lord Gardiner, tried to co-ordinate the varied proposals when he suggested to the 1967 conference of the National Marriage Guidance Council that divorce should be available on proof that a marriage had broken down irretrievably and that a matrimonial offence or a period of separation should be treated as evidence of breakdown. After further consultation with the Bishop of Exeter's group, the Law Commission reported: 'We are satisfied that if Parliament were to accept the principle of breakdown as the basis for divorce, practical and feasible proposals making use of the "separation ground" could be prepared.'[1] The Church of England dropped the idea of detailed inquests into marriage breakdown and the way was cleared for new divorce legislation. The stormy passage of the Bill through Parliament is described in Section III of this chapter.

II

Controversies surrounding marriage and divorce are so complex that any summary must fall into the trap of simplification. A number of quite separate kinds of consideration are involved. Further, one has the feeling that there is a gap between the arguments used and the driving force behind the arguments. In political debate it is common for what is said to be that which is thought to be the most acceptable and persuasive. Basic feelings and ideas are suppressed, sometimes consciously, for fear that they will detract from chances of success.

Theology and religion have faded in discussion about divorce. Church leaders accept that church and state are separate; that

[1] Report of the Law Commission for 1966/67, para. 75.

religious communities can make rules for themselves which they cannot expect the state to impose upon the whole population. In the particular case of divorce the Church of England finds theological justification for this approach in the explanation given by Jesus for the Mosaic permission of divorce: 'for your hardness of heart Moses allowed you to divorce your wives'. (Matthew, 19, 8; Mark, 10, 5.) Hardness of heart is interpreted as insensitivity of conscience, inability to apprehend the Creator's will. Thus, people who do not accept the Christian message must be allowed divorce.[1]

The traditional Christian view of sex and marriage has been based on St Paul's advice to the Corinthians:

'I say therefore to the unmarried and the widows, it is good for them if they abide even as I. But if they cannot contain, let them marry: for it is better to marry than to burn.'

I Corinthians, 7, 8–9.

He also singled out fornication as an especially grievous sin.

'Every sin that a man doeth is without the body. But he that committeth fornication sinneth against his own body.'

I Corinthians, 6, 18.

Thus celibacy was the ideal mode of existence. Sexual intercourse was a necessity for the continuance of the human race, but it should not be thought of as a source of pleasure. Even sex within marriage was often thought to involve some sort of defilement.

Now these attitudes seem so curious that their power over the centuries requires some explanation. Certainly they had unambiguous biblical authority. To contain sex within marriage produced stable family life and security for wives and children. The sexual urge was so powerful as to be greatly feared; therefore it had to be channelled and constrained. These are the obvious reinforcements for the Pauline doctrine. Psychologists would add that much pleasure can be derived from conscious self-restraint and an awareness of self-sacrifice. Further, the elderly are often the more dominant members of society and they can be envious of the sexual potency of the young and thus seek to restrain it. St Paul's message has become almost unheeded because of the decline of religious influence and also because sexual pleasure can be enjoyed without the pains and responsibilities of childbirth. In modern conditions St Paul became an embarrassment.

If a church is divided upon its teaching to the faithful, its impact

[1] See *Putting Asunder*, para. 12.

on the faithless will be further diminished: the disputes within the Established Church over the remarriage of divorced persons have scarcely increased its authority.[1] Quite apart from this weakness, the church–state relationship is a delicate one. Religious bodies want to have influence but they must avoid any impression of seeking to impose their brand of doctrine upon others. Equally, politicians with deep religious convictions cannot be expected to abandon them when called on to vote in the House of Commons, but they will frequently seek to justify their actions with arguments not overtly religious. Figures given in Chapter 9 show the opposition of Anglican and Roman Catholic Members to divorce reform, although there was little reference to religious teaching in parliamentary debates.

As theology fades, the main theme running through discussion on divorce is the need to maintain the stability of marriage. No one disputes that a happy marriage provides great comfort and satisfaction for the partners and love and security for children. Anything detrimental to this blissful arrangement is unfortunate. A law which permits the breaking of marriages may incite the breaking of marriages. Lord Redesdale, the sole dissentient on the Royal Commission of 1850, argued that a form of divorce which allowed the possibility of remarriage should be unobtainable. Such divorce, he argued, was a barrier to reconciliation, and the expectation of divorce sometimes increased the temptation to commit adultery.[2] Few will doubt the truth of these conclusions. The fears that the 1857 Act represented the thin edge of the wedge have been justified. Eighteenth-century England had accepted that an adulteress could not be permitted to disrupt the normal pattern of succession to large estates. Subsequently the middle class claimed a similar right and wives demanded equal treatment. Next the divorce law was attacked because it forced people into adultery or the pretence of adultery. Finally the whole concept of the matrimonial offence and the allocation of guilt and innocence were criticized as being unreal.

The case against Lord Redesdale was, and is, that his view is not acceptable to society. If divorce were not obtainable, people would live together in an unmarried state. Some do today – occasionally by choice but usually because the possibility of marriage is blocked. If the marriage law does not correspond to contemporary attitudes, then marriage law will be ignored. This is the truth which has to be faced. In a very real sense the advocates of divorce reform are seeking to strengthen the institution of marriage by reducing the number of extra-marital relationships and illegitimate children. Certainly there

[1] Cf. A. P. Herbert: *The Right to Marry* (Methuen, 1954).
[2] pp. 23–6; 1852–53 [1604], xl.

is no automatic correlation between the state of divorce law, the frequency of divorce and the incidence of unhappy and broken homes. Over the past thirty years divorce has become more common because of wartime upheavals and subsequently through the extension of legal aid.[1] The cost of legal proceedings, as a barrier to divorce, has gone. The social stigma of divorce has gone: a Prime Minister can have a divorce. There remain the psychological and financial stresses caused by disrupted family life and the opposition of a spouse who, at least in the eyes of the law, is an innocent party. These three problems formed the core of the discussion on the Divorce Bill.

Lady Summerskill obtained much publicity for her description of the Bill as a 'Casanova's Charter'. The fear is that middle-aged husbands would be encouraged to desert their middle-aged wives for younger figures and prettier faces. If marriage can be ended after five years' separation, even against the objections of the wife, then it may be argued that every wife is on five years' notice. Some defenders of female rights made great play with this theme. Yet it is unreal. Any marriage can be broken up without any notice: a husband (or wife) can leave the matrimonial home without any prior warning whatsoever. So long as the doctrine of the matromional offence prevailed, a deserted wife could insist on retaining the status of a deserted wife. Whether this is more desirable than the status of a divorcée is a matter of opinion.

The shock to children resulting from the break-up of their parents' marriage is commonly severe. Many subsequent difficulties and behaviour disorders may be traced back to this great smash in their lives. Is this a powerful argument against divorce where there are dependent children of a marriage? Or do children suffer less in a broken home as opposed to a home where parents constantly quarrel? A National Opinion Poll survey conducted in December 1967 showed that 61 per cent of those canvassed felt that given this choice it was better for a child to live with a single parent; 31 per cent considered the unhappy home to be preferable. Next month the Gallup Poll produced an even more definite result: 83 per cent favoured the single parent and only 10 per cent the unhappy home. The opinions show widespread support for the view that in conditions of marital stress, divorce, from the child's point of view, may be the optimum solution. Sir Jocelyn Simon, President of the Probate, Divorce and Admiralty Division, has argued that divorce should be unobtainable where parents have dependent children, but that otherwise divorce

[1] This is clearly shown in the Appendices to the Law Commission's report: *The Field of Choice.*

by consent should be allowed.[1] His suggestion went unheeded since it would focus bitterness and frustration upon blameless children.

Equally serious can be the financial consequences of divorce. Women may fear the loss of regular income and pension rights. A number of safeguards had already been provided by recent legislation; the Matrimonial Causes Act, 1955, the Matrimonial Homes Act, 1967, and the Maintenance Orders Acts, 1950 and 1958. The Divorce Bill itself added further safeguards by insisting that a court must approve the financial arrangements consequent upon a divorce as being fair and reasonable or the best that can be made in the circumstances. In addition, the operation of the Divorce Bill was postponed until January 1, 1971, so that further legislation on matrimonial property could first reach the statute book. Thus great efforts were made to meet the financial objections to divorce reform. Even so, legislation cannot fully meet the problem. If a man has but a modest income, any attempt to support two women and two families must produce an intolerable strain. Critics of the Divorce Bill objected that if a financial settlement was 'the best that can be made in the circumstances' it need not be fair and reasonable. Yet the extent of the problem can be exaggerated, for the majority of divorced women remarry. In any case, the economic difficulties start when a man leaves home; by the time a case comes to court a new standard of living will often have become established. Divorce does not itself create the material discomforts of deserted wives and children: on the contrary it may ease them somewhat if a divorce court is allowed to impose a fair and reasonable settlement on a decamping husband. The only other solution is for social security provision for deserted families to be made more generous.[2]

There remains the question, what principles should form the basis of divorce law? The Law Commission suggested two criteria:[3]

(a) To buttress, rather than undermine, the stability of marriage.
(b) Where, regrettably, a marriage has irretrievably broken down, to enable the empty legal shell to be destroyed with maximum fairness and the minimum bitterness, distress and humiliation.

To argue that divorce law should buttress marriage appears paradoxical. Yet it can do so through the encouragement of reconcilia-

[1] 'The Seven Pillars of Divorce Reform' in the *Law Society's Gazette*, June 1965, p. 344.
[2] Immediately this invokes opposing moral judgements – that the state should not subsidize immorality and that no moral principle is sound which inflicts suffering on the innocent.
[3] Cmnd. 3123, para. 15.

tion and by ensuring that law bears a reasonable relation to social opinion. Without question marriage remains a highly popular institution. A majority of divorced persons remarry. People marry younger and live longer, so the duration of marriage tends to increase. The number of weddings also rises. There is no firm evidence that marriage breakdown is increasing. By themselves, divorce statistics are misleading unless the greater number of marriages and the consequence of the availability of legal aid are taken into account.

Although the institution of marriage still flourishes, is it right that individual casualties should be treated by a process analogous to that of the criminal law, so that the status of a spouse depends upon 'guilt' or 'innocence'? This is the fundamental issue faced by the authors of *Putting Asunder*. They disliked the existing law because it generated a combination of falsity and hypocrisy with undefended divorce suits being handled like shelling peas. They wanted fuller consideration to be given to the termination of any marriage. Yet the case for the present system is not insubstantial. The matrimonial offence doctrine is well understood; it provides support for marriage in that an erring partner can never be certain of obtaining release; a spouse who wishes to remain married in a legal sense may do so unless he or she commits a matrimonial offence. The procedure fits well into our legal tradition in that the courts are attuned to the determination of guilt.

Yet the objections to the matrimonial offence concept are overwhelming and convinced the *Putting Asunder* group. When a marriage founders, it is rare for one party to be wholly to blame; the guilt and innocence distinction becomes unreal. Court procedure tends to become a farce and this brings law into disrepute. The need to establish an 'offence' in the technical sense leads to needless bitterness. Attempts at reconciliation are hindered since condonation of an offence limits the right to divorce. When adultery was made a ground for divorce it was widely regarded as a grievous sin; now this is no longer so. Increasingly, both parties to a divorce suit have committed adultery and this is no bar to a decree providing it is admitted. Often when a petitioner admits guilt, the respondent starts a cross-suit based on the admission. Dual 'guilt' brings the agreed reward – divorce. So the matrimonial offence doctrine permits divorce by consent but is a way designed to encourage maximum rancour and bitterness, which can cause additional hardship for children. Alternatively, where there is no consent, embittered spouses may prevent divorce: their legal partners then establish unrecognized unions which produce illegitimate children. Many of these unions are stable and harmonious and much firmer 'mar-

K

riages' than many orthodox ones. It could be claimed that the frustration felt by those who wish to marry but are not free to do so is a useful deterrent to those who contemplate breaking-up their own marriages. This argument would, indeed, be powerful were there firm evidence that such a deterrent exists. But, except where religious difficulties arise, there will always be the hope that divorce will be agreed if only because the discarded spouse may find a new partner.

As an alternative to the matrimonial offence, the breakdown of marriage concept has attracted increasing support. But it raises two immediate questions: how is breakdown to be judged, and is divorce without guilt and without consent an acceptable proposition? It has been noted that the Church of England report, *Putting Asunder*, proposed that breakdown be established through a careful enquiry by a divorce court. However, this process would undoubtedly accentuate recriminations as the parties to a divorce suit would have to show that their domestic life had been so disastrous as to place the marriage beyond redemption. The increase in personal bitterness would be entirely contrary to a main purpose of divorce reform and the interests of children could well suffer. The Law Commission also rejected the scheme as impracticable in terms of the availability of court facilities.

The Law Commission suggested three alternative bases for divorce law: breakdown without inquest; divorce by consent; separation – the period of separation required to be shorter where both parties wished for divorce. Stated baldly these alternatives are misleading. Breakdown without inquest must require some proof of breakdown, otherwise it becomes divorce by consent. If separation or the traditional matrimonial offences are accepted as conclusive evidence of breakdown, then again the result can be divorce by consent, albeit hedged about by some restrictions. But the phrase divorce by consent is curiously unacceptable. It is rejected as unthinkable by each committee or commission. The community, we are told, has a valid interest in marriage; it is not a matter for the partners alone. Consensual divorce is an obvious challenge to the stability of marriage, so it is something we must avoid, or pretend to avoid, at all costs. But divorce by consent need not necessarily give an unconditional right to divorce: the principle can be allowed to apply subject to time limits and approved financial settlements. If it implies no divorce without consent, it is a principle far more restrictive than the divorce legislation now adopted.[1]

[1] Cf. Sir B. McKenna: 'Divorce by Consent and Divorce for Breakdown of Marriage', 30 *Modern Law Review*, pp. 121–37.

Involuntary divorce is incorporated in the matrimonial offence doctrine because a 'guilty' party may be divorced against his or her will. The effect of the breakdown principle is to enlarge greatly the scope for involuntary divorce. If it be accepted that marriage should end when it is but an empty legal shell, then the end has to come whether both parties agree or not. Thus the breakdown principle is the truly radical principle.

III

As indicated above, the 1967 Bill was based on the breakdown of marriage principle, yet the standard matrimonial offences remained not as offences but as evidence of the breakdown of a marriage. Thus a petitioner has a *prima facie* right to divorce where the other spouse has committed adultery, has behaved cruelly, has deserted the matrimonial home two years previously, where the marriage partners have lived apart for two years and neither objects to divorce, and where one partner does object provided the separation has lasted five years. In all circumstances the court must be satisfied that the marriage has broken down irretrievably. Thus it is not sufficient to show that the respondent has committed adultery; the petitioner must also satisfy the court that he or she now finds it intolerable to live with the respondent. The court may also refuse divorce if to grant it would cause severe financial hardship. This Bill was drafted in the offices of the Law Commission and was not fully acceptable to some church opinion which had supported *Putting Asunder*. Instead of a court investigation into the state of a marriage, the Bill required the court to accept that a marriage had broken down in certain circumstances. This limited the discretion of the judge and tended to make divorce far more automatic than was intended by the authors of *Putting Asunder*. Since the vast majority of divorce petitions are undefended and automatic, it was inevitable that this automatic quality would remain after any reform that intended to liberalize the law. To argue that a single act of adultery should not be an inevitable passport to divorce is merely to insist on an increase in the amount of extra-marital intercourse. To urge that a court must be able to enquire into the possibility of salvaging a marriage is to ignore the fact that a marriage is dead long before the petition for divorce is heard by a court and often before the petitioner consulted a solicitor.

Although Leo Abse was the driving force in the Commons behind divorce law reform, he was unsuccessful in the 1967 ballot. The formal sponsor of the Bill was William Wilson (Lab. Coventry, South) who won fourth place in the draw. The Bill obtained a second reading on February 9, 1968, by 159 votes to 63. With this comfortable majority the Bill moved on to a Standing Committee where its supporters had a corresponding majority. However, the committee stage was long and difficult. Thirteen meetings were needed before the Bill passed through the committee stage. Ultimately two meetings a week were held (morning and afternoon on the same day) in an attempt to speed up progress. In spite of this effort, the Bill was not ready to be reported to the House until the end of May, by which date there was no private members' time available in the whole House. As the Government failed to provide extra time the Bill was lost.

Why did the Wilson Bill proceed so slowly? The obvious answer – that it was delayed by a filibuster – is not a fair explanation. Certainly opponents of the measure consumed a great deal of time in committee, but there is not much evidence of deliberate timewasting. The Divorce Bill was longer and more intricate than the other private members' bills examined in this book. The scope for discussion and amendment on points of detail was considerable. To hold thirteen committee sessions on a matter of this importance was not excessive. But apart from its complexity, two other factors retarded the Bill. It got off to a slow start. The second reading did not take place until February, three months after the opening of the session. The sponsor, William Wilson, could have claimed an earlier Friday, but did not do so in order, no doubt, to prepare more fully for the debate. The other reason is that the shades of opinion on the Standing Committee had a glorious but confusing variety. If the opponents of the Bill did not always agree with each other, nor did its supporters. While most of the Committee's time was taken up with amendments, often rather technical, which might have had the effect of restricting divorce, other amendments put forward by Dr Gray (Lab. Yarmouth) sought to facilitate divorce still further. Thus Dr Gray wanted unopposed divorce after desertion or separation to be subject to the delay of one year instead of two, and opposed divorce to be obtainable after three years' delay instead of five.[1] So while the Committee adopted the breakdown of marriage principle in Clause I without a division, the detailed application of the principle was attacked by those who wished it to be both more and less restrictive.

The ultimate reason why the Divorce Bill failed to pass in 1968

---

[1] This latter proposal, curiously enough, had the support of *The Times*, cf. leading article January 16, 1968.

is that the Government would not find time for it. In view of the precedents of capital punishment, homosexuality and abortion, this is a little surprising. Perhaps the Lord Chancellor, Lord Gardiner, the Minister most closely connected with the Bill, was less persuasive with his Cabinet colleagues than other Ministers had been in relation to the other Bills. The other difficulty was that the Divorce Bill did not stand alone, for the Sunday Entertainments Bill was in a similar plight. To provide facilities for one Bill and not the other would be to offer an obvious target for criticism: to aid both was certain to be expensive in terms of parliamentary time and possibly in terms of political support. It was also arguable – although an embarrassing theme for a Labour Government – that even if the Commons found time to pass the Bills before the summer recess it would be difficult to arrange for adequate consideration by the Lords.

Faced with non-co-operation from Ministers, the divorce reformers led by Leo Abse organized an effective campaign of protest within Parliament, especially within the Parliamentary Labour Party. It was intolerable, they argued, that a measure which had been extensively debated and which enjoyed not merely majority support but almost overwhelming support, should be delayed by the technicalities of the parliamentary timetable. Why should all the time and work invested in the Bill be wasted? Why should the Bill not be allowed to carry over from one session to another so that proceedings on a Bill in a new session could continue from where they had reached at the end of the previous session? Why should the Upper House not have a rather shorter summer recess in order to pass a measure desired by Parliament and which would bring comfort and relief to thousands of people? Quite substantial publicity was obtained for these views in the mass media. Inevitably they appealed to all those who felt that Parliament should where necessary amend its traditions to become a more effective vehicle for social change. There can be no doubt that this campaign, as Abse intended, had an effect on the decision of the Government to assist the Divorce Bill in the following parliamentary session.

Thus the scene was set for a resumption of the struggle in the 1968–69 session. Abse attended the private members' ballot in person so that he could go into instant action to persuade a highly placed Member to sponsor the divorce reform measure. But for him the ballot was a near disaster. Only the first eight in the draw could be certain of a full debate on second reading for whatever Bill they chose to introduce. None of the first eight names drawn was among Abse's firm supporters with the sole exception of John

Parker (Lab. Dagenham) who was already deeply committed to the Sunday Entertainments Bill. The ninth name was Alec Jones (Lab. Rhondda, West) who had been elected at a by-election in 1967. Abse hastened to persuade Jones to sponsor divorce reform.

The 1968 Jones Bill was almost identical in content with the 1967 Wilson Bill. There were, however, two changes which embodied amendments that had been agreed on the committee stage of the Wilson Bill. The provision that the court could refuse a decree where one party had attempted to deceive the court was dropped. The other difference was that the 'kiss and make up' period, in which marriage partners could live together again without affecting their right to divorce, was extended from six months to twelve; the period was reduced back to six months on the committee stage of the 1968 Bill. In terms of procedure the difference was that Jones had no certainty of securing adequate time to obtain a second reading. He chose to be the second measure down for consideration on December 6, 1968, coming after a relatively uncontroversial measure concerning employer's liability. The debate on divorce did not commence until 2.40 p.m., when a mere 80 minutes remained. Due to the custom of the House it was certain that the Speaker would not accept a closure motion after so short a time and the debate was adjourned without a decision. However, Abse had managed to persuade Ministers that the House must be allowed to come to a final decision, so the new Standing Order was operated which allows a Minister to move a motion permitting a morning sitting. Such a motion was subsequently agreed by 118 votes to 30.[1] The debate was accordingly resumed on the morning of Tuesday, December 17th, when the second reading was carried by 183 votes to 106.[2]

It will be noted that the balance of opinion was less favourable to the Bill than it had been in the previous session. There are a number of possible reasons. The tone of Abse's winding-up speech was firm and uncompromising, not designed to attract waverers. The day was Tuesday instead of Friday, so the attendance of Scottish Members was higher. Opponents of the measure had protested against the Government provision of additional time; this may have injected some party political feeling into the atmosphere and persuaded some wavering Conservatives to vote against. Finally, there is a slightly comic point. The Bill's sponsors had expected the Speaker to accept the closure motion about 12.45 p.m. and had warned their supporters to be available at this time. The Speaker,

[1] H. C. Deb, Vol. 775, cols 1045–8.
[2] *Ibid.*, cols 1133–6.

however, had a luncheon engagement and, as his deputy cannot accept a closure motion for a second reading, the vote was postponed until the Speaker's return and finally took place an hour later than expected. This miscalculation by those organizing support for the Bill may have had a little effect on the voting figures.

Inevitably, the personalities, arguments and attitudes involved in the Jones Bill tended to be the same as in the previous session. As before, the Bill needed thirteen sittings to pass through Standing Committee, but since an earlier start had been made the committee passed it by Easter. The attitude of the Minister looking after the Bill, Sir Arthur Irvine, the Solicitor-General, also became more helpful. He had abstained on the second reading of the Wilson Bill and his speech on that occasion could be regarded as mildly hostile; but he voted for the second reading of the Jones Bill. On both occasions the Government were formally neutral, but the personal attitude of the Government spokesman is still of importance. In the 1968–69 session a new and determined opponent of divorce reform appeared in the person of Bruce Campbell (Con. Oldham, West) who had joined the Commons after a by-election in June 1968. Daniel Awdry (Chippenham) replaced Sir George Sinclair[1] (Dorking) as the chief Conservative supporter of the Bill, and on both occasions the formal sponsor was assisted and guided by Leo Abse.

One wholly new factor in the 1968–69 session was the Matrimonial Property Bill sponsored by Edward Bishop (Lab. Newark) who had won third place in the ballot. This Bill sought to make a fundamental change in the law of property. It proposed that when a marriage ends in death, divorce or separation, the husband and wife would each retain anything they brought into the marriage and anything they were individually given or inherited during it: all other resources and property accumulated during the marriage would be split equally between husband and wife. The court was to be allowed to depart from these principles where their operation would be obviously unfair. These provisions would have a major effect on the financial position of many divorced persons, but they also raised questions of property law that had nothing whatever to do with divorce. Divorce reformers were in favour of Bishop's Bill except for those Ministers who argued that it was unworkable. Opponents of divorce reform were deeply divided. Some objected to the Bill perhaps because they feared it would undermine their

[1] Sir George had not changed his mind on divorce, but he became deeply concerned with the problems of race relations, and this occupied much of his time.

position. Lady Summerskill was so impressed by the value of the Matrimonial Property Bill that at one stage she indicated it might lead her to drop objections to the Divorce Bill.

Bishop's Bill provoked a major conflict within the Labour Party. The Law Officers argued that there were serious technical defects in the Bill and the problems of valuation that would arise would be completely unmanageable. The Law Commission was reviewing the whole field of the law of family property, and the Government view was that legislation must be postponed until the Commission had completed its study. Women's organizations were, however, in favour of the measure and the Labour Party has been traditionally sympathetic towards the feminist cause. So the Bill received overwhelming support from Labour back-benchers. Ministers were so determined to check this enthusiasm that an official whip was issued against the Bill – a two-line whip for Labour Members but a three-line whip for Ministers. This produced such a storm of protest at a meeting of the Parliamentary Labour Party that the Prime Minister, after a hasty consultation with the Lord Chancellor, announced that a free vote would be permitted after all. On January 24, 1969, the second reading was carried by 86 votes to 32.[1] After further negotiations with the Law Officers, Bishop agreed to withdraw his Bill in return for a promise of legislation in the following session.

These events necessarily had an impact on the Divorce Bill, for there was wide agreement on the need to provide additional financial safeguards for divorcées. In March the Solicitor-General informed the Standing Committee on the Divorce Bill that legislation on matrimonial property might be introduced next session and that it was the Government view that the Divorce Bill, if passed by Parliament, should not come into effect until the financial measure had been introduced. One of the leading opponents of divorce reform, Sir Lionel Heald (Con. Chertsey) immediately claimed that the Government now admitted what he had proclaimed for months, that the Divorce Bill provided inadequate protection for women divorced against their will under the five-year separation clause. He also argued that further consideration of the Divorce Bill should be delayed until the detail of the financial changes was available for consideration.[2] Not unnaturally the Bill's sponsors were not prepared to accept more delay and the proceedings on the Bill continued.

[1] H. C. Deb., Vol. 776, cols 801–96. Nine Ministers voted against the Bill and three voted for it.
[2] Letter to *The Times*, March 11, 1969.

The report stage occupied approximately five hours on Friday, April 25th, and a further two hours on the following Friday.[1] This time was entirely consumed by three new clauses. The first, proposed by the Bill's sponsor Alec Jones, strengthened the power of a divorce court to impose an equitable financial settlement before issuing a decree, and was carried by 86 votes to 22. The second, proposed by Sir Lionel Heald, sought to refuse divorce when a court was satisfied that the petitioner had attempted to deceive it and that the deception was serious in nature; this was defeated by 37 votes to 19. The third, proposed by Bruce Campbell, would have allowed couples before or after marriage to enter into a voluntary agreement that their marriage was a lifelong union terminable only by death. Where such an agreement had been made and a court subsequently accepted that a breakdown of marriage had occurred, the result would be a judicial separation and not divorce. This meant that there would be two levels of marriage and some couples would opt out of the normal application of the divorce law. Campbell's clause was still being debated when time ran out.

The debates on these clauses were all long-winded. Often the Chair had to request Members to address themselves more closely to the specific proposal under discussion. Twice while the first new clause was being considered the unofficial whip for the Bill, Peter Jackson (Lab. High Peak), attempted to move the closure: on the first occasion the Chair refused to accept the motion and on the second Jackson failed to secure the attendance of the necessary hundred supporters. There was a lack of spirit in the debates. It was expected that the Government would make extra time available if necessary. The sponsors were resigned to the fact that more time would be needed; their opponents were determined to ensure that it was.

The Government duly announced that an all-night sitting would be held on June 12, 1969, to allow the House to come to a decision on the divorce measure. Sir Lionel Heald thereupon tabled a motion of protest. He had two complaints. First, that the Government were giving priority to the Divorce Bill over other private members' Bills:[2] second, that the Government were pretending to neutrality and taking no responsibility for a measure they were assisting. Ministers decided that this challenge must be met, so on the evening

[1] H. C. Deb., Vol. 782, cols 814–98, 1821–52.
[2] This priority had a dual aspect. Other private members' Bills were not offered the opportunity of an additional sitting. Further, Friday, June 13th, was allocated to private members' Bills, but since the Divorce Bill still occupied the House at 11 a.m., the business arranged for that day had to be abandoned.

of Thursday, June 12th, Sir Lionel's motion was debated – and defeated by 166 votes to 62 – before the argument on divorce was resumed at 1.5 a.m.[1] During the night and the following morning many amendments were debated, most of which sought to limit the scope for divorce. Seven of the amendments were put to the vote and defeated: on five occasions the vote was preceded by a successful procedural motion that the question be put. Throughout this period thirty to forty staunch opponents of the Bill were present. For the sponsors the vital need was not simply to out-number their opponents but to keep a core of one hundred supporters on hand so that, when necessary, authority could be obtained to hold a division. They succeeded. The highest opposition vote, 58, was in support of an amendment to delete the qualification 'or the best that can be made in the circumstances' from the court's power to impose an equitable and satisfactory financial settlement as a condition of divorce. This demonstrates again that the biggest obstacle faced by reformers was not religious but concern about the material well-being of families broken by divorce.[2] Finally, the third reading was obtained on the Friday afternoon by 109 votes to 55.

The House of Lords gave the Bill a second reading by 122 votes to 34. Lady Summerskill's description of the measure as a Casanova's Charter was countered by the Lord Chancellor with the information that in New Zealand, where a similar law had been in effect for fourteen years, no less than 40 per cent of the petitioners for divorce were women. Two features of this debate are notable – the size of the majority in favour and the split in the ranks of the bishops. Five bishops voted in favour, three against, while the Archbishop of Canterbury, who was present, abstained. There is no clear correlation between the division of opinion in the Established Church over the Divorce Bill and High Church/Low Church attitudes. High Churchmen are less favourable towards the concept of divorce, but they are also more critical of state supremacy over the church and thus more willing to accept distinctions between the law of the church and the law of the state.

A large number of amendments were put down for examination at the committee stage. This occupied three days, but the debate was sharp and businesslike, with no suspicion of a filibuster. Divisions

---

[1] H. C. Deb., Vol. 784, cols 1797–2074.

[2] On this occasion seven members voted in favour of the termination of debate and in favour of the amendment: they were P. Channon (Con. Southend, West); J. Hunt (Con. Bromley); R. Maxwell-Hyslop (Con. Tiverton); B. Millan (Lab. Glasgow, Craigton); R. Mitchell (Lab. Southampton, Test); J. Nott (Con. and Nat. Lib. St Ives) and P. Tapsell (Con. Horncastle).

were challenged on a number of amendments; only one amendment was carried by a contested vote, although other minor changes in the Bill were made without disssent. The one significant amendment concerned divorce after two years' separation; by 65 votes to 61 it was agreed that this should require the consent of the respondent, not merely the absence of objection. It is possible that this alteration will delay divorce in cases where a respondent feels unable, for conscientious reasons, to 'consent' to divorce although willing to abstain from objection. The other main attempts to amend the Bill can be summarized briefly. Deletion of the provision that the traditional matrimonial offences should constitute proof of breakdown of marriage was defeated by 54 to 106 (this would have adopted the *Putting Asunder* formula rejected by the Law Commission). Extension of the period of separation required before divorce by consent is permitted from two years to three was defeated by 34 to 89. Elimination of divorce after five years' separation, where one party objects, was defeated by 35 to 85. Deletion of the word 'grave' from the condition that a respondent can object to divorce where it would inflict grave financial hardship was defeated by 70 to 95. A requirement that financial provision for the respondent should be 'fair' instead of 'fair and the best that can be made in the circumstances defeated by 41 to 69. One other amendment, accepted without a division, postponed the operation of the Bill until January 1, 1971, in order that the new legislation being prepared by the Law Commission might become law before the new pattern of divorce became effective.

In the Lords it is possible for amendments to a Bill to be moved at the third reading stage although, by convention, such amendments should refer to proposals made at an earlier stage of the proceedings and postponed for further consideration. One such change was moved by Lord Dilhorne which provided that a respondent could object to divorce on the grounds that it would cause severe financial hardship *only* in the case of a divorce sought under the five-year separation rule. Had this change not been made it would have been possible for a respondent whose conduct had caused the break-up of a marriage to avoid divorce: an impecunious husband might have been unable to get a divorce from a spiteful adulteress. The Lords accepted Lord Dilhorne's third reading amendment without a division.

Thus the Lords made three significant changes in the Bill. One, referring to the date of operation, was of merely temporary significance. Of the other two, one tended to make divorce more difficult in some cases while the other removed a possible barrier to divorce.

The Commons accepted all these alterations without much demur on October 17, 1969. Indeed, with the end of the parliamentary session but a few days away, there was no time for further argument.

IV

The question remains – why was the Divorce Bill campaign so long and difficult? The ground had been well prepared by the publication of *Putting Asunder* and the spadework of the Law Commission. *Putting Asunder* at least blunted opposition from the Established Church. Formal Roman Catholic objection was inevitable, but by no means all Catholic Members joined the opponents in Parliament. Public opinion polls showed firm majority support for reform. Alastair Service, chief lobbyist for the Divorce Law Reform Union, encouraged both Gallup and the National Opinion Polls to organize surveys on the divorce issue because he was confident that the results would be favourable. Thus the Gallup survey in January 1968 showed that 70 per cent approved the proposition that a husband and wife who have lived apart for two years should be entitled to a divorce if both agreed to it; 17 per cent answered 'no' and 13 per cent 'don't know'. 56 per cent supported divorce after five years' separation when only one party wished for it; 26 per cent answered 'no' and 18 per cent 'don't know'. The N.O.P. results were less favourable to agreed divorce after two years but more favourable to divorce without agreement after five years. In face of these figures it is difficult to argue that the Bill was slowed down by the force of public opinion.

A large number of women's organizations were deeply concerned by the Bill and their views were pressed in the Commons by Sir Lionel Heald. They were, however, not united in their views. The most important and influential organization, the National Council of Women, was essentially concerned about the financial position of divorced women and stressed that few men could afford to support two families. The Mothers' Union, the National Board of Catholic Women, the Medical Women's Federation and the Council of Married Women opposed the Bill on wider grounds: they argued *inter alia* that two years' separation was an insufficient period to provide proof of irretrievable breakdown of marriage, and they objected to divorce without agreement since it would enable a defaulter to benefit from his wrongdoing. But even these bodies did not dispute the principle of Clause I, that breakdown of marriage should be the basis of divorce law. So female dissatisfaction was divided. Nor was it presented effectively. Notices were issued to the press but there was no vigorous lobbying of Parliament.

In Parliament itself the resistance to the Bill was not highly organized. Again this may be because the opponents were not fully agreed among themselves. Some were against divorce *per se*; some accepted the basic principle of the Bill but wished to have particular clauses amended. It was also clear that there was little hope of building up a majority against the measure. Apart from the second reading of the Jones Bill, the total anti-vote never exceeded 60. The main hope was to try to secure amendments through delaying tactics, yet the delay was not a blatant filibuster but skilful use of the opportunities of protest offered by the intricacies of parliamentary procedure.

Organization in support of the Bill was much more intensive. Leo Abse was the dominant figure. His colourful personality, his boundless energy, his contacts with the press and his close acquaintance with some Ministers were all of great importance. Abse was described to me by one of his associates as 'a publicity campaign in himself'. Peter Jackson did much whipping of Members in support of reform. Outside Parliament the pressure group directly concerned was the Divorce Law Reform Union. This had been a relatively small and impoverished body but was greatly strengthened by a new recruit, Alastair Service, who moved on to the divorce question having previously assisted with the cause of abortion. The D.L.R.U. held a reception to launch the Wilson Bill. MPs were circulated to determine probable supporters. A brief was prepared for second reading debate and a whipping letter was sent to Members known to be sympathetic. Subsequently a letter of thanks was sent to Members who voted for the second reading. As concern developed about the economic consequences of divorce, the D.L.R.U. hastily prepared a pamphlet on the financial security of divorced women: this was a cheaply produced but highly informative document produced after some assistance from the Ministry of Social Security. The D.L.R.U. was surprised by the reaction to this document of some solicitors, who, it seemed, had been giving mistaken advice for years. Abse and Service both stimulated press notices that were generally favourable in tone. In particular, they stirred up a considerable volume of protest when the Wilson Bill failed for lack of time. Thus divorce reform was promoted by an inexpensive but highly effective campaign.

To return to the question posed above – why was the parliamentary campaign so protracted? The pressures of opinion and, indeed, organization tended to favour the Bill. Yet the delay had two main causes. The technicalities and the flukes of the parliamentary time-table helped to destroy the Wilson Bill. The other and fundamental difficulty was the intricacy of the subject. It had far wider ramifications than the other social issues discussed in this book. Apart from religious and moral controversy, questions were raised involving legal procedure, child welfare, social security and property law. The limited ration of time allowed for private members' Bills can scarcely be expected to accommodate a measure that arouses such a galaxy of argument. It is also the case that divorce law has a major personal impact on more people than the other Bills discussed in these pages. Probably the number of women having an abortion will exceed the number having a divorce, but abortion is a concealed and personal affair, while divorce is public and involves usually more than two people. These considerations, plus the immense difficulties facing any major legislation promoted by a back-bencher, explain the delay. The passage of the Divorce Reform Act also illustrates the truth of Abse's view that the only way to achieve social reform in a parliamentary context is to persevere, to nag and nag, to keep nagging away.

Chapter 8

Sunday Entertainment

I

The Fourth Commandment in the past has had a major impact on the pattern of social life in Britain. For those whose religious faith has been based upon a strict interpretation of the scriptures, the preservation of the Sabbath has been a dominant concern. To set Sunday apart from the normal routine served a number of purposes. For one day each week the message of church and chapel could go forth unimpeded by competing claims on the time and the energy of the populace. In industrial areas the deadly monotony of a seven-day working week was largely avoided. Sunday introduced an element of variety and, as attendance at religious ceremonies declined, it produced more leisure. As living standards improved, there followed a demand to use leisure time for recreation and entertainment of various kinds. Necessarily this created a conflict with existing Laws on Sunday observance and with religious opinion that insisted on the stern application of these laws.

The Lord's Day Observance Society was founded in 1831. Originally an Anglican organization it has, in the twentieth century, become associated with chapel rather than church. It is one of the oldest, best known and most active pressure groups in British politics. It has, according to the Crathorne Committee, about 35,000 members and receives subscriptions from 2,000 local churches and chapels – all Protestant. It is committed to opposing commercial encroachments into Sunday as a national day of rest and to promoting Sunday as an occasion for worship and Christian service. It has a system of district organizers whose task is to keep alive enthusiasm for the cause by speaking in churches or at public meetings and also to prevent activities contrary to the Sunday observance laws by reporting them to the police authority or by threatening to initiate legal proceedings. Whenever any attempt is made to liberalize the law, the L.D.O.S. mounts a massive campaign to preserve the *status quo*. J. D. Stewart has remarked that the L.D.O.S. should be grateful to those who try to change our Sunday laws as the Society needs a vigorous campaign of this kind about every five years to keep it in a healthy condition.[1] It has a long tradition of

[1] *British Pressure Groups* (O.U.P., 1958), p. 136.

stimulating correspondence with MPs from local supporters. Further, it has the great tactical advantage, as compared with most of the other pressure groups discussed in this study, that it is trying to maintain the law and not to change it.

The question of Sunday observance is, of course, wider than Sunday entertainment, for it includes, e.g. employment and trading. This chapter deals solely with the controversy over Sunday entertainment. Yet it is noteworthy that the Fourth Commandment prohibits explicitly all Sunday work. The full force of this edict has never been accepted because of the need to maintain essential services on Sunday. There can be differences of opinion upon the definition of essential services, but this aspect of the argument has tended to fade away. What remains is the conflict over sport and entertainment. Critics of the Lord's Day Observance Society can argue that it is concerned not so much with the Fourth Commandment as with the imposition of a puritan attitude towards pleasure on at least one day a week.

Much of the Sunday observance legislation has become archaic and has been disregarded for a long time. An Act of 1625 declared:

'. . . the holy keeping of the Lorde day, is a principall part of the true service of God, which in very many places of this realme hath beene and now is pfaned and neglected by a disorderlie sort of people, in exercising and frequenting bearebaiting, bullbeiting, enterludes, comon playes and other unlawfull exercises and pastimes . . . there shallbe no meetinge assemblies or concourse of people out of their owne parishes . . . and that every pson or psons offending in any the p'misses, shall forfeit for every offence three shillinge foure pence, the same to be employed and converted to the use of the poore of the parish where such offence shalbe comitted. . . .''

In 1677 another Act 'for the better Observation of the Lord's day commonly called Sunday' decreed *inter alia*:

'. . . that all and every person and persons whatsoever shall on every Lords day apply themselves to the observation of the same by exercising themselves thereon in the dutyes of piety and true religion publiquely and privately and that noe tradesman, artificer workeman labourer or other person whatsoever shall doe or exercise any wordly labour business or worke of their ordinary callings upon the Lords day or any part thereof (workes of necessity and charity onely excepted). . . .

'. . . that if any person or persons whatsoever which shall travel upon the Lords day shall be them robbed that noe hundred nor the inhabitants thereof shall be charged with or answerable for any robbery soe committed but the person or persons soe robbed shall be barred from bringing any action for the said robbery, any law to the contrary notwithstanding. . . .'

These two Acts, and a few other minor measures dealing with the same topic, were repealed in 1969 as part of the Statute Law (Repeals) Act. The effective legislation, which is the cause of the controversy, is a measure passed in 1780 to combat the profanation of Sunday. The central provision reads as follows:

'that . . . any house, room, or other place, which shall be opened or used for publick entertainment or amusement, or for publickly debating upon any subject whatsoever, upon any part of the Lord's Day . . . and to which persons shall be admitted by the payment of money, or by tickets sold for money, shall be deemed a disorderly house or place. . . .'

Had it not been for the Lord's Day Observance Society it is more than probable that this Act would also have fallen into disuse. Its scope has been limited by subsequent statutes; many ingenious devices are used to evade its provisions; its occasional application arouses irritation. Yet still it remains.

The original purpose of the Act appears to have been the suppression of 'disputations' on religious and other matters, rather than to eradicate entertainment.[1] Opponents in 1780 argued that the effect was to interfere with freedom of speech. In the nineteenth century the law was not always enforced. The position varied in different regions of the country; what was accepted in London would be condemned in Wales. When the newly-formed London County Council took over responsibility for licensing music and dancing in 1889, no action was taken against Sunday music and lectures. These events grew in popularity. But five years later, in Leeds, two persons who had lectured on a Sunday were prosecuted by the L.D.O.S. and the case failed only on a technicality. Following this case Lord Hobhouse made two unsuccessful attempts to persuade the House of Lords to pass amending legislation to permit lectures and musical performances on Sunday provided that they were not organized for the pecuniary profit of the promoters.

Development of the cinema introduced a fresh element into the problem. The 1909 Cinematograph Act required cinema premises to

---

[1] Report of the Crathorne Committee, para. 12: 1964–65, Cmnd. 2528, xxiii.

L

be licensed by the local authority mainly for the purpose of securing adequate fire prevention arrangements. Soon the licensing powers were being used to control opening times and the type of films shown. Many cinemas began opening on Sunday, and in 1916 the London County Council added to its licences a requirement that profits from Sunday shows should be paid to selected charities. This situation continued until 1930 when London theatre interests decided to contest the legality of the L.C.C. licences. The High Court ruled that Sunday cinemas were contrary to the Act of 1780.[1] The Labour Government introduced a Bill to legalize existing practice; this proved highly controversial but was given a second reading on a free vote by 258 to 210. No further progress had been made when the Government was overwhelmed by the international economic crisis. The new National Government, preoccupied by economic problems, regarded the sabbatarian controversy as an irritating deflection from its main task. It therefore produced another Bill to legalize for twelve months existing practice in relation to Sunday cinemas, concerts and lectures. This measure was easily passed – but with the whips on – and gave breathing space for a fuller consideration. Next year the Sunday Entertainments Act was passed which again virtually legalized the *status quo*.[2] Where local practice had been to have Sunday concerts and cinemas, these were to continue. Concerts were to be controlled by the local licensing authority. Application for Sunday cinemas in fresh areas would require the support of the local authority, backed by a local referendum and the consent of Parliament. The subsequent polls on this issue have provided a focus of activity for the L.D.O.S.; usually the sabbatarian cause has been defeated.

Theatres, variety shows and dancing on Sunday were still prohibited. Yet means were found to limit the effect of the law. The formation of a club evaded the law because a club gathering was not open to the public. A comedian could tell a joke provided he used no stage properties. Some of the results were absurd. A singer could not don a kilt to render 'Annie Laurie' unless he happened to be a Scot – which made it national dress and not a stage property. It was also possible to charge, not for admission, but for a programme or a reserved seat. Similarly, it was not possible to charge for admission to a sporting fixture on Sunday. This helped the development of amateur sport and club coffers, especially of cricket clubs, were swollen by car park charges and voluntary contributions from spectators.

[1] *R. v. L.C.C. ex parte the Entertainments Protection Association* (1931) 2 K.B. 215.
[2] The second reading vote was 237 to 61.

During the Second World War the Government proposed that theatres be permitted to open on Sunday for the benefit of servicemen on leave and away from home. Actors were divided on the issue. S.T.O.P. (Sunday Theatre Opposition Party) took one view while C.A.S.T. (Campaign of Actors for Sunday Theatres) took the other. It was decided that the decision should be subject to a free vote in the Commons, which thereupon ruled by 144 votes to 136 that the theatres remain closed. This incident provides powerful evidence of the strength of sabbatarian feeling. (It is also true that the average age of Members during the war was unusually high and that many of the younger Members were absent on war service.) The Festival of Britain caused a similar conflict. A Bill to allow several exhibitions associated with the Festival to open on Sunday received a second reading by 364 votes to 128, but an amendment ts exclude the amusement part from Sunday opening was carried by 389 votes to 134. The negligible Government majority in the 1950 Parliament may have made Members more susceptible to constituency pressure. Of the 45 Members who had majorities of less than 1,000 only 2 voted for Sunday opening of the amusement park: these highly marginal seats provided 1½ per cent of the supporters of Sunday amusement but 9 per cent of its opponents.[1]

The first major challenge to Sunday observance law came in 1953 with the Sunday Observance Bill sponsored by John Parker (Lab. Dagenham). This sought to repeal existing legislation and to allow theatres and cinemas to open subject to local option and a contribution to charity from profits; sports, circuses and fun-fairs were to be free from control in relation to Sunday opening. The L.D.O.S. retaliated with a great campaign and a monster petition was organized and, when presented to the Commons, it was said to contain 512,735 signatures. Their reward was a handsome victory, for the Bill was defeated by 281 votes to 57 and a proposal by Eric Fletcher (Lab. Islington East) that a Royal Commission be appointed was defeated by 172 votes to 164. The Government opposed the idea of a Commission on the argument that the issue was one to be settled by Members on a free vote.

Denis Howell[2] provoked the next major parliamentary discussion by moving a motion asking for a Select Committee to review the law on Sunday observance. Howell was a football referee who had been active in the development of amateur Sunday football. The

[1] Letter in *The Economist*, December 23, 1950, from Philip Williams and David Butler.

[2] Member for Birmingham, All Saints, 1955–59, and Birmigham, Small Heath, since 1961, Minister for Sport in the Wilson Government.

Home Office attitude by this time, March 1958, had become a little less obstructive; the Joint Under-Secretary indicated that he thought that a committee could do no more than reflect the cleavage in public opinion on the subject, but agreed that a committee should be appointed if the House so decided. At the end of the debate the motion that the question be now put was carried by 54 to 31 but, since this fell short of the 100 votes needed to obtain the closure, the motion, in a formal sense, was not voted upon and the question lapsed.

After the 1959 Election there was modest but steady pressure in the Commons for the initiation of an official enquiry.[1] The Wolfenden Report on Sport and the Community issued in 1960 was mildly in favour of reform.[2] It was not hostile to participation in Sunday sport, although it was opposed to an extension of professional sport on Sunday. It also observed that no one should be handicapped through unwillingness to play games on Sunday. After much delay the Home Secretary (R. A. Butler) announced in July 1961 the appointment of a Departmental Committee to review the law on Sunday Observance. The Committee had a slightly unusual composition for a departmental committee in that Parliament provided a majority of the membership. The chairman was Lord Crathorne, better known as Sir Thomas Dugdale, and four of the remaining seven members were drawn from the Commons. Many shades of Christian opinion were represented on the Committee which was certainly not composed of zealots for reform.[3]

The Committee deliberated for over three years and its report appeared in December 1964. Evidence was collected from a wide range of sources. The British Council of Churches and the Roman Catholics urged that the traditional character of Sunday should be preserved for the Christian community and for the well-being of national and family life. The Welsh Council of Churches put the same viewpoint more forcibly; its representatives wanted active encouragement of worship in Wales and were opposed to any relaxation of the law. The Lord's Day Observance Society wanted legislation strengthened to prevent evasions: the Society argued that liberty of some individuals had to be curbed for the benefit of the community. Other non-religious bodies supported the maintenance

[1] E.g. H. C. Deb., Vol, 616, col. 171; Vol. 621, col. *137*; Vol. 626, cols 1570-1; Vol. 629, cols *74-5*. (Italics indicate written answers.)

[2] Paras 225-7, 230. This body had been established in 1957 by the Central Council for Physical Recreation to recommend measures for the development of sports and outdoor activities in order that they 'may play a full part in promoting the general welfare of the community'.

[3] Cf. comment in *The Economist*, July 22, 1961.

of the separate character of Sunday and stressed the undesirability of work on that day. Equally, there was wide acceptance of the need to smooth out anomalies in the law and that there was an increasing gap between the law and current practice. The Association of Chief Police Officers argued that some aspects of the law were obsolete and unenforceable. Clearly, law which is unenforceable and derided brings the whole concept of law into disrepute. The recommendations of the Committee reflected this mixture of religious, social and practical considerations.

Its work can be divided broadly into four sections, entertainment, sport, trading and employment; the last two of these fall outside the present study. On entertainment the views of the British Council of Churches were potentially influential but its evidence failed to give a clear lead: 'We should not in general regard Sunday theatres, cinemas and similar performances as undesirable in principle from the point of view of the audience. There is no theological reason why the theatre should be in a different position from other such entertainments. We should, however, regard as highly objectionable any large expansion of these facilities because of the extra Sunday labour involved.' The Lord's Day Observance Society was, in contrast, explicit and forthright. It was totally opposed to Sunday entertainment. It wished the law to be changed so that cinemas would be forced to close on Sunday; the declining attendance at cinemas and the lack of interest in local polls on the subject of Sunday cinemas were used as arguments to support their position. The Crathorne Committee were equally forthright in rejecting the L.D.O.S. view. Instead, the Committee proposed that the 1780 Act be repealed so that all entertainments permissible on weekdays should be permissible on Sundays except between the hours of 2 a.m. (3 a.m. in the West End of London) and 12.30 p.m.

The Committee felt, no doubt correctly, that the character of Sunday was affected more by the control of sporting activities than by restricting entertainment. Sporting organizations were deeply divided in their attitude to Sunday. Against any change in the law were the Football Association, the Football League, Rugby Union and the National Greyhound Racing Society. In favour of some relaxation of the law were the Rugby League, the British Boxing Board of Control, the Jockey Club, the National Hunt Committee, the R.A.C., the Auto-Cycle Union and the English Table Tennis Association. The Committee managed to meet the views of a majority of these bodies by proposing that Sunday sport be prohibited only if the players or participants were remunerated for taking part. No betting should be allowed at race courses on Sunday. In all, the report was far more radical than might have been expected from the composition of the Committee. However, it appeared at a moment of great political uncertainty. The Labour Government had recently been elected with a negligible majority; the next Election could come at any time. Naturally, politicians sought to avoid a fresh outburst of sabbatarian controversy even if it was starting to lose some of its vigour.

Six months before the publication of the report the Commons had had an inconclusive debate on a Bill to amend the Sunday Observance law of 1625. This measure was introduced by Sir John Barlow (Con. Middleton and Prestwich): it was an unballoted Bill for which some time became available through a fluke of the parliamentary time-table.[1] A particular incident in Sir John's constituency had aroused his concern. A bowling club had been warned that to play a bowls match on Sunday would break the law if a charge were made for admittance, if betting were allowed, and if people were allowed to play who did not live in the parish. Officials of the club accepted the first two conditions but were not able to satisfy the third, so the match was cancelled. The inspector had used the 1625 Act which forbade people to travel outside their own parish to engage in any kind of sport on a Sunday; this provision Sir John wished to repeal. The Lord's Day Observance Society had circulated Members to whip up opposition to this attempt to make the law correspond with reality. Inevitably it was argued that no changes should be made in the law until the Crathorne Report was available. More curious was the view that the existence of obsolete law was a matter of no consequence because it was ignored and, if an attempt were made to enforce it, then a jury could be trusted to refuse to convict. These propositions combine the theory of legal moralism with a disregard for the sanctity of law.

To revert to the Crathorne Report debated by the Commons in February 1965.[2] The motion was in a neutral form 'to take note' of the report and there was no division. The tone of the speeches, with notable exceptions, was broadly sympathetic. Ministers avoided giving any clear indication of the Government attitude, although the Secretary of State for Wales, George Thomas, in the winding-up speech, did stress that implementation of the report would leave some anomalies – Rugby Union could be played but not Rugby League, while Wimbledon could have tennis but not speedway.[3]

[1] H. C. Deb., Vol. 696, cols 837–86.
[2] H. C. Deb., Vol. 706, cols 858–964.
[3] In 1965 professional players were still excluded from the All-England Tennis Championships.

Subsequently, the Home Secretary, Sir Frank Soskice, informed the Commons that legislation would have to come through private members' procedure and no undertaking could be given to provide government time.[1] This timidity was doubtless influenced by the Government's exiguous majority.

Fresh efforts to pass legislation were stimulated by the report. The first attempt came from the Upper House. In November 1966 Lord Willis introduced a Sunday Entertainments Bill which was prepared with the help of official draftsmen. It did not cover the whole field of Sunday observance but merely sport and entertainment. It was also limited to England and Wales. The Crathorne recommendations were followed with two main exceptions. First, the starting time for entertainments and sports was delayed from 12.30 p.m. to 2 p.m.; on this item the Bill was more restrictive than Crathorne. Second, the Bill made no mention of the proposed ban on professional sport. A second reading was obtained without a division; a mere two out of fourteen speeches were wholly hostile. At the committee stage there was a single vote when an amendment that Wales be omitted from the operation of the Bill was rejected by 9 votes to 28. On the report stage there was again a single vote; the Bishop of Leicester moved a new clause to define more closely the type of spectacle that would be allowed on a Sunday, but this clause was defeated by 79 votes to 33. There was no time available in the Commons to consider the Bill which therefore lapsed. As a trail-blazer Lord Willis had been extremely successful and one might have expected a similar Bill would soon pass through the House of Commons.

William Hamling (Lab. Woolwich, West) sponsored the Willis Bill in the following session. Initially, his prospect of success was poor; with the ninth place on the ballot, his Bill would have restricted time for the debate, so the Chair was certain not to accept a motion that the question be put. Thus it seemed highly probable that the Bill would be talked out. For this reason the attendance at the second reading debate was thin. As four o'clock approached John Parker was speaking: he was discussing the situation of the Jews in Babylonia and its influence on Sabbatarian doctrine. He managed to create the impression he was talking the Bill out himself and sat down a few seconds before four o'clock. No one rose to continue the debate. The Chair called a division. The second reading was carried by 29 votes to 18.[2] It was a superb piece of parliamentary gamesmanship, for the Bill's opponents had been taken completely by surprise. At the crucial moment they were, quite literally, speechless.

[1] H. C. Deb., Vol. 715, cols 1791–2.
[2] H. C. Deb., Vol. 755, cols 1931–2.

The committee stage was not unduly prolonged and was completed in four sittings. One amendment was carried contrary to the wish of the sponsors: this was not specifically sabbatarian in character for it decreed that Sunday work should earn double pay or a day off in lieu of double pay.[1] A challenge to professional sport on Sunday was defeated by 11 votes to 8. Two amendments designed to check noise and defend the peace of worshippers were defeated by the casting vote of the chairman.[2] The exclusion of Wales from the Bill was lost by 7 votes to 5, but subsequently a provision was added that Wales and Monmouth should have a local poll on the lines of the Sunday drinking law. Meanwhile, a motion had been put down on the Commons Order Paper urging the Government to promote legislation on the basis of the Crathorne Report – i.e. Hamling's Bill minus the acceptance of professional sport.

At the report stage the Bill ground to a halt and was destroyed. Two whole Fridays were devoted to the measure but little progress was made. In part this was because the sponsors could not muster the hundred votes needed to force a decision on any amendment. The determined opponents of the Bill numbered no more than thirty, but this was enough to obstruct progress. And since the sponsors could rally little more than twice this number, it seems that the vast majority of Members were either unconcerned over the issue or were determined to evade it. The second inconclusive Friday was May 3, 1968, and the Bill was not put down for further consideration until May 24th. Both the intervening Fridays were also to be devoted to private members' Bills. However, other Bills were already down for consideration on these days, *inter alia* the Theatres Bill. Had the Sunday Entertainments Bill been added to the Order Paper on these days, it is certain that its opponents would have mounted a filibuster against other measures which might have endangered their safe passage. This was the pattern of events on May 24th when determined filibustering by Sir Cyril Black (Con. Wimbledon) eliminated any hope of further advance without government assistance through the provision of extra time. The Divorce Bill was in a similar position. In spite of protests, Ministers took no action and the battle was to be resumed in session 1968–69.

It had become clear that a crucial objection to fresh legislation was concern about noise and disturbance. Professional sport – at least some of it – attracts large crowds. An assembly of a large

[1] This was deleted at the report stage.
[2] In case of a tie the Chair must vote in such a way that the question can be reconsidered. An amendment defeated in committee can be debated again at the report stage.

number of people is always liable to be detrimental to the peace and serenity of the area where they congregate. In particular, the behaviour of crowds at football matches was becoming a major social nuisance. If there is trouble on Saturday afternoon, why duplicate the possibility of trouble on Sunday afternoon? Once a week was enough. This type of reasoning, nothing to do with the basic philosophy of the Lord's Day Observance Society, placed the future success of the Bill in jeopardy, so when the Bill was reintroduced a fresh clause was added to attempt to satisfy the 'noise' objection. The clause allowed a local authority to apply to the magistrates for an order prohibiting Sunday use of any premises for competitive sport if residents in the vicinity had been unreasonably disturbed by such use on a Sunday. A magistrates' order would have effect for three years.

John Parker drew the third place in the 1968 private members' ballot. However, this piece of good fortune was immediately offset by a serious tactical error. He chose the eighth and last 'second reading' Friday for the Sunday Entertainments Bill, so that it did not come before the Commons until the very end of February 1969. The reason was that Parker hoped that the Bill could be passed through the Lords before his second reading date; he would then have 'picked' up the Lords Bill and obviated entirely, or drastically reduced, the need for discussion in the Upper House after the Commons had passed the Bill. Unfortunately for Parker, the rules of procedure do not permit a private member to adopt a Lords Bill in this way. The result was that several valuable weeks were wasted and the chance of a successful filibuster greatly increased.

Led by Sir Cyril Black, the Defenders of the Sabbath rallied strongly for the second reading debate.[1] Only eight out of twenty-one speeches were clearly in favour of the Bill. At the end three divisions took place. The motion that the question be now put was passed by 113 to 84: the second reading was carried by 104 to 95: a motion to refer the Bill to a committee of the whole House was defeated by 85 to 71. The small majority on second reading ensured a narrow majority of supporters on the standing committee and thus further reduced the prospect of sending the measure to the statute book. The division also illustrates a constitutional oddity of how Members can influence the content of legislation which does not affect their own constituencies. Scotland and Ulster were excluded from the Sunday Entertainments Bill but their Members were entitled to vote on it.

[1] H. C. Deb., Vol. 778, cols 2069–174.

Vote on Sunday Entertainments Bill
Second Reading 28.2.1969[1]

Area	Aye	No	Absent
England	104	76	327
Wales	1	5	30
Scotland	1	9	61
Ulster	0	7	4

It will be noted that the proportion of absentees was lowest from Ulster. Scottish Members often return home on Thursday night if this is possible in order to deal with constituency business. The absence of Welsh Members was due to an agreement to stay away in return for the Welsh option clause in the Bill. Taking only the votes of English and Welsh Members the vote for the Bill was 105 to 81, a much more substantial majority than the Bill actually received. There may be a case for Scottish and Welsh nationalism: these figures suggest there is also a case for English nationalism.

The sponsors did manage to get the Bill allocated to Standing Committee B instead of C, which is the normal committee for private members' legislation. This ensured that meetings could be held twice a week and not once. Excluding the chairman, the Committee had nineteen members, ten Labour and nine Conservatives. All the Labour Members favoured the Bill except two, E. Bishop (Newark) and W. Wilkins (Bristol, South); all the Conservatives opposed it except C. Morrison (Devizes) and J. Hunt (Bromley). The average age of the supporters was forty-six, that of the opponents fifty-four. This age gap has additional significance since the average age of Labour Members elected in 1966 was eighteen months *higher* than that of the Conservatives. Also curious was the geographical character of the Committee. Wales which was affected, and doubtless very concerned, was unrepresented: Northern Ireland, not affected, did provide one Member, Captain Orr (U.U. Down, South) who played a major part in the proceedings.

The committee stage was completed after nineteen sittings, some of which lasted much longer than the normal 2½ hours. The nineteenth meeting lasted from 4.15 p.m. to 11.6 p.m. During all this time only one major change was made when the provision for local option in Wales was struck out. Strangely enough, this was a victory for the Bill's opponents. The option scheme had been introduced by the sponsors to minimize objections from Welsh Members. Sir Cyril Black and his colleagues hoped, doubtless with good reason, that the rejection of the compromise would stiffen Welsh resistance

[1] The figures do not total 630 as some seats were vacant.

to the whole Bill on the report stage and third reading. It would be tedious to review other details of the committee proceedings. Some time was lost due to the inability to maintain a quorum; much time was lost in arguments over the times of committee meetings. In short, the proceedings degenerated into a filibuster. Not merely were the speeches of the opponents unduly long and wandered away from the issue under debate, but new clauses were introduced – for example, to restrict pool betting on Sunday – which were outside the purpose of the Bill. The filibuster succeeded because by the date of the final sitting, July 15, 1969, all the time available in the Chamber for private members' Bills had been used and, indeed, the House was almost ready to rise for the summer recess. Thus even had the Government been minded to provide additional time for the Sunday Entertainments Bill, the pressure of the calendar would have made this difficult to arrange.

II

Opinions will differ as between Christians and non-Christians on the significance of Sunday. Opinions also differ among Christians as to how Sunday should be observed and how far Sunday observance should be enforced by law. To form a scale of conduct for oneself is to frame a personal preference; to argue that your scale, or some part of it, be imposed upon others by law, raises immediately a wide range of issues about conscience, liberty and law. The extreme Sabbatarian sees no difficulty. The Lord's Day Observance Society reflects a simple faith: that the law should recognize and reinforce the fact that Britain is a Christian country and that it is a Christian duty to bear witness to the Lord on the Sabbath Day. Any secular activity is out of place on the Sabbath. Commercial exploitation of the Lord's Day must be resisted, and any extension of secular activity on that day is a bit more of the thin edge of the wedge leading to a total defilement of Sunday.

Such a trend of thought quickly loses touch with reality. Modern industrial society cannot shut down one day in seven for spiritual contemplation. Essential services must be maintained. Some work must be done on Sunday. Over the years public demand has encouraged the provision of a wider range of facilities and Sunday trading has become more extensive. But sport and entertainment can scarcely be brought within any definition of 'essential'. Thus for some people it is reasonable to argue that an actor should not be required to perform on a Sunday although, regrettably, some policemen must go on duty.

Should the proponents of a particular religious theory be permitted to impose their views on others? This question has a seventeenth-century flavour. The triumph of religious toleration should point the way to an emphatic negative response. Yet the religious zealot sees things differently. Truth has been revealed to him. It is his duty to prevent sin and to save souls. If to stop the work of the Devil it is necessary to restrict liberty, then liberty must suffer. This brand of doctrine is not accepted by most active Christians. The churches recognize that not all people are Christian, that some adhere to other faiths and that some are irreligious. Thus the British Council of Churches specifically repudiates the attitude of the Lord's Day Observance Society. It recognizes that only a minority attend religious services and that a minority should not attempt to dictate to others how Sunday should be spent. Equally, the B.C.C. is keen to preserve the special character of Sunday provided that this can be achieved without acts of religious intolerance.

The pattern of argument over Sunday entertainment has been neatly reversed. A concern for family life and the preservation of amenity has taken the place of the Fourth Commandment. If bread-winners are forced to work – or perform – on Sunday, their family can never have a day together. An actor or a professional sportsman is in a different position from many other workers in that Sunday duty cannot be performed on a rota basis. Further, persons with less specialized skills who object to Sunday work can more easily move to another job with more congenial hours: a milk roundsman can become a bread roundsman. Thus the theme of liberty emerges in another form. It is no longer a question of a religious minority imposing its own standard on society; instead it is claimed that society should not be so selfish as to impose on particular professions a manner of work that is disruptive of normal family life. Again on the issue of amenity, the liberarian approach has a new guise. The assembly of large crowds causes noise and disturbance, especially when crowd behaviour is bad. Those who are effected by the vigour of football fans can claim, to use Mill's terminology, that the fans engage in other-regarding action. Here is a clear and simple conflict of interest. Football enthusiasts want to enjoy themselves: other people may want peace and quiet undisturbed by rowdiness. An obvious compromise is to have crowd enthusiasm on Saturday and peace on Sunday. Such a compromise has no necessary connexion with religion.

This trend of thought could lead to legislation on Sunday entertainment on the lines of the Crathorne Report. It is quite unacceptable to both extremes of opinion on Sunday observance. Those who wish for a secular society wish to see Sunday treated as any other day:

what is permissible on a weekday should be equally permissible on Sunday. At the other end of the spectrum the Lord's Day Observance Society opposes secular activities on Sunday: it does not object to Sunday sport or entertainment merely because they create noise or give rise to employment. Accordingly the Society has used its influence *against* attempts to limit the freedom given by the Sunday Entertainments Bill. When Lord Willis' Bill was before the Lords the L.D.O.S. wrote to peers objecting to amendments to exclude Wales and professional sport from the Bill and argued that these amendments would create anomalies and stimulate pressure for further changes in the law. For the L.D.O.S. the only satisfactory outcome was the rejection of the whole measure.

The L.D.O.S. had little support at national level from other religious organizations. The British Council of Churches preferred a Crathorne-style compromise but made no public stand on the Sunday Entertainments Bill. In spite of its isolation the L.D.O.S. is highly organized. Each candidate at a general election is asked by the Society to state his or her views on Sunday observance: the responses enable the Society to determine which Members are most likely to be sympathetic to their cause. These Members can then be approached in the hour of need – when legislation is in prospect which will threaten Sunday. The Society writes to Members and peers whenever legislation is reaching a crucial stage. Monster petitions were presented to Parliament praying against the Parker Bill of 1953 and the Hamling Bill of 1967. Supporters of the Society are asked to write to their local Members urging opposition to any liberalization of the law. £3,000 was collected by the Society for the campaign mounted against the Hamling Bill.[1]

At the local or 'grass roots' level there has been significant resistance to the Bill, not all of which has been stimulated through the L.D.O.S. The Baptists have also been active. The Baptist Union has said that it supports the statement of policy issued by the British Council of Churches, but it is also true that Baptists are hostile to the idea of Sunday theatres and they have suggested that restraints on Sunday sports should cover payments by spectators and payments to players. The Welsh Baptists wanted Wales excluded from the Bill altogether. One Labour Member for a socially mixed and politically marginal Midlands constituency had 130 letters objecting to the Bill, by no means all from religious fanatics: no single constituency can be wholly typical but perhaps this one is more typical than most.

On the other side of the controversy there was no equivalent organization to stimulate support for the Bill. The National Secular

[1] The L.D.O.S. journal, *Joy and Light*, No. 271, p. 164.

Society naturally approved of the measure, but it is a relatively weak body and has wider interests than Sunday observance. Most national sporting bodies were in favour and in April 1968, at a meeting in the Long Room at Lords Cricket Ground, various sports joined together in a formal demonstration of support for Sunday freedom, at least after 2 p.m. Bodies represented included the British Amateur Athletic Board, the British Boxing Board of Control, the British Show Jumping Association, the British Horse Society, the M.C.C., the R.A.C., the Auto-Cycle Union, the Royal and Ancient Golf Club, the Football Association, the Football Association of Wales, the Football League and the Rugby Football League. A dissenting voice came from Rugby Union, which recognized that it was impossible to stop Sunday games but said it would not encourage them. The only other major body opposed to Sunday events was the English Amateur Swimming Association: the A.S.A. in Wales was 'rather in favour'[1] of holding events on Sunday. Hockey was also a little out of line with other sports in that it favours Sunday play after 12.30 p.m. not 2 p.m.

An attempt to whip up support for the Parker Bill was made by the Theatres' National Committee headed by Emile Littler. The theatre owners are strongly in favour of Sunday opening. For half a century they have resented what was felt to be the privileged position of cinemas on Sunday. The anomalies in the law regarding concerts and club performances are also irksome. And at a time when many theatres have closed, the extra business that Sunday could bring is seen in some places as a condition of survival. Accordingly a meeting was held in January 1969, attended by many of the sports organizations, theatrical organizations and trade unions from the world of entertainment. Those present were urged to encourage the bodies they represented to write to Members pressing support for the Sunday Entertainments Bill and, in particular, to ask them to be present when the Bill came up for second reading. However, the entertainment business is not wholly unanimous in its attitude. The trade unions have some concern about the conditions attached to Sunday work. Especially, there is a deep cleavage of opinion on the subject in Equity, the actors' union. A fair summary of the situation is that the entertainment business is largely in favour of Sunday performances while the sporting world is almost united in favour of Sunday events.

Public opinion has supported Sunday entertainment and by an increasing majority. A comparison of three Gallup polls is instructive.

[1] Denis Howell, Minister for Sport: Standing Committee C on the Sunday Entertainments Bill, session 1967–68, col. 71.

Places of entertainment like theatres and cinemas to open on Sunday?

% responses

	April 1958	*Feb. 1965*	*Jan. 1968*
Approve	50	56	74
Disapprove	39	37	11
Don't Know	11	7	15

Professional sport on Sunday?

	April 1958	*Feb. 1965*	*Jan. 1968*
Approve	46	53	63
Disapprove	41	39	18
Don't Know	13	8	19

There is no great difference in attitude between England and Wales regarding professional sport. The percentage of positive approval is almost the same in both countries although the opposition is stronger in Wales and the Don't Knows many fewer. Age is the most significant factor: 81 per cent of the 16–24 age group favoured Sunday sport but only 32 per cent of those above 65. Only among elderly Welsh people was there a clear majority against the Sunday Entertainments Bill.

Why, then, did the Bill fail in 1968 and again in 1969? The explanation must involve personal, institutional and wider socio-logical factors which often interact on each other. The immediate answer is that the Government failed to provide extra time. But for what reason? In contrast to the other Bills discussed in this study, the second reading majorities in favour of the Sunday Entertainments Bill had been very small. The vigour of the opposition in the 1969 Standing Committee delayed the Bill for so long that by the time the Bill emerged from committee the parliamentary session was moving towards its end and the provision of extra time would have been difficult to arrange. It is also believed that one member of the Cabinet was strongly opposed to the Bill and this could have affected the attitude of the Government. Again at a personal level, one must record that opponents of the Bill showed great energy and tenacity; they met together to plan amendments which would permit the ventilation of every conceivable objection to the measure. On the other side, the sponsors displayed little of the political skill of Leo Abse and David Steel which had helped other controversial measures to the statute book. The second reading of Parker's Bill was delayed by a tactical error. Some supporters of the Bill allowed themselves to be drawn too easily into detailed arguments in committee and thus provided more debating points for their opponents and further slowed down progress. Ultimately, extra meetings of the Standing Committee were arranged to enable the Bill to complete its committee stage, but this move was delayed and more time was wasted. Even the title of the Bill was ill-chosen. Instead of the Sunday Entertainments Bill it could well have been a Sunday Observance (Amendment) Bill, and this would have placed emphasis on freedom rather than enjoyment: freedom is morally superior to enjoyment. Above all, the sponsors failed to enlist the sympathy of many Members who can normally be expected to assist liberal and progressive causes. Perhaps this was due to a feeling that Sunday observance was not an important issue; that it was an old man's quarrel harking back to the 1930s and beyond; that there was no real public demand for the Bill because most people are able to do what they want to on Sundays. The argument used forty years ago in support of Sunday cinemas, that the alternative was the public house or the street corner, has no application to the Parker–Hamling Bill. There is no doubt that Sunday is generally regarded as a weekly opportunity for recreation and pleasure and that the modern inventions, notably the motor-car, radio and television, have effectively circumvented the restrictive legislation of earlier centuries. As a result there is no strong feeling about the restraints that remain, and no virile pressure group exists to counteract the Lord's Day Observance Society. The tide of modern life has by-passed Sunday observance legislation to such an extent that relatively few people care greatly if it stays or not.

In contrast to abortion, homosexuality and theatre censorship, there has been no administrative difficulty in applying the law on Sunday observance. Partly this is due to the public character of entertainments and sporting fixtures; partly it is due to the simplicity of the 1780 Act. The public nature of sporting events also means that the general interest is more obviously, and perhaps more legitimately, concerned with their control than is the case with personal matters. Thus, where noise and crowds are involved, arguments about liberty can be made to cut both ways. On the noise and nuisance aspect, the compromise offered by the Bill's sponsors, the prospect of control by magistrates, did little to placate their opponents, no doubt because their chief opponents were implacable. The crucial compromise, over professional sport, the sponsors refused to make. Had the Bill incorporated the essence of the Crathorne proposals there is little doubt that it would have passed. Some theatres would have opened and amateur sport would have received a considerable fillip.

Yet much of the explanation above is negative rather than positive.

It tends to show why the Bill failed to arouse enthusiasm rather than why it aroused hostility. Clearly, the great stimulus to opposition to any attempt to liberalize law relating to Sunday has been the L.D.O.S. The Society has prevented existing law from falling into disuse; it has persistently lobbied Parliament; it has done its utmost to gain public support. Some Members who led the opposition to the Sunday Entertainments Bill keep in close touch with the Society. It would be easy to ascribe the defeat of the Bill to the influence of the L.D.O.S.

Such a view is too simple. The Society's message may still be well received by some ageing congregations of an evangelical frame of mind. It seems primitive and extreme in the more sophisticated world of Westminster. Indeed, the Society seems to be regarded there as an uncomfortable and embarrassing ally. The Society has no Members on its executive committee; no Members are named as Vice-Presidents. This is fairly unusual for a pressure group so intensely concerned with attempts to influence legislation at the parliamentary level. Conservative Members will tend to dislike the Society's criticism of royalty, leading church dignitaries and the Roman Catholic Church. Its attacks on commercialization of the Sabbath do not fit easily into a philosophy of freedom for private enterprise. Further, the Society is quite willing to criticize Members who assist its cause in Parliament on the ground that their support for sabbatarian principles is half-hearted and incomplete: two of the most determined opponents of the Sunday Entertainments Bill at the committee stage, Peter Mills (Con. Torrington) and Captain Orr (U.U. Down, South) were subsequently criticized in this vein by the Society's magazine *Joy and Light*.[1]

Nevertheless, the activity generated by the Society had an effect. The letters to Members which it stimulated may have encouraged some Members mildly sympathetic to the Bill to absent themselves from the second reading debate. It remains true, however, that the L.D.O.S. has been successful only because other factors have been at work. Apart from noise and nuisance considerations there has been quiet but strong religious objections to the introduction of a 'Continental Sunday' from many who would not uphold the rigorous doctrine of the L.D.O.S. Some Conservative Members also opposed the Bill as another item in the catalogue of left-wing permissive legislation promoted by private members' Bills. To a slight degree the fate of Parker's Bill can be attributed to a backlash effect arising from the other measures discussed in this book. But the vital factor is that of differential abstention. When the party whips are off, the

[1] No. 273, p. 195.

M

normal compulsion on Members to attend Parliament is removed. Whether a Member attends at all is likely to depend on the strength of his feelings about the business. Those Members who objected to the Sunday Entertainments Bill were more strongly motivated than those who supported it.

Chapter 9

The Voting Analysed

The average division list from the House of Commons is not an exciting or revealing document. It will faithfully reflect the size of a Government's majority. If the issue is not of the highest importance, the whips of the two main parties will have agreed to 'pairing' arrangements which permit an equal number of Members of both parties to be absent for reasons of health, business or possibly pleasure. Pairing reduces the number of Members voting but leaves the size of the Government majority intact. The divisions become of interest when they show evidence of party disunity – of a revolt among Government back-benchers or of fragmentation of the Opposition.

On a free vote there is a dramatic change. Members are under no party pressure to support a particular policy: they are under no party pressure even to attend Parliament. The division lists offer a vivid insight into their attitudes. This chapter is devoted to an analysis of the crucial divisions on the issues of conscience examined in this book.[1] There are three sections of the analysis, First, the votes of Members on each of five[2] issues are related to the social character-istics of Members. Second, the extent of participation is examined – how far did Members bother to turn up and vote – again with reference to social characteristics. Third, the voting on each topic is compared to that on each of the other topics. The most critical division on each of the five issues has been selected for detailed study. Normally, this would be the second reading division. However, on Abortion the third reading has been selected because the majority in favour of the Bill was smaller and the vote represented a more considered attitude to the Bill than the second reading vote. The 1968–69 Divorce Bill is chosen in preference to the Bill in the previous session because the latter did not become law. The 1968–69 Sunday Entertainments Bill is chosen in preference to that of 1967–68 because the number voting upon it was substantially higher. All figures in this chapter include tellers.

[1] The detailed numerical analysis has been carried out by my research assistant, Mrs Margaret Fuller. Only the major results of her work are presented here.

[2] Theatre censorship is excluded as it caused no division in the Commons on either the second or third reading.

TABLE 1

The Divisions Analysed

Subject	Date	Sponsor	Reading	Ayes	Noes
Capital Punishment	21.12.64	Silverman	Second	357	172
Homosexuality	5. 7.66	Abse	First[1]	246	102
Abortion	13. 7.67	Steel	Third	169	85
Divorce	17.12.68	Jones	Second	185	108
Sunday Entertainment	28. 2.69	Parker	Second	106	97

The term 'capital punishment' in Table 1 is used for the sake of brevity: the subject of the Bill was the abolition of capital punishment. Unless this is kept in mind the figures in all the tables in this chapter can be misleading. The figures relating to capital punishment also differ from those on the other four Bills in that the capital punishment vote was held in the 1964 Parliament while the others were decided in the 1966 Parliament. The party balance of Members resulting from the 1964 Election was not the same as the outcome of the 1966 Election and, of course, there is some difference in social

TABLE 2

Voting by Party

	Labour	Conservative	Liberal
		Voting Aye	
Capital Punishment	268	81	8
%	84·8	26·6	88·9
Homosexuality	184	51	11
%	50·8	20·2	91·7
Abortion	130	32	7
%	36·0	12·6	58·3
Divorce	154	24	6
%	43·9	9·2	50·0
Sunday Entertainment	83	22	1
%	23·7	8·5	8·3
		Voting No	
Capital Punishment	1	170	1
%	0·3	55·9	11·1
Homosexuality	33	69	—
%	9·1	27·3	—
Abortion	23	62	—
%	6·4	24·4	—
Divorce	20	87	1
%	5·7	33·2	8·3
Sunday Entertainment	26	68	2
%	7·4	26·1	16·7

[1] Ten-Minute Rule Bill.

characteristics between the Members elected. There are also minor changes in the composition of Parliament as time passes due to by-elections; again these will be reflected in the tables below.

Although the party whips are off duty on issues of conscience, the first task is to examine the relationship between party affiliation and opinion on these questions. Table 2 shows clearly that Labour and Liberal Members were heavily in favour of the reforms while Conservative Members were hostile. Only on homosexuality was the balance of Conservative opinion other than overwhelmingly conservative. (The percentage figures Tables 2–9 always refer to the percentage within a category of Members voting in a particular way: the percentage figures for Aye and No votes do not total 100 as some Members were absent.)

Another important influence on opinion is age.

TABLE 3

Voting by Age Groups

		Under 35	35–44	45–54	55–64	65+
			on January 1, 1969[1]			
			Voting Aye			
Capital Punishment		2	77	101	107	70
	%	40·0	68·1	55·8	51·7	56·9
Homosexuality		17	83	76	56	14
	%	73·9	54·6	40·6	30·1	17·5
Abortion		11	58	54	37	9
	%	45·8	37·4	28·9	20·1	11·4
Divorce		13	55	57	44	16
	%	48·2	34·2	29·8	24·7	22·5
Sunday Entertainment		6	29	33	30	8
	%	22·2	18·0	17·5	16·8	11·4
			Voting No			
Capital Punishment		3	26	53	64	26
	%	60·0	23·0	29·3	30·9	21·1
Homosexuality		—	15	28	36	23
	%	—	9·9	15·0	19·4	28·7
Abortion		3	18	30	27	7
	%	12·5	11·6	16·0	14·7	8·9
Divorce		3	19	45	27	14
	%	11·1	11·8	23·6	15·2	19·7
Sunday Entertainment		3	22	27	33	12
	%	11·1	13·7	14·3	18·5	17·1

[1] Because the ages of Members are calculated with reference to a single base date, this table overestimates ages in relation to the votes on capital punishment (held on 21.12.64), homosexuality (5.7.66) and abortion (13.7.67).

Again the message is clear. Younger Members were far more heavily in favour of reform.[1] The distinction is particularly notable in the case of homosexuality. Without question, party and age are the two best general predictors of opinion on issues of conscience. A young Labour Member is highly likely to be in favour of change: an elderly Conservative Member is highly likely to support the *status quo*.

Table 4 contrasts the voting record of male and female Members. It appears to show that the women were markedly more favourable to change than men except on Sunday entertainment. In a sense the table is misleading because there is proportionately a higher number of women Members in the Labour Party: at the 1966 Election, 26 women were elected, 19 of them Labour. Thus the women were favourable to reform, not because of their sex, but because nearly three-quarters of them were Labour supporters. As compared with men, their relatively low absentee vote for the abortion vote (48 per cent) is also noteworthy.

Religious belief must have a major influence when a decision has to be made which has great moral implications. Yet some Members are a little uneasy about voting on the basis of personal religious convictions. In Britain every religion is a minority religion. Every Member knows that only a minority, sometimes a small minority, of his constituents will belong to the same church as he does. Of course, if a Member has clear and vigorous opinions on an issue of conscience he will not be deterred from voting merely by the knowledge that he belongs to a religious minority. But if his sympathies are less firmly established, the knowledge that many constituents have different views can make it easier to abstain.

It is impossible to obtain full information about the religious affiliations of Members. Some Members carry their faith like a banner; a few may conceal it; others avoid public ascription to a faith, probably because they have none. Religious belief or disbelief has been attributed to roughly half the Members, some of whom are deeply religious and some not: the intensity of belief cannot be known. The other half must be treated as 'No Information'. Thus the figures in Table 5 are less complete and less satisfactory than those in the other tables. Yet it seems reasonable to assume that Members who proclaim their convictions are the strongest believers and that the 'No Information' group are apathetic or mildly agnostic. Except on capital punishment their abstention level was slightly higher than among Members as a whole.

[1] The number of Members in the lowest age-category for the capital punishment vote is too small to be significant.

TABLE 4
Voting by Sex

	Voting Aye		Voting No	
	Male	Female	Male	Female
Capital Punishment	337	20	116	6
%	56·2	69·0	27·7	20·7
Homosexuality	235	11	99	3
%	39·0	44·0	16·4	12·0
Abortion	160	9	81	4
%	26·5	36·0	13·4	16·0
Divorce	175	10	104	4
%	29·1	38·5	17·3	15·4
Sunday Entertainment	102	4	94	3
%	17·0	15·4	15·7	11·5

TABLE 5
Voting by Religion

		No information	Roman Catholic	Anglican[1]	Free Church	Jew	Atheist/ Agnostic
				Voting Aye			
Capital Punishment		193	18	58	41	23	24
	%	54·7	69·2	41·1	77·4	79·3	88·9
Homosexuality		110	13	46	24	21	32
	%	37·5	40·6	28·7	38·1	65·6	66·7
Abortion		78	2	29	18	15	27
	%	26·3	6·2	18·2	28·6	46·9	57·4
Divorce		88	3	32	20	13	29
	%	28·9	9·4	20·6	32·3	41·9	65·9
Sunday Entertainment	%	49	3	12	6	13	23
	%	16·2	9·7	7·7	9·8	41·9	51·1
				Voting No			
Capital Punishment		103	3	60	4	1	1
	%	29·2	11·5	42·6	7·5	3·5	3·7
Homosexuality		45	8	40	8	1	—
	%	15·4	25·0	25·0	12·7	3·1	—
Abortion		31	18	30	2	3	1
	%	10·5	56·3	18·9	3·2	9·4	2·1
Divorce		45	13	39	7	4	—
	%	14·8	40·6	25·2	11·3	12·9	—
Sunday Entertainment		38	4	35	17	1	2
	%	12·6	12·9	22·6	27·9	3·2	4·4

As to be expected, Table 5 shows strong Roman Catholic opposition
to the Abortion Bill and, to a lesser extent, the Divorce Bill. The
Anglican support for hanging is perhaps a little more surprising. On
Sunday entertainment, support for the Bill came from disbelievers

[1] Includes Church of England, Church in Scotland, Church in Wales.

and Jews, opposition from Free Church and Anglican Members, while the Roman Catholics stayed away. The notable feature of the figures for Anglican Members is the almost equal division of opinion on all issues save Sunday entertainment.

Tables 6 and 7 show the relation of education to opinion. Once again there is a tendency for the categories of educational experience to reflect party affiliation. With one exception the 41 Members whose education was limited to elementary standard were Labour supporters and 26 of them were over fifty-five years of age. The public schoolboys are predominantly Conservative. A comparison of these two categories will show that Members whose education was restricted to the elementary level were more in sympathy with the various reforms – save the homosexuality measure:[1] here is another indication that opinion on this question was heavily influenced by age, since the elementary education group are older.

TABLE 6
Voting by Schooling

		Elementary	Secondary	Public School	Private
			Voting Aye		
Capital Punishment		39	196	119	3
	%	84·8	68·3	41·0	50·0
Homosexuality		12	134	98	2
	%	26·7	43·6	36·0	50·0
Abortion		9	99	60	1
	%	20·9	31·7	22·2	25·0
Divorce		15	115	54	1
	%	35·7	37·0	19·8	33·3
Sunday Entertainment		8	62	36	—
	%	19·0	20·0	13·3	—
			Voting No		
Capital Punishment		—	47	124	1
	%	—	16·4	42·8	16·7
Homosexuality		9	42	51	—
	%	20·0	13·7	18·8	—
Abortion		4	27	53	1
	%	9·3	8·7	19·6	25·0
Divorce		7	32	69	—
	%	16·7	10·3	25·4	—
Sunday Entertainment		2	36	58	1
	%	4·8	11·6	21·5	33·3

[1] The percentage of the public-school educated voting for abortion reform was slightly higher than the percentage of elementary schoolboys, but the percentage of the former voting against was twice as high.

TABLE 7

Voting by Higher Education

		Oxbridge	Other University	Other Higher Education	None	Forces
				Voting Aye		
Capital		119	81	20	132	5
Punishment	%	50·9	69·8	74·1	58·7	18·5
Homosexuality		101	65	17	58	5
	%	42·4	47·8	56·7	27·7	33·3
Abortion		68	36	13	49	3
	%	28·4	25·9	41·9	23·9	20·0
Divorce		53	51	19	58	4
	%	22·3	36·2	61·3	28·7	25·0
Sunday Enter-		39	28	4	32	3
tainment	%	16·6	20·0	12·9	15·8	18·7
				Voting No		
Capital		77	18	4	53	20
Punishment	%	32·9	15·5	14·8	23·5	74·1
Homosexuality		27	18	4	47	6
	%	11·3	13·2	13·3	22·5	40·0
Abortion		37	13	1	29	5
	%	15·5	9·4	3·2	14·2	33·3
Divorce		44	19	2	39	4
	%	18·5	13·5	6·5	19·3	25·0
Sunday Enter-		34	23	3	32	5
tainment	%	14·5	16·4	9·7	15·8	31·3

The category of Members in the higher education table most favourable to reform is that grouped under the rubric 'Other Higher Education' which covers technical colleges, teacher training colleges and correspondence courses. With seven exceptions these are Labour Members. At the other extreme come the 28 Service Officers, believers in social discipline and opponents of the permissive society; all these Members are Conservatives. The effect of Service experience on attitudes towards capital punishment is dramatic. Oxbridge graduates tended to be less favourable to reform than non-Oxbridge graduates, and here again is a party difference: non-Oxbridge graduates tend to be Labour Members.

The classification of occupations in Table 8 requires some explanation. It is based on a Member's means of earning a living immediately before election to Parliament. 'Professions' include law, medicine, accountancy, teaching, central and local government service including the armed forces. 'Workers' include miners, railway clerks and other wage-earning activities. The miscellaneous group includes farmers, housewives, journalists and white-collar workers. With two exceptions the 'workers' are Labour Members. The great majority of 'business' Members are Conservative. Table 8 shows that the 'workers' were strongly opposed to capital punishment but that they had more doubts about homosexuality.

TABLE 8

Voting by Occupation

		Professions	Business	Workers	Miscellaneous
			Voting Aye		
Capital Punishment		141	49	77	90
	%	54·9	43·4	77·0	56·6
Homosexuality		117	37	29	63
	%	44·8	33·9	29·9	39·1
Abortion		74	24	22	49
	%	28·1	22·2	22·9	30·2
Divorce		86	22	30	47
	%	32·6	19·8	31·9	29·6
Sunday Entertainment		48	16	17	25
	%	18·2	14·7	17·9	15·8
			Voting No		
Capital Punishment		79	46	3	44
	%	30·7	40·7	3·0	27·7
Homosexuality		28	28	21	25
	%	10·7	25·7	21·6	15·5
Abortion		32	21	7	25
	%	12·2	19·4	7·3	15·4
Divorce		39	25	12	32
	%	14·8	22·5	12·8	20·1
Sunday Entertainment		37	29	6	25
	%	14·1	26·6	6·3	15·8

Table 9 divides the country up into regions in order to analyse voting by area. Any attempt to distinguish regions is open to detailed geographical objections. For the present purpose England has been divided into five parts, North West, North East, Midlands, South West and South East. The South East region has been drawn broadly in recognition of the dominance of London over the cultural values of a large part of the country, and it covers all counties to the south and east of Cambridgeshire, Huntingdon, Buckinghamshire, Oxfordshire and Hampshire. The South West runs from Lands End to include Gloucestershire, Wiltshire and Dorset. The North West comprises Cumberland, Westmorland, Lancashire, Cheshire and

Skipton. The North East comprises Northumberland, Durham and Yorkshire (except Skipton). All the remainder of England has been allocated to the Midlands and forms a wide band from Herefordshire to Lincolnshire.

TABLE 9

Voting by Region

		N.W.	N.E.	Midland	S.W.	S.E.	Scotland	Wales	Northern Ireland
					Voting Aye				
Capital		54	55	61	18	99	41	27	2
Punishment	%	64·3	66·3	63·5	41·9	48·5	57·7	75·0	16·7
Homosexuality		32	27	43	17	97	18	12	—
	%	38·1	32·5	44·8	39·5	47·5	25·3	34·3	—
Abortion		20	19	29	11	72	10	7	1
	%	23·8	22·9	29·9	26·2	35·1	14·1	20·0	8·3
Divorce		28	20	27	14	65	18	13	—
	%	33·3	24·1	28·1	32·6	31·7	25·4	37·4	—
Sunday		8	19	12	5	60	1	1	—
Entertainment	%	9·5	22·9	12·8	11·9	29·4	1·4	2·8	—
					Voting No				
Capital		14	10	22	19	83	13	4	7
Punishment	%	16·7	12·0	22·9	44·2	40·7	18·4	11·1	58·3
Homosexuality		13	14	13	9	31	18	1	3
	%	15·5	16·9	13·6	21·0	15·2	25·3	2·9	25·0
Abortion		17	8	10	8	31	9	1	1
	%	20·2	9·6	10·3	19·0	15·1	12·6	2·9	8·3
Divorce		17	7	17	8	36	17	1	5
	%	20·2	8·4	17·7	18·6	17·6	23·9	2·9	45·5
Sunday		14	8	8	5	41	9	5	7
Entertainment	%	16·7	9·6	8·5	11·9	20·1	12·7	13·9	63·6

This table invites a variety of comment. It shows the extent to which support for the Sunday Entertainments Bill was concentrated in South East England. The same area was also the most favourably disposed to the Bills on abortion and homosexuality. Scottish Members were remarkably hostile to reform. At the 1966 Election only 20 of the 71 Scottish Members elected were Conservative, so the proportion of Liberal and Labour Members for Scotland was higher than that for the Commons as a whole. The South West is notable for its support of capital punishment. A comparison of the North West and the North East shows the former to be more tolerant of homosexuality and the latter of Sunday entertainment.

None of the Bills studied here applied to Northern Ireland, and those on homosexuality, divorce and Sunday entertainment did not extend to Scotland. This did not prevent Scottish and Ulster Members voting where their sympathies were heavily engaged, and their action in the division lobby had a significant effect on the size of the majority in favour of the second reading of the Parker Sunday Entertainments Bill. The fact that their own constituents were not affected – at least immediately – did not seem to have any impact on the presence or absence of Members. Thus the absence rate for Scottish Members was much higher on the Abortion Bill, which included Scotland, than on the homosexuality and divorce measures that did not. The significant factor is the day of the week: the abortion vote was on a Friday, whereas the other two votes were on Tuesdays.

The percentage of absent Members in any group delineated in the above tables can, of course, be found by adding the Aye percentage to the No percentage and deducting the result from 100. But the extent of participation in these conscience votes is of such importance as to require further examination. In the following set of tables Members are analysed in terms of their attendance record in the division lobbies with reference to party, age, etc. The tables cover 595 Members who were entitled to vote in all four critical divisions in the 1966 Parliament. Capital punishment is excluded from this set of calculations, for to include it would reduce significantly the total of Members entitled to vote on all issues. So the possible attendance record varies between four and nought. It should be stressed again that there are many reasons for not voting. A Member may be sick, have other official business or decide he does not wish to commit himself on a particular subject. Occasionally there are a few Members actually present in the Palace of Westminster who decide not to vote; the word 'attendance' in the table headings below refers to attendance in the division lobby, not attendance at Parliament.

The higher attendances of Labour Members are the more remarkable – some would say more creditable – when it is remembered that up to ninety Labour Members held office in the Government and so had much heavier calls upon their time.

TABLE 10
Attendance by Party

Party		Attendances			
		0	1	2	3	4
Labour		51	89	92	74	32
	%	15·1	26·3	27·2	21·9	9·5
Conservative		45	64	79	48	8
	%	18·4	26·2	32·4	19·7	3·3
Liberal		—	1	7	3	1
	%	—	8·3	58·3	25·1	8·3

Table 11 shows a higher level of activity among the younger Members.

TABLE 11
Attendance by Age[1]

Age group		Attendances				
		0	1	2	3	4
Under 35		—	3	11	8	1
	%	—	13·0	47·8	34·8	4·4
35–44		19	35	51	32	13
	%	12·7	23·3	34·0	21·3	8·7
45–54		24	45	48	50	11
	%	13·5	25·3	27·0	28·1	6·1
55–64		35	50	53	26	12
	%	19·9	28·4	30·1	14·8	6·8
65+		19	21	15	9	4
	%	27·9	30·9	22·1	13·2	5·9

But there is little difference between men and women.

TABLE 12
Attendance by Sex

		Attendances				
		0	1	2	3	4
Male		96	145	171	120	39
	%	16·8	25·4	30·0	21·0	6·8
Female		1	9	7	5	2
	%	4·2	37·5	29·2	20·8	8·3

What effect does religious persuasion have on the attendance records of Members? The short answer is that the irreligious Members are the most active. Lowest participation comes from Anglican and Free Church Members, but as between the two groups rather separate influences may be at work. The Free Church group has a high proportion of Members from Wales and Scotland and the distance between Westminster and their constituencies affects attendance (see Table 13). The same explanation cannot apply to Anglicans. It may be that some Anglicans, especially Conservative Anglicans, were uncertain how to vote and avoided the dilemma by abstention. It has been shown that Conservative Members were generally hostile to these reforms, yet all the measures, save perhaps the Sunday Entertainments Bill, has received some support from church leaders and influential church publications.

[1] As at January 1, 1969. See footnote to Table 3, remembering that capital punishment is excluded from Table 11.

Analysis by schooling, Table 14, shows the lowest attendances for those with only elementary education. The Members in this group are the older Labour Members and the effective influence here is probably age rather than level of formal education.

TABLE 13
Attendance by Religion

Religious Group		Attendances				
		0	1	2	3	4
No information		56	75	79	49	18
	%	20·2	27·1	28·5	17·7	6·5
Roman Catholics		1	8	11	8	2
	%	3·3	26·7	36·7	26·7	6·6
Anglican[1]		23	40	57	30	3
	%	15·1	26·1	37·2	19·6	2·0
Free Church		9	23	15	9	4
	%	15·0	38·3	25·0	15·0	6·7
Jews		5	4	4	14	4
	%	16·1	12·9	12·9	45·2	12·9
Atheist/Agnostic		3	4	12	15	10
	%	6·8	9·1	27·3	34·1	22·7

TABLE 14
Attendance by Schooling

		Attendances				
		0	1	2	3	4
Elementary		11	11	10	4	5
	%	26·8	26·8	24·4	9·8	12·2
Secondary		45	80	85	58	23
	%	15·5	27·5	29·2	19·9	7·9
Public School		40	62	83	63	12
	%	15·4	23·8	31·9	24·2	4·7
Private		1	1	—	—	1
	%	33·3	33·3	—	—	33·3

Two categories emerge from the higher education analysis, Table 15, as the most active participants on the issues of conscience, the other higher education group and the Forces group. These two groups have nothing in common except a high level of motivation: the 'other higher education' Members were stimulated by enthusiasm for the various reforms, while the Forces Members were spurred on by hostility to them (see Table 7).

[1] Includes Church of England, Church in Scotland, Church in Wales.

TABLE 15

Attendance by Higher Education

		Attendances			
	0	1	2	3	4
Oxbridge	38	62	65	48	13
%	16·8	27·4	28·8	21·2	5·8
Other University	19	34	39	32	8
%	14·4	25·8	29·5	24·2	6·1
Other Higher Education	4	6	7	9	3
%	13·8	20·7	24·1	31·0	10·4
None	35	50	62	30	16
%	18·1	25·9	32·2	15·5	8·3
Forces	1	2	5	6	1
%	6·7	13·3	33·3	40·0	6·7

TABLE 16

Attendance by Occupation

		Attendances			
	0	1	2	3	4
Professions	43	62	71	56	17
%	17·3	24·9	28·5	22·5	6·8
Business	16	22	32	24	8
%	15·7	21·6	31·4	23·5	7·8
Workers	18	31	24	14	5
%	19·6	33·7	26·1	15·2	5·4
Miscellaneous	20	39	51	31	11
%	13·2	25·7	33·5	20·4	7·2

Table 16, based on occupational categories, shows the lowest attendances from Members in the 'workers' classification. This is another reflection of the tendency noticed already for the older Labour Members with limited formal education not to respond so readily when the division bells ring.

The traditional view that Scottish Members have the poorest attendance records is not wholly supported by Table 17, for the rate of Welsh absenteeism is greater. However, the difference is due to the decision of many Welsh Members to abstain on the Sunday Entertainments Bill.[1] Members from the North West were more energetic than those from the North East. But the most active participants were Members from the southern half of England, particularly the South East: no doubt this is a consequence of the convenience of having a constituency and a home nearer to Westminster.

[1] See p. 170.

TABLE 17

Attendance by Region

		Attendances				
		0	1	2	3	4
North West		12	25	19	20	5
	%	14·8	30·9	23·4	24·7	6·2
North East		17	27	22	12	3
	%	21·0	33·3	27·2	14·8	3·7
Midlands		14	25	28	16	3
	%	16·3	29·1	32·6	18·6	3·4
South West		6	7	14	13	—
	%	15·0	17·5	35·0	32·5	—
South East		22	35	60	49	29
	%	11·3	17·9	30·8	25·1	14·9
Scotland		14	21	22	11	—
	%	20·6	30·9	32·3	16·2	—
Wales		11	9	10	2	1
	%	33·3	27·3	30·3	6·1	3·0
Northern Ireland		1	5	3	2	—
	%	9·1	45·4	27·3	18·2	—

The remaining tables in this chapter relate the attitude of Members on each issue to their attitudes on each of the other issues. In this way it is possible to measure how far views on one issue are related to views on the others. Tables 18–23 must be read *vertically*. The square where a subject concides on both the vertical and horizontal axes shows how Members voted in the crucial division on that subject. Remaining figures in this vertical line show how Members voting in the division voted on other topics. It will be seen that the tables are a partial mirror image. To take an example: the two squares comparing capital punishment and homosexuality show the same totals of Aye and No votes, but they do not show the same figures for absence. The number of Members voting on capital punishment who were absent from the homosexuality vote is not the same as the number of Members voting on homosexuality who were absent from the capital punishment vote. It will also be noticed that the total of Members voting on any subject (A) does not always coincide with the total shown in the further analysis of how this group of Members voted on any other subject (B). This is because the analysis of voting on B excludes Members who left Parliament since the vote was taken on A due to political defeat, death or resignation. Alternatively, where the vote on B was prior to the vote on A, the analysis of B necessarily excludes Members who were not yet elected to Parliament. This distinction is of greatest importance in relation to capital punishment because the decision on this question was taken in the 1964 Parliament whereas all the other decisions were made in the 1966 Parliament.

Tables 18 and 19 show that Members favourable to reform on one issue are generally favourable to reform on others. Equally, those who oppose change in one sphere generally oppose it in others. There are some exceptions. Those who opposed the Bills on homosexuality and abortion were fairly evenly divided on their attitude to capital punishment. The opponents of abortion reform and Sunday entertainment were also divided in their attitude to homosexuality. Also notable is the high absentee rate for the Sunday entertainment vote – except among the opponents of capital punishment. The other significant feature is the great fluidity in the groups of Members supporting and opposing the various Bills. Those who supported measure A were more likely to support than oppose measures B, C, D, E, but the probability that they would support B, C, D, E was roughly equal to the probability that they would be absent when these measures were voted upon. The analogous statement is true for the opponents of measure A.

When the figures for comparative attitudes are broken down as between Labour and Conservative Members the picture becomes more complex. Tables 20 and 21 relating to Labour Members do not show the same tendency to offer general opposition to reform. Labour opponents of Bills on homosexuality, abortion, divorce and Sunday entertainment were in favour of the abolition of capital punishment because, with a single exception, the Party was unanimous on this issue. Rather more surprising are the figures relating to the opponents of Sunday entertainment: a significant majority were in favour of the homosexuality and abortion Bills and they were equally divided on divorce. The Labour Members supporting reform show a much higher degree of consistency. A similar, but not quite so high a degree of consistency, is to be found among Conservative opponents of change (Tables 22 and 23). It is in the middle-ground of politics where attitudes are complex. Thus the Conservative supporters of a particular reform often did not support others, just as Labour opponents of one measure did not necessarily object to others. It will be seen that Conservative supporters of the abolition of capital punishment were almost equally split over abortion and that a majority opposed the Divorce and Sunday Entertainment Bills. Conservative supporters of homosexuality reform were evenly split on divorce.

N

TABLE 18
Comparative Attitudes: all Members

		Capital Punishment		Homo-sexuality		Abortion		Divorce		Sunday Entertainment	
		Aye	No	Aye	No	Aye	No	Aye	No	Aye	No
Capital	Aye	357		152	40	101	29	110	26	63	23
Punishment	No		172	13	46	13	34	10	51	10	43
	Abs.			15	14	6	23	12	13	12	13
Homo-	Aye	152	13	246		110	21	114	16	64	20
sexuality	No	40	46		102	8	25	12	34	8	27
	Abs.	125	71			50	39	53	51	32	46
Abortion	Aye	101	13	110	8	169		92	4	59	11
	No	29	34	21	25		85	5	43	4	30
	Abs.	185	83	115	67			86	55	42	53
Divorce	Aye	110	10	114	12	92	5	185		57	9
	No	26	51	16	34	4	43		108	3	39
	Abs.	167	67	108	52	71	37			46	49
Sunday	Aye	63	10	64	8	59	4	57	3	106	
Enter-	No	23	43	20	27	11	30	9	39		97
tainment	Abs.	216	74	152	63	96	51	118	66		

TABLE 19
Comparative Attitudes: all Members
by percentages

		Capital Punishment		Homo-sexuality		Abortion		Divorce		Sunday Entertainment	
		Aye	No	Aye	No	Aye	No	Aye	No	Aye	No
Capital	Aye	100		61·8	39·2	59·8	34·1	59·4	24·1	59·4	23·7
Punishment	No		100	5·3	45·1	7·7	40·0	5·4	47·2	9·4	44·3
	Abs.			6·1	13·7	3·5	27·1	6·5	12·0	11·3	13·4
Homo-	Aye	42·6	7·6	100		65·1	24·7	61·6	14·8	60·4	20·6
sexuality	No	11·2	26·7		100	4·7	29·4	6·5	31·5	7·5	27·8
	Abs.	35·0	41·3			29·6	45·9	28·6	47·2	30·2	47·4
Abortion	Aye	28·3	7·6	44·7	7·8	100		49·7	3·7	55·7	11·3
	No	8·1	19·8	8·5	24·5		100	2·7	39·8	3·8	30·9
	Abs.	51·8	48·3	46·7	65·7			46·5	50·9	39·6	54·6
Divorce	Aye	30·8	5·8	46·3	11·8	54·4	5·9	100		53·8	9·3
	No	7·3	29·7	6·5	33·3	2·4	50·6		100	2·8	40·2
	Abs.	46·8	38·9	43·9	51·0	42·0	43·5			43·4	50·5
Sunday	Aye	17·6	5·8	26·0	7·8	34·9	4·7	30·8	2·8	100	
Enter-	No	6·4	25·0	8·1	26·5	6·5	35·3	4·9	36·1		100
tainment	Abs.	60·5	43·0	61·8	61·8	56·8	60·0	63·9	61·1		

TABLE 20
Comparative Attitudes: Labour Members

		Capital Punishment		Homo-sexuality		Abortion		Divorce		Sunday Entertainment	
		Aye	No	Aye	No	Aye	No	Aye	No	Aye	No
Capital	Aye	268		119	26	85	17	99	16	57	12
Punishment	No		1	—	1	—	—	—	—	—	—
	Abs.			9	6	5	3	8	2	9	6
Homo-	Aye	119	—	184		88	12	98	5	52	12
sexuality	No	26	1		33	4	6	6	8	4	3
	Abs.	104	—			37	4	46	6	26	11
Abortion	Aye	85	—	88	4	130		78	—	52	7
	No	17	—	12	6		22	2	9	2	5
	Abs.	146	1	84	23			72	10	28	14
Divorce	Aye	99	—	98	6	78	2	154		50	5
	No	16	—	5	8	—	9		19	1	5
	Abs.	122	1	73	17	50	11			32	16
Sunday	Aye	57	—	52	4	52	2	50	1	83	
Enter-	No	12	—	12	3	7	5	5	5		26
tainment	Abs.	167	1	110	24	68	15	98	13		

TABLE 21
Comparative Attitudes: Labour Members
by percentages

		Capital Punishment		Homo-sexuality		Abortion		Divorce		Sunday Entertainment	
		Aye	No	Aye	No	Aye	No	Aye	No	Aye	No
Capital	Aye	100		64·7	78·8	65·4	77·3	64·3	84·2	68·7	46·1
Punishment	No		100	—	3·0	—	—	—	—	—	—
	Abs.			4·9	18·2	3·8	13·6	5·2	10·5	10·8	23·1
Homo-	Aye	44·4	—	100		67·7	54·5	63·6	26·3	62·6	46·1
sexuality	No	9·7	100·0		100	3·1	27·3	3·9	42·1	4·7	11·5
	Abs.	38·8	—			28·5	18·2	29·9	31·6	31·3	42·3
Abortion	Aye	31·7	—	47·8	12·1	100		50·6	—	62·6	26·9
	No	6·3	—	6·5	18·2		100	1·3	47·2	2·4	19·2
	Abs.	54·5	100·0	45·6	69·7			46·7	52·6	33·7	53·8
Divorce	Aye	36·9	—	53·3	18·2	60·0	9·1	100		60·2	19·2
	No	5·9	—	2·7	24·2	—	40·9		100	1·2	19·2
	Abs.	45·5	100·0	39·7	51·5	38·5	50·0			38·5	61·5
Sunday	Aye	21·3	—	28·3	12·1	40·0	9·1	32·5	5·3	100	
Enter-	No	4·5	—	6·5	9·1	5·4	22·7	3·2	26·3		100
tainment	Abs.	62·3	100·0	59·8	72·7	52·3	68·2	63·6	68·4		

TABLE 22
Comparative Attitudes: Conservative Members

		Capital Punishment		Homo-sexuality		Abortion		Divorce		Sunday Entertainment	
		Aye	No	Aye	No	Aye	No	Aye	No	Aye	No
Capital	Aye	81		27	14	13	12	7	10	5	10
Punishment	No		167	13	45	13	31	10	47	10	42
	Abs.			6	7	1	10	4	10	3	7
Homo-	Aye	27	13	51		15	9	10	11	11	7
sexuality	No	14	45		68	4	19	6	25	4	24
	Abs.	21	67			13	32	7	41	6	34
Abortion	Aye	13	13	15	4	32		10	4	6	4
	No	12	31	9	19		60	3	31	2	25
	Abs.	36	81	27	43			11	43	14	36
Divorce	Aye	7	10	10	6	10	3	24		6	3
	No	10	47	11	25	4	31		84	2	33
	Abs.	43	66	30	35	18	26			14	32
Sunday	Aye	5	10	11	4	6	2	6	2	22	
Enter-	No	10	42	7	24	4	25	3	33		68
tainment	Abs.	45	70	33	38	22	33	15	49		

TABLE 23
Comparative Attitudes: Conservative Members
by percentages

		Capital Punishment		Homo-sexuality		Abortion		Divorce		Sunday Entertainment	
		Aye	No	Aye	No	Aye	No	Aye	No	Aye	No
Capital	Aye	100		52·9	20·6	40·6	20·7	29·2	11·9	22·7	14·7
Punishment	No		100	25·5	66·2	40·6	51·7	41·7	55·9	45·5	61·8
	Abs.			11·8	10·3	3·1	16·7	16·7	11·9	13·6	10·3
Homo	Aye	33·3	7·8	100		46·9	15·0	41·7	13·1	50·0	10·3
sexuality	No	17·3	26·9		100	12·5	31·7	25·0	29·8	18·2	35·3
	Ans.	25·9	40·1			40·6	53·3	29·2	48·8	27·3	50·0
Abortion	Aye	16·0	7·8	29·4	5·9	100		41·7	4·8	27·3	5·9
	No	14·8	18·6	17·6	27·9		100	12·5	36·9	9·1	36·8
	Abs.	44·4	48·5	52·9	63·2			45·8	51·2	63·6	52·9
Divorce	Aye	8·6	5·9	19·6	13·9	31·2	5·0	100		27·3	4·4
	No	12·3	28·1	21·6	36·7	12·5	51·7		100	9·1	48·5
	Abs.	53·1	39·5	58·8	51·4	56·2	43·3			63·6	47·0
Sunday	Aye	6·2	5·9	21·6	5·9	18·7	3·3	25·0	2·4	100	
Enter-	No	12·3	25·1	13·7	35·2	12·5	41·7	12·5	39·3		100
tainment	Abs.	55·5	41·9	64·7	55·9	68·7	55·0	62·5	58·3		

Chapter 10

Legislation Without Party

I

Controversy over particular private members' Bills can lead easily to controversy over the whole procedure for back-bench legislation. Those who suffer defeat in a political tussle are tempted to argue that the rules of political battle are unfair. The losers cry 'Foul'. A certain amount of activity on these lines has been stimulated by recent legislation on issues of conscience.

The argument about the value of private members' Bills is not new. The 1930 Select Committee on Procedure heard opposed opinions. Mr Winston Churchill thought it should be made difficult 'for all sorts of happy thoughts to be carried on to the statute book'.[1] The Labour chief whip thought that time spent on private members' Bills was 'very largely wasted'.[2] Lloyd Goerge was more favourable because he felt that the procedure offered an opportunity to discuss new ideas and new topics.[3] Writing towards the end of the 1930s, Harold Laski was hostile. He argued that if a matter were important enough to require legislation, then responsibility for the legislation should rest upon the Government; that in any case legislation will not pass unless the Government approves of it. The private member as a sponsor of legislation was in a hopelessly weak position: A. P. Herbert had been forced to accept damaging amendments to his Divorce Bill and 'the truncated measure which resulted will probably prevent the serious rationalization of the marriage laws for many years to come'.[4] This is a searing criticism. Yet it ignores two vital points. If a government wishes to evade a moral issue, the private member is the only alternative source of initiative within the rules of parliamentary procedure. Secondly, it is at least as valid to claim that a limited reform prepares the way for subsequent and wider reform as it is to claim that limited reform impedes subsequent and more radical change – especially on matters affecting religious belief and social values where behaviour patterns change slowly.

Critics of back-bench legislation can argue that it produces bad

[1] *Procedure on Public Business*, Special Report, q. 1530, 1930–31 (161) viii.
[2] *Ibid.*, q. 718.
[3] *Ibid.*, q. 893.
[4] *Parliamentary Government in England* (Allen & Unwin, 1938) p. 166.

laws and/or that the time spent on it could be better used in another way. The latter view used to be popular in left-wing circles. The private member was thought to be a nineteenth-century irrelevance. Once a Labour Cabinet was elected with a clear majority in the Commons it must then set about the task of achieving socialist reconstruction of the country. No time could be spared for the trivia which back-benchers might wish to see on the statute book. Essentially this was Laski's view and the view of the Attlee Labour Government in the immediate post-war years. But experience bred disenchantment. By 1948 the energy of the Government was seen to flag and the possibility that back-benchers could contribute usefully to the total of legislation became difficult to deny. So in 1948 time was again made available for private members' Bills after a gap of nine years, and Sir Ivor Jennings' comment was increasingly acceptable: 'The fact that much Government legislation is either vote-catching or of a departmental character renders desirable the provision of time for other measures.'[1]

The challenge since 1967 to back-bench legislation is quite different in character. The objections are right-wing rather than left-wing. Nothing is heard about trivial time-wasting; instead the complaint is that the Government allows back-benchers to have glorious and irresponsible freedom to force through changes in the basic fabric of our social life. Five separate yet complementary arguments in this approach can be distinguished.

1. The Government is succeeding in obtaining the passage of controversial laws without accepting responsibility for them.
2. Measures are passed at a stage when insufficient study and debate has been devoted to the issues involved.
3. Constituents do not know the views of parliamentary candidates on non-party issues: Members, therefore, have no mandate.
4. Important votes on private members' Bills are taken on Fridays or in all-night sittings when attendance is low.
5. Private members' Bills are badly drafted and do not – in the case of complex measures – operate as intended.

These propositions will be considered in turn.

1. The Government is succeeding in obtaining the passage of controversial laws without accepting responsibility for them. This is the basic challenge. It is claimed that permissive social legislation is unpopular with many electors, including government supporters; that were the Cabinet to espouse these causes openly it would lose

[1] *Parliament* (Cambridge U.P., 2nd edn, 1957), p. 373.

support; that because these causes are keenly pressed by many Labour Members, the Cabinet has let them go ahead while dodging responsibility.[1] No back-bench initiative that arouses great passion can succeed unless the Government arranges extra time and this, it is argued, implies not merely neutrality but covert support. The counter-argument is that the supply of extra time merely allows the Commons to reach a decision; a Bill allowed such a facility might be successful or it might be defeated. In fact, all the measures allowed extra time have passed. No doubt this is because Ministers have judged correctly the broad wishes of the House. If a government aided a Bill that failed it could be accused of pushing it or of wasting Members' time.

The main issue, however, is Laski's theme that all legislation should be government legislation. Here one must face the fact that British parties, if not class parties, are differentiated by their economic policies rather than by moral attitudes. It is 'bread and butter' issues which excite the electors; votes are won and lost over matters of material well-being. Immigration is the only social controversy likely to have a significant impact on voting behaviour.[2] Capital punishment and a few other issues could have a slight effect where a Member had played a prominent role in a campaign for reform. But attitudes on these social questions traverse economic divisions and take second place to them. If our party system resembled more closely a European model, it might be that social issues could fit neatly into the established party complex. A Roman Catholic party with a generally conservative, private enterprise approach to economic issues could be expected to oppose legislation on abortion and divorce, but to support Sunday entertainments, the abolition of capital punishment and the reform of the law on homosexuality. Britain does not happen to have that kind of Conservative Party. Religious differences are submerged in a two-party system. Any government, Conservative or Labour, must offend some of its supporters if it dares to approach issues of this nature. The consequent inaction can breed festering social problems. The alternative is to set aside the party dimension and for Parliament to decide as a Parliament and not merely as a body recording Cabinet decisions.

[1] A development of this thesis is that the Government gave a green light to back-benchers on social issues to provide an outlet for their crusading energies and so divert them from criticism of government policy. But left-wing opposition to ministerial policy has continued unabated and most Members closely concerned with the measures discussed in this book are not, and never have been, noted for extreme political opinions.

[2] David Butler and Donald Stokes: *Political Change in Britain* (Macmillan, 1969), Ch. 15.

Responsibility moves away from Cabinet to Parliament. This is not a new or revolutionary tendency but a movement towards older ways.

2. Measures are passed at a stage when insufficient study and debate has been devoted to the issues involved. This is an obvious line of attack against any proposal for reform. Any subject may be illuminated by further research: levels of knowledge can always be improved. Public participation in any discussion is always incomplete and fuller discussion and understanding will always be desirable. Unless law is to be treated as immutable, at some stage decisions must be taken and votes determine the outcome. But the plain fact is that Parliament does not rush ahead on conscience issues. All the measures discussed in this book were preceded by a report of some kind. Capital punishment had a Royal Commission. Departmental committees had considered homosexuality and Sunday observance. A Joint Select Committee had reviewed theatre censorship. The Law Commission had reported on the divorce laws. Documents had been issued by the Established Church on homosexuality, abortion and divorce. It seems probable that no private member's Bill on an issue of conscience could succeed without some preliminary enquiry of this kind. The one Bill that failed to pass, that on Sunday entertainments, is the one that departed most clearly from the recommendations of the preceding studies. Indeed, except in the case of abortion, the claim that further study was needed did not become an important strand in the argument. Abortion was the one case where the law was changed without some support from an *official* enquiry.

3. Constituents do not know the views of parliamentary candidates on non-party issues: Members, therefore, have no mandate. Without question, this statement is correct. But is it relevant? It has been argued above that the electorate is more concerned with economic issues than other issues. To put this in another form, electors are more concerned with party issues than non-party issues. Votes are cast on party lines because parties differ on matters which are felt to be most important. It is ridiculous to suppose that many voters would change their allegiance because a candidate said he would vote this way or that on a private member's Bill. In reality, the level of public knowledge of party policies is low. Opinion studies have shown repeatedly the limitations of public understanding and the extent to which people do not agree with the policies of the party they support. No parliamentary candidate can foresee all issues that will be presented to Parliament in the coming four or five years. No parliamentary candidate should be willing to guarantee that his views will not change in the light of changing circumstances. The British tradition of democracy is based on representation, not on the unfree

actions of mandated delegates. The public can express opinions on any issue through pressure groups, the mass media and personal communication with their elected representatives. But the decisions remain with Members. Voters who are displeased with Members have a possibility of redress at the next General Election. Even then, almost all will make a choice in accordance with an individual perception of *party* principles or programmes.

4. Important votes on private members' Bills are taken on Fridays or in all-night sittings when attendance is low. In general, this statement is accurate. Yet due to various curiosities of parliamentary procedure it is not wholly true in relation to the five divisions analysed in Chapter 9.

Subject	Date of division	Day of week	Time	Members voting[1]
Capital Punishment	21.12.64	Monday	11 p.m.	529
Homosexuality	5. 7.66	Tuesday	4 p.m.	348
Abortion	13. 7.67	Friday[2]	11.45 a.m.	254
Divorce	17.12.68	Tuesday	1.50 p.m.	293
Sunday Entertainment	28. 2.69	Friday	4 p.m.	203

It is difficult to maintain that any of these divisions were held at an unreasonable hour. Members who absented themselves did so for a variety of reasons. A few may have decided to take full advantage of the lack of a party whip and to have time off; others were ill or had urgent business elsewhere; many will have decided that they did not wish to commit themselves on the particular issue; occasionally Members are present but abstain deliberately. Those who do vote are those who feel most strongly about the subject and, one hopes, are those most fully informed about it. Is there any advantage to be gained by filling the division lobbies with extra Members who care less and know less about the issue to be decided? A great benefit of legislation without party is that it offers Members freedom, not merely in terms of how to vote but whether to vote at all.

The criticism that Members do not bother to vote can be linked with Proposition 2 that decisions are taken with inadequate preparation. This raises the further question of how far existing law has been the result of careful deliberation in Parliament. Both theatre censorship and Sunday observance were based on eighteenth-century statutes which were passed largely for reasons that today are totally unacceptable, i.e. political and religious intolerance. The law on

---

[1] Including tellers.
[2] Thursday sitting carried on overnight.

homosexuality was, indeed, a late-night rush, virtually undebated. Abortion law had become uncertain and depended upon judicial decisions rather than parliamentary decisions. Only in the cases of capital punishment and divorce could the existing law be said to be the result of full consideration by a democratic assembly. But law is accepted as legitimate in Britain because it is the law, not because of the conditions under which a law was made. In any case, a private member's Bill which survives all the obstacles offered by parliamentary procedure has at least as good a claim to validity in democratic terms as the law which it replaces.

5. Private members' Bills are badly drafted and do not – in the case of complex measures – operate as intended. As major items of back-bench legislation now can get the help of official parliamentary draftsmen, this complaint tends to lose its sting. It has, however, been pressed in the case of abortion reform, particularly since the Act came into effect. As Parliament spent many hours examining the precise wording of the Bill it cannot be accused of inattention. The situation is that opponents of abortion reform have tried to stir up hostility to the new Act partly by claiming that Parliament did not intend it to work as it is working. How far this is true must be a matter of opinion. What is certain is that any legislation, including government legislation, may not have the effects intended; major examples are the gaming laws, the breathalyser law and the Race Relations Act. Any fresh statute may have surprising results which have no necessary connexion with drafting or the inadequacy of back-benchers.

So far this discussion has been concerned with the House of Commons. Yet the Lords still have a potentially important role in legislation. Exactly what the consequences would be if the Lords threw out a private member's Bill that had passed the Commons cannot be foreseen: it would depend upon the character of the Government and the attitude of the Government to the Bill. At one stage in the proceedings on the Abortion Bill, when the Lords had passed restrictive amendments, there was some speculation about a constitutional struggle between Lords and Commons. The amendments were subsequently rescinded and my impression is that the constitutional aspect of the matter had little to do with the Lords' change of mind. No doubt in earlier decades the Upper House would have strenuously opposed all the legislation discussed in this book. However, since the Life Peerages Act, 1958, and particularly since the advent of the Labour Government in 1964, the nature of the active membership of the Lords has changed. There is still a great Conservative majority that can be assembled if Tory whipping is vigorous, e.g. the rejection in 1969 of Government proposals on the reshaping of parliamentary constituencies. But on most occasions the Lords now provide a broad cross-section of opinion. On homosexuality and Sunday entertainment they have been more progressive than the Commons. Taking the six case-studies together, the Lords, on balance, have assisted rather than impeded reform.

Normally, another important influence on legislation is the Civil Service. Ministers rely on their permanent advisers for technical expertise and the benefit of their administrative experience. On issues of conscience the role of the official is restricted; it is not his task to guide the moral values of a Minister. This does not mean that the civil servant ignores all issues of conscience. The Home Office was deeply concerned about the relationship between the death penalty and the morale of the police force. The Ministry of Health had to take account of the effect of the Abortion Act on the National Health Service. The Lord Chamberlain's Office lost a part of its duties with the abolition of theatre censorship. Nevertheless, since we do not seek moral leadership from the Civil Service, its impact on such issues is restricted. Perhaps this is one reason why Mr Ronald Butt has urged the need for a Law Ministry or Ministry of Justice. To quote his article in *The Times*:[1] 'A Law Ministry would be useful because for many Bills dealing with social or moral matters there is no Ministry which is now logically or directly connected with them.' Yet is it so terrible that there are still aspects of human experience that do not come under the surveillance of a Minister and his staff?

The absence of party discipline, combined with an element of withdrawal by the Civil Service, creates an influence vacuum at Westminster. How is it filled? One might expect the democratic pressure of opinion to become more important. Yet the results of opinion polls have little effect on policy; capital punishment and Sunday entertainment provide two examples. Public opinion is often too abstract, too unorganized and too imprecise to be an effective political agent. For opinion to matter it must be reasonably specific and be expressed by persons of authority. Authority may derive from status or knowledge. Members of the Commons take note of the opinions of their constituents because they have the status of voters, and the view of a group of voters is necessarily more weighty than that of one individual. Members are especially concerned with the views of leading personalities in their local party organization because of the status of these people within the party hierarchy. This suggests that Members are highly sensitive to constituency opinion.

[1] October 23, 1969.

But sensitivity does not imply submission. The tradition of British representative government is expressed in the words of Burke.

'Certainly, gentlemen, it ought to be the happiness and glory of a representative to live in the strictest union, the closest correspondence, and the most unreserved communication with his constituents. Their wishes ought to have great weight with him; their opinion, high respect; their business, unremitted attention. It is his duty to sacrifice his repose, his pleasures, his satisfactions, to theirs; and above all, ever, and in all cases, to prefer their interest to his own. But his unbiased opinion, his mature judgement, his enlightened conscience, he ought not to sacrifice to you, to any man, or to any set of men living. These he does not derive from your pleasure; no, nor from the law and the constitution. They are a trust from Providence, for the abuse of which he is deeply answerable. Your representative owes you, not his industry only, but his judgement; and he betrays, instead of serving you, if he sacrifices it to your opinion.'

Certainly, the spirit of Burke is invoked by any Member in trouble with constituency supporters. It is difficult to find clear evidence that Members have bowed to constituency pressure, partly because Members may be reluctant to make this kind of admission. It is also impossible to distinguish the chain of causation. If Scottish Members are hostile to homosexuality and Welsh Members to Sunday entertainment – is this due to constituency pressure or because representatives from Scotland and Wales are more likely to hold such views. If the latter explanation be adopted, constituency pressure becomes nothing more than a reinforcement mechanism. It was argued above that few votes will be won or lost on conscience issues, partly because such items are of secondary importance in a contest dominated by political parties and partly because the vast majority of electors will not know the views of candidates on non-party issues. Even so, it would be an error to write off constituency opinion entirely. A Member may rarely be persuaded to vote against deep personal convictions; he may be persuaded to vote when he has no strong feelings; he may also be persuaded to abstain when local pressure is contrary to his own mild inclination. The third of these possibilities can help to explain the fate of the Sunday Entertainments Bill. This example also demonstrates that if Members do adjust to active local opinion they may sometimes act against trends in public opinion. Active opinion is not necessarily majority opinion.

Pressure groups and the enthusiams of individual Members largely fill the influence vacuum surrounding issues of conscience. Names of

Members who played a leading role in these matters have been recorded above: much depends on the political skill of the sponsors of Bills and that of their opponents. The nature of pressure groups varies greatly. Some are formed to struggle for a cause. Others have a *raison d'être* far removed from the political scene but are drawn into it by the contents of proposed legislation. The Abortion Law Reform Association, the Society for the Protection of the Unborn Child, the Divorce Law Reform Union and the Homosexual Law Reform Society were all created to fight for a cause. The Lord's Day Observance Society is not quite in the same category since its activities are not so concentrated on attempts to influence legislation. The women's organizations and the sporting bodies are wholly different; normally they do not deal with politicians and the law. It is not surprising that their political impact is so weak. Potentially the strongest organizations on issues of conscience are the churches, in spite of a decline in religious belief and church attendance. The Church of England has assisted with law reform on the subjects of homosexuality, abortion and divorce. Yet, in general, the voice of organized Christianity is diminished by divisions within the faith and by divisions within particular churches. Even Roman Catholic opinion is not as clear and firm as it was ten years ago. This relative weakness of organized religion increases the opportunity for campaign-oriented pressure groups.

The task of campaigning bodies is to influence opinion in Westminster and outside. Especially where sex is involved the group must first establish the respectability of its cause. Once a body of educated opinion recognizes the existence of a problem and the case for statutory reform, then Members will become interested. When a campaign reaches the parliamentary stage, outside bodies tend to become less important as the necessary organization and negotiation must generally be done by Members themselves.

One firm generalization about the influence of pressure-groups emerges from the six case-studies: the greater the public interest in an issue, the more numerous the organizations concerned with it, the less significant will be any campaign designed to affect the form of legislation. The weapons available to a group seeking reform are information and argument. Where mass interest is aroused the group will have inadequate resources to influence the flood of opinion – and perhaps of emotion. Further, the more widespread a discussion the more varied the levels at which it will be conducted and the information which a campaign group can supply tends to be less heeded. In these circumstances a campaign makes less impact on the public; the impact on Westminster is also lower since parliamentarians are subjected to a wider array of competing pressures. Capital punishment stimulated such public interest that no *ad hoc* campaign could have more than a limited effect on either public opinion or the legislature. Discussion on divorce was quieter; the issues were more complex; nevertheless, they were debated by a wide range of organizations. The Divorce Law Reform Union played some part in these discussions, but it was insufficiently strong to have a major effect. As one moves towards the topics with a lower coefficient of public involvement, the campaign-groups become more significant. The Lord's Day Observance Society had some impact on events through the activity it helped to generate at constituency level. The Abortion Law Reform Association and the Homosexual Law Reform Society worked quietly and effectively to mould the opinion of influential persons. Of all the groups noticed in this study, A.L.R.A. has been the most influential. Finally, at the other end of the involvement spectrum from capital punishment, comes theatre censorship. Here few people were concerned. The theatre is a minority taste. Intellectuals did not launch a crusade for their freedom: to do so might have stimulated opposition. So there was no campaign group on the A.L.R.A. model. Instead, a few people in positions of influence took the necessary initiatives. Pressure was there, but not in the commonly recognizable form.

Whether it is of advantage to a campaign group to excite public consciousness must depend on an estimate of the state of opinion if aroused. Those who oppose capital punishment know from the opinion polls that the more controversy they can create the greater the pressure on Parliament favouring their cause. Conversely, some of the L.D.O.S. successes in enforcing Sunday observance law have been partially counter-productive in that they have aroused hostility to the Society. On non-party questions, one other rule for campaign groups to follow is that their activities around Westminster should be discreet: pressure that is too obvious is disliked. Particularly on moral issues a Member wants to be, and be thought of, as the guardian of his own conscience.

II

What institutional changes could usefully be made to facilitate parliamentary examination of matters which fall outside the normal channels of party policy and departmental insistence? Mr Butt's proposal for a Ministry of Justice was noted above. The notion is of respectable antiquity, and a fair case can be made for it. The Haldane Committee on the Machinery of Government urged that such a Ministry be established to take responsibility for the administration of justice.[1] Harold Laski approved the concept in his *Grammar of Politics*.[2] In *Law Reform Now*,[3] edited by Andrew Martin and Gerald Gardiner, subsequently Lord Chancellor in the Wilson Government, the establishment of a Law Commission was suggested which would advise on matters of law reform; the chairman of this body was to be both a Member of the Commons and a Minister of State in the Lord Chancellor's Department. The common theme of these proposals is that a Minister should be directly answerable to the Commons on matters of law reform: such an arrangement might well stimulate wider interest in legal codification and modernization. But Mr Butt wants a Ministry of Justice to 'take over and frame satisfactorily' any private member's Bill which had obtained a second reading so that the Ministry could shape it according to the pattern of public opinion inside and outside the House. This is an extraordinary proposition. It is the duty of Ministers to propose measures they feel to be justified, not measures which they think will prove popular. The force of public opinion should make itself felt through constituency pressure on Members, not through Ministers' opinion of the state of public opinion. Mr Butt agreed that if the sponsor of a Bill disliked the version put forward by the Minister of Justice, he could go ahead with his original measure, but he would be faced by a hostile Minister so his chances of success would be substantially reduced. Clearly, this was Mr Butt's intention. He seems to dislike the situation where Parliament accepts the task of deciding a moral issue while Ministers and civil servants tend to wait on the sidelines.[4]

Under the Law Commissions Act, 1965, a Commission was appointed to advise the Lord Chancellor on questions of law reform. The Commission is an independent body of lawyers: their programme of work is agreed with the Lord Chancellor. Their reports may become the subject of government legislation or they may be adopted by back-benchers and reach the statute book via the ballot procedure. *The Field of Choice* was the major influence on the form of the Divorce Bill. While much of this activity is relatively technical and non-controversial, it is inevitable that the Commission will sometimes stray into the realm of policy. If it is asked to advise on the

[1] 9230, 1918, Cd. pp. 63–78, xii.

[2] Allen & Unwin, 1925.

[3] Gollancz, 1963, pp. 8–10. See also A. Martin: *Methods of Law Reform* (1967), an inaugural lecture at the University of Southampton.

[4] Mr Butt also suggested that the Minister of Justice should be 'overtly political but not essentially party-political'. How could this be done without destroying the collective responsibility of the Government? See *The Times*, October 23, 1969.

optimum legal method of carrying out policy X, where X is a matter of dispute, the subsequent report inevitably will be regarded as a partisan document. Is the present shape of the Law Commission better than the Martin/Gardiner idea of 1963 which envisaged that the Commission would be headed by a Minister? I think it is. A Minister as chairman would be tempted to dodge issues that split his party and the Cabinet. Advice from the Commissioners that the chairman found embarrassing would, presumably, not be published. Now the Law Commission has a greater measure of freedom. Its proposals are set apart from the party dimension. As with reports from Royal Commissions and other advisory bodies, Parliament can adopt the suggestions of the Law Commission or it can reject them.

Is it possible to devise reforms which would help rather than hinder parliamentary consideration of issues of conscience? The ballot procedure to decide priorities for private members' Bills is an obvious target for criticism. The luck of the draw may give top places to Members with idiosyncratic ideas which are unlikely to win the support of the House. Should this happen, it is arguable that valuable time and opportunities have been wasted. An alternative procedure would be for Members to table Bills in the form of motions: priority for the Bills could then be determined by the number of signatures of support each attracted. Thus the most popular Bills would go to the head of the queue and would have an excellent chance of becoming law. Judged by a productivity criterion of the number of laws passed, there can be no doubt that such a procedure would give the best results. But the new statutes would not necessarily be the most valuable. The danger is that the majority party would dominate the proceedings, perhaps by design, perhaps not. Minority intersts would tend to be squeezed out. And this would be sad. Unorthodox minority opinions can only become relatively orthodox majority opinions if they can be freely ventilated and their advocates are given a fair chance to persuade others. Popular ideas and non-controversial items already have an advantage over unpopular ideas in that they can more easily find a sponsor: there is no need to make this advantage absolute.

Professor Ramsay Muir suggested to the Select Committee on Procedure in 1930 that allocation of time for private members' Bills should be determined by a committee which would choose the Bills it felt were most worthy of discussion.[1] This idea merely creates fresh difficulties. Upon what criteria could a committee fix priorities? If it preferred Bills with the widest support, it would, as argued above, discriminate against minority interests and new ideas. If it adopted

[1] p. 256, 1930–31 (161), viii.

any other method, the committee could be accused of pushing forward personal preferences or, more probably, holding back personal *bêtes noires*. The ballot may be an imperfect technique, but its shortcomings are less serious than those of the alternatives.

A useful change in the ballot procedure would be to bring forward the date from November to July (except in the first session of a new Parliament) so that the draw would be held at the end of the previous session.[1] This would have a dual advantage. Members would have more time to prepare their measures and it would become easier to provide them with assistance from the official parliamentary draftsmen. It is highly desirable that Members successful in the ballot should have such help: the practical difficulty at present is that work on private members' Bills is concentrated in the first few weeks of each session when there is also much drafting work to be done in the preparation of government measures. If the 'drafting season' for private members' Bills could be extended, this pressure would be eased. The other benefit is that a July ballot would allow the formal first reading of balloted Bills to take place on the first Friday of the session and second readings could commence a month earlier than at present. There are minor objections to this plan. Members returned at autumn by-elections would not be able to enter a ballot until the following summer. The other snag is that in July it might not be clear whether a measure going forward in the present session was, or was not, going to succeed: therefore it could fail to find a sponsor in the following session due to uncertainty whether a sponsor would be needed. In practice, by the middle of July it is usually possible to make a shrewd guess about whether a particular Bill will succeed. And it would always be possible for a Member to keep his options open until the end of the session. On balance, a July ballot would be an improvement.

The main difficulty facing private members' Bills is shortage of time: this is just one aspect of a general shortage of legislative time. Two solutions are possible: to speed up business and to make more time available. If speeches were fewer and shorter, more rapid progress could be made. But the Commons has always resisted the imposition of a time-limit on individual speeches. Nor is it reasonable to expect Members who object to a measure to list their objections in staccato fashion. While the rules of debate permit the possibility of a filibuster, there is a general desire in the House that business should proceed in a reasonable manner: a Member who occupies an

[1] This idea was suggested to the Procedure Committee in 1965 by the Study of Parliament Group: Select Committee on Procedure, Fourth Report: 1964-65 (303) viii.

O

excessive amount of time tends to lose sympathy. The need is to maintain freedom for adequate discussion without suffering from an abuse of that freedom. The technique devised to secure this happy mean is the closure motion which is accepted at the discretion of the Speaker but which also requires both a majority in the division lobbies and a hundred affirmative votes. One proposal to reduce obstruction is to lower the figure of one hundred. Is it too high? One hundred is no more than 16 per cent of the whole House. If a measure is sufficiently controversial to stimulate at least some sign of a filibuster, is it unreasonable that 16 per cent of Members must turn up in support of a Bill to ensure a safe passage to the statute book? In my view the number should not be changed.

At the committee stage a filibuster by a minority can be countered by a resolution passed by the majority that the committee should meet more frequently or hold longer sessions. Government by exhaustion is not a satisfactory arrangement. The alternative technique to ensure that business does proceed is a guillotine or timetable motion which allocates a maximum number of hours of debating time to so many clauses of a Bill. The guillotine is occasionally used for government legislation and always arouses Opposition protest. It is at present improbable that the Commons would agree to the extension of this device to private members' time.[1] However, anyone who has studied the verbatim record of the committee stage of the 1968/69 Sunday Entertainments Bill is liable to conclude that even for back-benchers' Bills the use of the guillotine may sometimes be justified. At the report stage the prospect is that arguments on matters of detail will be repeated which have already been fully aired in committee. Yet where legislation is not based on party ideology such repetition is more acceptable because it is less certain that the view of the whole House will be the same as that of the committee. The only safeguard against deliberate time-wasting is a greater willingness on the part of the Chair to accept the closure motion.

The alternative method of helping private members would be to provide them with more time. Since the ration of Fridays allowed for back-bench Bills was increased as recently as 1967, it is difficult to argue for a further increase granted the heavy competing claims

---

[1] The Select Committee on Procedure for the session 1958–59 proposed that a business committee be established to consider all Bills sent to standing committee after second reading and to report to the House the date by which each Bill should be reported back from standing committee. 'Thereafter it should be open to the Government in respect of a Government Bill or to the Member in charge of a private member's Bill to move a motion instructing the standing committee in the sense of the report, or the amended report, of the business committee.' para. 7, 1958–59 (92), vi. No action was taken on this proposal.

for parliamentary attention. What is needed is not more time *per se* but more time in particular circumstances to remove bottlenecks. Normally there is but a single Standing Committee to deal with private members' Bills which have to queue up to receive attention. If this queue becomes too long or moves too slowly because the Committee is delayed by a complex or contentious measure, then a second or third such committee should be established. The normal objection to extra committees, that it is difficult to man them, should not apply here with its usual force: if a group of Members feel sufficiently strongly on a topic to sponsor a Bill – or oppose a Bill – on a subject, then they should be willing to attend a committee formed to discuss it in detail. At present the queue may sometimes be dodged with the assistance of the Government whips, but this is an unsatisfactory solution and brings ministerial neutrality into question.

A second and sometimes greater bottleneck is the report stage on the floor of the House. Here the principle should be firmly established that where a Bill has survived its second reading and committee stage in something near its original form, then the Government should provide an opportunity for the Commons to come to a decision. This can be done without the sacrifice of government time but through extra or extended sittings. On a number of occasions the Wilson Government has made such arrangements, but these have been allowed by grace and favour, not as of right. Could such a right be established – on a conventional basis – then the position of a Member sponsoring a Bill would be greatly strengthened. Indeed, time might well be saved. At present the point of a filibuster is the hope that a Bill will drop because it runs out of time; failing that, if the Government finds extra time, one can try to pin some element of responsibility for the Bill on to Ministers. If it were known that extra time would be made available if necessary, albeit at inconvenient hours, then the incentive to waste time would partially disappear.

It is sometimes argued that Bills which fail to complete their parliamentary journey during one session of Parliament should be allowed to continue in the next session (except when a new Parliament has assembled) from the stage already reached. Time that had been spent on the Bill would not, as now, be wasted. In the summer of 1968 this reform was urged by some supporters of the divorce and Sunday entertainment measures. The present sessional 'cut off' does seem arbitrary and unnecessary. Yet in the case of controversial private members' Bills it is not clear that a 'carry-over' system would help. Under existing rules no facilities would be available for measures brought up from the previous session. If time were taken from the

ration of sixteen Fridays for Bills winning in the ballot, then the
chances of these Bills in succeeding sessions would diminish with the
development of a hopeless log-jam of private members' measures.
The alternative would be extra time provided by the Government as
suggested above; but if this is to happen, far better for it to be done
at the end of the session than for the issue to be delayed, perhaps for
several months. A sessional carry over could substantially increase
the influence of Lords' amendments. The Government does now
arrange time at the end of the session to iron out differences between
the Houses on private members' legislation. The tyranny of the
timetable forces issues to a conclusion: either a Bill passes or
alternatively it fails and has to await full re-argument. To allow
'carry over' from one session to another would remove the sense of
urgency and could well increase delays to legislation rather than
reduce them.[1]

III

So far this analysis has been concerned with private members' Bills.
But it is not inevitable that moral issues are discussed through this
channel. It would be quite possible for a government to take the
initiative while disclaiming interest in the outcome. The Government
could bring a measure before Parliament; stress that it accepted no
responsibility for the Bill; announce that its supporters would have
a free vote; so establish firmly that the decision to be made was a
decision for Parliament alone. Douglas Houghton, when Chairman
of the Parliamentary Labour Party, urged that Ministers should be
willing to allow such parliamentary freedom.[2]

What type of problem is suitable for this form of non-party
treatment? To reply 'issues of conscience' is unhelpful. The phrase
lacks precise definition. It can refer to issues dominated by moral
considerations: it can refer to issues where the parties have no
policy. Should adoption, animal welfare and the preservation of
amenity be thought of as matters for individual conscience? The

---

[1] Cf. evidence of the Chief Whip, John Silkin, to the 1966–67 Select Committee
on Procedure: Sixth Report of the Committee (539) q. 439. The Committee
proposed that a 'carry over' arrangement be allowed for Bills subject to the
procedure for second reading by committee. A Minister may propose a motion
that a Bill be sent to a committee for second reading, but the motion will fail
if twenty Members rise to object. Thus this procedure applies solely to non-
controversial measures and has no relevance to issues of conscience. The
Committee's proposal to allow sessional 'carry over' for uncontroversial Bills
has not been accepted.
Letter to *The Times*, June 24, 1969.

same question can be extended to an endless range of topics. In practice, a matter becomes an issue of conscience when it is convenient for the parties to treat it as such. The scope for non-party legislation must depend on the attitude of the major parties: anything which stimulates party controversy is necessarily excluded. Government and Opposition must be willing to agree on a free vote. Otherwise Ministers stand on the sidelines in a pose of neutrality while the Opposition tries to create a party row. Equally, if the Government has a declared policy it cannot allow its supporters a free vote because, as with capital punishment, the position of Ministers becomes impossible should their advice be rejected. Thus for non-party legislation the freedom from whipping must apply to all Members.

There are two other conditions. Non-party decisions are not suitable for legislation which has major implications for public expenditure. The Government cannot abdicate from its responsibility for our national finances; it must approve policies which add significantly to the burdens on the Exchequer, particularly in regard to the distribution of financial benefits. The second requirement is that the policy framework of a Bill must come from an independent, non-ministerial source. No government should frame detailed legislation and then proclaim indifference to it. Various kinds of body can review the need for change in the law and shape proposals with sufficient precision to enable them to be made the basis of legislation. Royal Commissions, Departmental Committees, the Law Commission and Parliamentary Select Committees already provide advice that is sometimes translated into Bills. It has been shown that such bodies have played an influential role in preparing the way for private members' Bills, notably on theatre censorship and divorce. Government and Opposition should be more willing to agree that legislation based on such reports should be introduced into Parliament and considered freely upon its merits.

R. H. S. Crossman, when Leader of the House of Commons, proposed to the Select Committee on Procedure that committees be established to consider proposals for future legislation. The Committee accepted the suggestion.[1] Such committees would enable Members to hear the views of experts and of interested parties which are now submitted to government departments and may never come directly before Parliament at all – at least not in any formal sense. Thus fully informed the committees could work out the broad lines of any future legislation. Small groups of back-benchers would thus have a clear role in policy-making: the increase in their influence would be a direct consequence of the detailed attention they had

[1] para. 14 and p. 26 1966–67 (539).

devoted to their subject. Normally the report of such a committee would provide the basis of legislation introduced in government time, although obviously the Government would retain a veto. For a committee's report to be persuasive it would have to be virtually unanimous or be based upon a majority view that cut across party allegiance.

The idea of pre-legislation committees was welcomed by those who felt that Members should play a real part in policy formation. However, no such committee has yet been appointed, apparently because of a shortage of Members willing to serve.[1] The idea should be revived. The difficulty of recruiting Members would be eased if, as with stage censorship, the committees were drawn from both Houses of Parliament.

But is it really possible for Parliament to play a more constructive role in law-making? J. S. Mill's dictum must not be forgotten: 'a numerous assembly is as little fitted for the direct business of legislation as for that of administration'.[2] Ninety years later Professor J. A. G. Griffith regarded the task of Parliament in legislation as 'examination, criticism and approval'.[3] It is quite clear that Parliament as a whole cannot master the details of a problem or draft complicated proposals for new legislation. Initial spadework must always be done by small groups of people with specialized knowledge and skill. The task for Parliament is to accept or reject the main heads of proposals prepared in this way. Here I am in entire agreement with Mill and Griffith. My argument is simply that the preparatory work does not necessarily have to be done within Government Departments or be presented by Ministers to Parliament on the basis that the prestige of the Government is linked to the fate of the draft legislation.

Criticism of Parliament is rife. In part, this is due to a new and dangerous dissatisfaction with democracy. In part it is because the public have a mind-picture of an assembly controlled by party organizations that is too easily obedient to the Government's will. Academic reformers have sought to provide Members with a more positive role in the process of governing. The most common suggestion is that they should be more active in the scrutiny of the work of Government Departments and in the discussion of policy problems at a stage prior to the announcement of official policy. This is

---

[1] The pressure of committee work on Members has increased greatly in recent years: see Select Committee on Procedure p. 247 1968–69 (410).

[2] *Representative Government* (1861) Ch. 5.

[3] See his penetrating article, 'The Place of Parliament in the Legislative Process', *Modern Law Review* (1951), Vol. 14, pp. 279–96 and 425–36.

the pattern of argument in favour of specialized select committees. No doubt, Members could develop these functions to the public advantage and their own satisfaction. But such committee work, however useful, will not excite the public imagination or do much to change the general image of our legislature.

Parliament will attract news coverage, popular interest and support if it discusses topics which capture wide attention and if it is seen to act with some degree of independence. Since 1966 the Commons have been more independent. Government back-benchers have voted against their leaders more frequently. Some major government initiatives have had to be abandoned. In particular, the scheme to reform the House of Lords was defeated by an *ad hoc* coalition of back-benchers from both sides of the House. Such events, although embarrassing to Ministers, give Parliament a sense of purpose. So also do controversial private members' Bills. There are those with conservative inclinations who regret the raising of controversial topics. What can be forgotten is that the law that reformers try to change is itself controversial. And no vigorous society can have a permanent moratorium on disputed moral questions. This book has tried to show that these issues of conscience – questions regarded as suitable for individual rather than party determination – have received careful attention from Parliament and many other organizations. They have also aroused more public interest than the common run of legislation, partly because of the subject-matter and partly because the outcome has been unpredictable. Before the second reading debate on the 1968–69 Divorce Bill the Speaker asked Members who wished to join in the debate to let him know privately whether they were for or against the Bill, as otherwise he could not ensure a balanced debate.[1] His request illustrates sharply the abnormal freedom and reality of the subsequent discussion. When the whips are off, Parliament has a new vitality. Members are forced to think for themselves about the questions at issue. Legislation without party puts Parliament at the heart of the decision-making process. This is a healthy advance for democratic values. It is also good for society as it enables problems to be faced that would otherwise be avoided.

[1] H. C. Deb., Vol. 758, col. 810.

Index

P

GEORGE ALLEN & UNWIN LTD

Head office:
40 Museum Street, London, W.C.1
Telephone: 01-405 8577

Sales, Distribution and Accounts Departments
Park Lane, Hemel Hempstead, Herts.
Telephone: 0442 2344

Athens: 7 Stadiou Street, Athens 125
Auckland: P.O. Box 36013, Northcote Auckland 9
Barbados: P.O. Box 222, Bridgetown
Beirut: Deeb Building, Jeanne d'Arc Street
Bombay: 103/5 Fort Street, Bombay 1
Calcutta: 285J Bepin Behari Ganguli Street, Calcutta 12
P.O. Box 23134, Joubert Park, Johannesburg, South Africa
Dacca: Alico Building, 18 Montijheel, Dacca 2
Dehli: 1/18 B Asaf Ali Road, New Dehli 1
Hong Kong: 105 Wing on Mansion, 26 Hankow Road, Kowloon
Ibadan: P.O. Box 62
Karachi: Karachi Chambers, McLeod Road
Lahore: 22 Falettis' Hotel, Egerton Road
Madras 2/18 Mount Road, Madras 2
Manila: P.O. Box 157, Quezon City D-502
Mexico: Libreria Britanica, S.A., Separio Rendon 125, Mexico 4, D.F.
Nairobi: P.O. Box 30583
Ontario: 2330 Midland Avenue, Agincourt
Rio de Janeiro: Caixa Postal 2537-Zc-oo
Singapore: 36c Prinsep Street, Singapore 7
Sydney, N.S.W.: Bradbury House, 55 York Street
Tokyo: C.P.O. Box 1728, Tokyo 100-91

CONSTITUTIONAL BUREAUCRACY

HENRY PARRIS

This is the first book to provide a general account of administrative growth in nineteenth-century Britain. The result of ten years' work, it challenges accepted notions of the nature of government during the period. It is largely based on unpublished records and fills a surprising gap in the literature.

Students both of politics and history will be glad to have an account of the great formative period in British government, particularly as we stand on the threshold of major reforms which lead to a reconsideration of first principles. It will also interest civil servants and all those taking part in the controversy over the efficiency of British administration.

The author defines his main qualifications for writing it as an obsession dating from his undergraduate days with the paradox that, in nineteenth-century Britain, the great majority of people preached *laissez-faire* whilst energetically practising government growth and intervention. In addition he has undertaken extensive preliminary studies in the development of particular departments, such as the Board of Trade and the Home Office.

'. . . this book is invaluable . . . a good piece of documentary history, well researched.' *Irish Independent*

'In the course of his argument Mr Parris accumulates a fascinating amount of evidence about the way things actually happened.' *The Economist*

'Interesting and thoroughly researched.' *New Society*

'. . . can be confidently recommended . . . The documentation is extremely full . . .' *The Times Literary Supplement*

'A most readable general account of administrative growth in nineteenth-century Britain. The book will be of interest to students of political history and public administration.' *International Review of Administrative Sciences*

LONDON · GEORGE ALLEN & UNWIN LTD